A SIMPLE REVOLUTION
The Making of an Activist Poet

Judy Grahn

aunt lute books
san francisco

Aunt Lute Books
P.O. Box 410687
San Francisco, CA 94141
www.auntlute.com

Cover design: Amy Woloszyn, Amymade Graphic Design
Cover photo: Judy Grahn 1973 West Coast Lesbian Conference in LA,
Photo by Chana Wilson
Text design and typesetting: Amy Woloszyn, Amymade Graphic Design

Senior Editor: Joan Pinkvoss
Managing Editor: Shay Brawn
Production: Ellen French, Chenxing Han, Aileen Joy, Alexa Kelly, Jada Marsden, Soma Nath, Kara Owens, Erin Petersen, Shaun Salas

This book was funded in part by grants from the Sara and Two C-Dogs Foundation, the Vessel Foundation, and Horizons Foundation.

Library of Congress Cataloging-in-Publication Data

Grahn, Judy, 1940-

 A simple revolution : the making of an activist poet / Judy Grahn

  p. cm.

 Includes bibliographical references and index.

 ISBN 978-1-879960-87-9 (acid-free paper)

 1. Grahn, Judy, 1940- 2. Women poets, American--Biography. 3. Lesbians--Biography. 4. Gay liberation movement--Biography. 5. Protest movements--United States--History--20th century--Biography. I. Title.

 PS3557.R226Z46 2012

 811'.54--dc23

 [B]

                            2012037980

Printed in the U.S.A. on acid-free paper

10 9 8 7 6 5 4 3 2 1

To all brave radicals
past, present, and future

PREFACE

A memoir rests on a foundation of memory, that oozy and changeable bog, constructed more of feelings than sequences of events. Sorting for "reality" means conducting research, careful lists, double and triple checking. And still I can't seem to spell names correctly. More double checking, someone to come in behind me with an eye for detail, sentence structure, accuracy that matches intention.

I wanted to fill out the picture of my life in the 1970s more fully than one person can, because it was such a collective experience. It seemed inaccurate, and even arrogant to try to tell a group story using only my own limited memory. What if I garbled and misrepresented?

So I interviewed people, about twenty of them, drawing on their recollections, and pulling a few direct statements into the body of my own telling. I also have carefully mapped some Bay Area lesbian households, as they constituted a geography of interconnection, a kind of interlocking urban village, for a particular area and era of time.

Sometimes I joke that this book becomes in places a "multiple personality memoir." But in the end the perspective is mine, guided by my hopes that I have contributed to a fuller picture of the contributions of Northern California women to the mass movements of the Seventies, that younger folks find meaningful truths in this account, and that I have faithfully served that demon-lover: activist art.

Judy Grahn

A SIMPLE REVOLUTION

CHILD OF THE WIND

"We have to go to the press right now, something very bad has happened—we've been vandalized." I looked up, startled at the urgency in my lover's face as she burst into the living room.

The press was on Market Street in Oakland. The year was 1977. I felt numb and unreal as we walked through the factory-sized plant we had so painstakingly built up. The other press members were already inside the cavernous building. They walked with us through room after room, showing us the devastation, the blood drained from their faces. We stepped carefully over thick trails of black ink. The gooey stuff pooled on stacks of freshly printed books and saturated our precious papers. A wide heap of shredded graph paper and film, two feet high, lay outside the darkroom—the early production stages of six books. The black rollers of our printing presses, usually gleaming, were covered in abrasive, grainy powder.

Who did this? Everyone had a different idea, but all agreed it was a violent attempt to annihilate our enterprise, the largest women's press in the country. We stared at each other. We talked fast. Was it the FBI? Was it cops? How did they get past the alarm system? What should we do? My heart began to beat fast as my numbness flowed into heightened fear.

Casey stepped forward. "No matter who they are, they might come back. We have to guard our plant."

"They might set fire to it next time," someone else said, ratcheting up the tension.

"We have a rifle and a pistol," Casey said. "We'll take turns staying up all night, two at a time."

So the next night I found myself in the darkened building, sitting side by side with my lover on a thin pallet. We shivered on the cold cement floor, staring at the dancing shadows of the leaves through the skylight, waiting for something more sinister to show its face. I wondered how, after I had given up guns, decided that violence did not suit our revolution at all, how was it that I held a rifle across my lap?

Chicago, 1949

I looked around in a dither. We were in a room filled with human heads that came into focus one expressive, unique face at a time. As I craned my neck and stood on tiptoe, my eight-year-old eyes absorbed the variety like food for my expanding heart. How one set of eyes was totally round, the next person's eyes were modulated with almond shaped eyelids, the next had eyelids with an extra fold near the nose, like mine, yet not like mine, as the skin tones varied as much as the shapes. And the hair! I had never seen such amazing hair, now shaped into butterfly wings, now kinky short and held in place with a thin string of beads, now braided, spilling down an imaginary back. How had creation accomplished this? Who were all these folks and where did they live?

I wanted to know them all. How did they speak? What were they thinking about?

My mother and I, a modestly dressed white woman and a bright-eyed white tomboy, had just walked into "The Hall of the Races of Man" at the Field Museum of Natural History in Chicago in early 1949. This was one of two places my mother took me before we left Chicago—the other being the Brookfield Zoo. She wanted me to remember something of what the great city had to offer.

"Look, Judy," my mother said with great excitement. "Here are people who live everywhere on earth, all the people who live here on the planet. Isn't this amazing?"

Well, not quite everyone. But here in the huge museum room, over a hundred fascinating faces and a few bodies of individual women and men beamed into life, sculptures of human beings from across the globe, each unique in shape, color, expression, age, and emotion.

"Can you imagine making all these pieces?" My mother's black eyes were wide with wonder. The sculptures were splendid, even miraculous, and aroused in me a powerful desire to know all the beautiful faces on earth, to actually meet these shining people. A dark-skinned man standing with his bare feet apart, holding a bow, a brown-skinned woman intently scanning the horizon of a marketplace or a sheep herd or a fishing village, a light-skinned woman with her hair piled in mountain-shaped waves or hung long in braids. The sculptor's fingers had shaped their individuality into the forms, making normal the dignity of their lives, of their work. Lives and work so completely different from anyone we knew in Chicago.

We had made the trip to the museum in downtown Chicago on the El train from our homogenous neighborhood of recently arrived working-class people whose ancestors were all European, like my father, who had been born in Sweden. All I knew were men who worked in factories, wore long-sleeved clothing and heavy coats, in contrast to the dark-skinned man leaning on a spear or the intensely alert woman, a headband on her brow, naked to the waist, with a baby on her back.

This was a thrilling opening of my sense of the variety of human lives in place on the earth. I remember the statues as wax, though later learned that their maker, Malvina Hoffman, used bronze; nevertheless she captured a luminescent quality of skin tone that gave the people depicted an uncanny interior light. In my memory they glowed with a life fire from not only Hoffman's brilliant sculptor's eyes and hands, but also from the handwork of bees in delivering up the wax.

Trapped in a disturbed mind and a small life in a one-bedroom apartment with an angry husband, angry teen-age son and daughter, plus me, my mother's imagination loved to escape into the world at large, and seldom had the opportunity. Just to get us to the museum would have required herculean effort on her part. Exceedingly shy, more often deaf than not, preoccupied by interior messages and terrors, she made her own interpretations of reality. While to my father, the craftsman, it would have mattered a great deal whether the sculptures were bronze or wax, to my mother and me it did not; what mattered was the excitement they roused, the yearning to know and love. This newly awakened desire would last my entire life.

THE MOVE

Life in Chicago through the Great Depression and World War II had been hard on my parents and now, in 1949, we were leaving. My father had already gone ahead to a very different part of the country, far from blazing steel mills, noisy brick apartments and icicle winds off Lake Michigan. With my sister newly married and my brother gone to Kentucky, my parents and I were going to the high desert of New Mexico, a place of cowboys and cactus, fifteen hundred and sixty miles south and somewhat west of Chicago, a place called "Las Cruces," "The Crosses." Not remotely similar to our brick apartment in the towering and industrialized concrete world on the far south side of Chicago.

Growing up I would come to know the wind in two very different wildernesses. As a young child I knew the Chicago wind, the wind off Lake Michigan in winter. You have to turn your back on that bad breath because if you try to look that goddess wind in the face, she will crack your teeth and turn you to stone. She is the closest to Medusa, the gargoyle, I have ever experienced.

That wind, whose effects are so clear on the outside, turning umbrellas inside out and driving birds thousands of miles to the south, now comes inside your tender little body. The wind is slender like a narrow metal sword. The wind lunges. And that is deeply frightening. The organs, the blood, the bones shudder in their tiny permeable cells, totally vulnerable: "Oh please don't freeze my lungs." The winds of the Southwest, I would soon experience, were entirely different beings.

MAKING MEANING OF FAMILY LESSONS

As a child, my names fascinated me, and I wanted to know what they meant. Some people carve their names in the wooden school desks. I wrote mine over and over in pencil. Learning that Judith was a fierce warrior woman in the Bible was exciting and significant to me, as was my father's surname. Grahn means "evergreen tree" he would say, fingering his moustache. In former times the name had been longer, "Grahnquist" or "branch of the evergreen tree." Where did the quist go? "Some sergeant took it away a few generations ago," he responded, "some drillmaster in the Swedish army found it too hard to say and shortened it." My grandfather had been a member of the king's guard in Sweden, a point of family pride.

My love of names was connected to love of words, and their power to evoke emotion. My father loved poetry and gave me the great lifesaving gift by reciting it to me, showing me how to read, speak, and hear it. He had three or four small, very plain, bound books of poetry—with blue, black, or rose covers indistinguishable from hymnals—but inside the covers were workers' voices speaking to ordinary people, in poetry by Robert Service and Carl Sandburg. Sandburg had gone to the same school in Galesburg, Illinois, as my father, though he was twenty years older, and was also the son of Swedish immigrants, and also carried the middle name August. Like my father, he quit school after the eighth grade, and traveled "out west" before returning to Illinois. Sandburg was a social democrat, and his work rang with the real needs of working people who did not yet have union protections of any kind. He wrote of urban workers whose veins bled out and whose faces showed hunger and deprivation. He was optimistic about social change and understood the pride that workers have or want to have in their work and in the place of their being and in the product they are making, no matter what the conditions. He used a heroic, oracular voice in some of his work.

My father read Sandburg's poem "Chicago" to me, and as a child I too would read aloud in bold tones: "Hog Butcher for the World / Tool Maker, Stacker of Wheat / Player with Railroads and the Nation's Freight Handler / Stormy, husky, brawling…" And the accumulative consonants would snap against my palate, resonating the chambers of my ears with the sheer vibratory power of words. But what were "painted women under the gas lamps" and how were they related to "stormy," "brawling"…? Later, I would realize he meant storms of poverty and what they force people to sell.

I loved Sandburg's attitude, the forthright descriptions, the pride, the working-class content—people like my parents!—and the formality. I loved, too, the poet's taking on the voice of a whole city, a grand personification, a speaking in behalf of millions of people, and a rolling up of their singular occupations into metaphors of industry itself. How would a poet come to do that, I wondered? How much would he need to know, did a moment arrive when he knew he was capable of speaking for so much? The Chicago poem helped me appreciate the city long after we had left, the value of the lives of people hunched in thick coats against both wind and mean destiny. The poem helped me forgive the meanness of children of factory workers (of whom I was one), schoolyards carpeted with small sharp stones that bit into your knees and hands and made you spill out in red rivulets, the rackety thrill of riding the El, scratched by its inevitable eye-catching cinders, the foglike deathreek of the stockyards in summer, and the raw concrete of the grassless streets.

What the drastic factory conditions of the 1940s did to my sensitive parents, did to any of the "husky," "brawling" steelworkers and their dependent wives, became more clear to me over the course of my unfolding life and relationship with them.

That my father Elmer wanted out of that factory life was evident from his incessant gambling; craps and poker games ate his salary, and my sister once described him coming home with a teddy bear instead of money, proudly giving the carnival prize to my mother as though it were a greater achievement than any mere paycheck. As foolish as this makes him sound, however, he was also active during the twenties and thirties as a labor organizer. My brother once told me that he had been a leader of men then, that men had respected him and listened to him.

That he didn't do well in the life of upward scrambling was evident not only from his getting fired from his job in a Chicago steel factory, but also in the phrase he used so often, "gilly galloo bird," as something one did not want to be. "These gilly galloo birds in the government don't know how to run anything!" Slam the newspaper down. "A gilly galloo bird, you know what that is, don't you?" He would twinkle his eyes at me, while my mother stirred warningly in her chair. He would look at her, then finish, "A gilly galloo bird flies around the world so fast he flies backwards." This didn't make sense to me. When I was a teenager he would tell it the real way, when my mother was not around: "The gilly galloo bird was a bird who wanted to fly really, really fast. He flew so fast, he flew faster and faster, until he flew all the way around the world" (long pause, bright eyes fixed on mine) "and he flew up his own ass."

With that graphic image, I got it, we can get carried away by our own self-importance, but steady slow pace wins the race.

And this slow pace, the patience of the craftsman, was evident in my father's woodcarving. He taught me the art of woodcarving. Whenever he got fired, he would sit on the edge of his bed, his black hair combed slick with water, his cardboard box of tools pulled out. He would bring home found objects—bits of plastic and wire, string, wooden orange crates. He taught me which are the most appropriate kinds of wood: white and yellow pine for carving; oak, birch, and mahogany for furniture; redwood splinters too much to carve or sand. He showed me how to hold the little tools, the Exacto knives, the carefully sharpened pocket knife. How to aim away from your own flesh. How to make slow, small, shallow cuts, raising tiny curls of wood that fell to the floor in a light pile that scattered when you walked over it. Small cuts, found materials, the rest in one's mind: how to make something. From nothing. From an idea and a feeling.

He taught me how to make some of the tools from nothing as well, like the tiny hand drills with wooden handles. With these drills he made post holes through the base of the tiny cannons, so they swiveled in the portholes of the foot-long Spanish galleon we made together when I was fourteen. With the jig he made of flat wood and carefully spaced nails, I took dark waxed string and wove the lines, lines the real-life sailors of history would have clambered hand over foot to go from the bulwarks of the main deck to the tall masts with their spars, or "yards," to furl and unfurl the sails. Tying tiny knot after tiny knot I made the rope ladders, called "ratlins" (rat lines).

Later, my father read to me the ballads of Robert Service, and the chants of Vachel Lindsay, and I read them out loud by myself, absorbing the capacity of working-class voices to render ordinary people's experiences, even the harshest of them, into something dignified and artful. I also loved the beautiful poetic voice of Robinson Jeffers, who wrote with such bittersweet passion of the mysteries of life, both creature and human, in California.

But it was the English poets and a few Americans, chiefly Edgar Allen Poe, that I studied for form. John Donne touched my heart. I loved poets who wrote long dramas, and I memorized sections of Shakespeare, and all of Samuel Taylor Coleridge's *Rime of the Ancient Mariner*.

Elmer's last job in Chicago had been at Ingersoll's steel factory, where he had become shop steward by the time they laid him off in 1948—for drinking, my mother hinted. He then sat on the side of his bed for six months, whistling and holding his head in his hands, thinking about what to do.

He and my mother had raised three children in the one-bedroom apartment near Palmer Park on the far South Side. By 1948, the angry teenagers had matured. I was still at Pullman elementary on Forestville, near 111th Street. Recently his best friend, also named Elmer but called "Elm," had moved with his wife to the southernmost tip of New Mexico. Elm had written a letter optimistic about my father's chances of getting a white-collar job with the college there.

Two weeks before my sister's wedding, he took the train down to New Mexico, and a few weeks later, he sent for my mother and me to join him. While my father was gone and before my mother and I took the train to New Mexico, I was in the hospital with a severe bout of strep throat, and in my fever I dreamed of our trip. The dream consisted of two cowboy boots, one leaning upon the other. The boots were intriguing but they had a dreadful cast, that sense of green-yellow ugliness that sometimes seeps in with fever.

Elmer was optimistic when my mother and I arrived on the train and moved into the garage apartment with him. He dressed in his dapper Chicago clothes and went out to get a white-collar job. While waiting for his dream job to materialize, he returned to being a cook, the occupation he had before working in a factory. He also bought red-brown, ankle high Wellington boots, a light grey Stetson hat, and a string tie, determined to fit into the desert culture and its romantic vision of tough but tender-hearted cowboys, fiercely independent Apaches, powerful Spanish dons, renegade sheriffs, and the exalted outlaw Billy the Kid. The county itself was romantically named, Doña Ana, Lady Anne. Elmer August Aleric Grahn, fresh from the wilds of Chicago, grew a salt-and-pepper beard, trimmed into a triangle like the one Buffalo Bill had worn. My father became a character in his own Western drama, polishing the Wellingtons to an impossible gloss, posing with his chin in the air while my mother took a Kodak snap. Still, the white-collar job did not materialize.

The town we had moved to, Las Cruces, had sidewalks only in some parts of town. Our new neighborhood had both sidewalks and a cornfield plowed by a man and a mule. No longer sheltered and separated by bricks and concrete, we were now in contact with nature in entirely new ways.

MOUNTAIN DANCERS

Ping! Ping! Ping! I awakened in the middle of the night to fat drops of water falling on my face. The August monsoon had come. My mother was dashing between the living room and the kitchen. Rain drummed thunderously onto our flat tin roof. Streams of water were first dripping, then streaming vigorously through the edges of the white ceiling tiles, as she rushed to put pots, bowls and cups under the leaks; at leak thirteen she ran out of vessels and began with towels. She was exceedingly upset, while my father guffawed and pulled at his moustache and I laughed with delight.

How astounding, how unthinkable, that here in this desert place the rain could come right into our house, down onto me where I slept in the living room, that we could not keep it out, that it made the lovely *ping!* sound and then filled the vessels to overflowing in the long downpour. Mixed with adobe soil and the leaves of desert plants, the smell of the rain was delicious, musky and complete, like the most sumptuous dish cooked up by nature of a summer's night. I soon learned that you could smell the rain happening miles away, its sensual flower brought on the breath of the foreshadowing wind.

My father had rented a structure he later referred to contemptuously as a cinderblock shack—a garage apartment built with very little exact measurement, and as though out of odds and ends, by our landlord, Colonel Roberts. The badly hung windows did not keep out the weather and the walls didn't line up squarely at the corners, so on a bright day you could see light in the crack at the northeast corner. The adobe south wall, with its natural insulation, was defeated by the other three cinderblock walls and the roof, which was corrugated tin and full of nail holes. The square asbestos tile covering the ceiling was stained brown from leaks, the floor of the tiny kitchen sloped alarmingly, and there were doors only on the single closet and the minuscule bathroom. The whole thing was under three hundred and fifty square feet, an oven in the summer and a drafty freezer in the winter. No wonder my mother was unhappy at first, and as fall came on, my father was getting cynical and restless. The craftsman, the hunter, the gambler, the would-be white-collar worker, all thwarted. The man who had come so far to change his life (in the middle of it) was finding the landing hard.

I, on the other hand, had come awake; everything prior to New Mexico seemed like a long, alarming sleep.

In December of that first year, 1949, our neighbors took their daughter Kay and me to Tortugas Pueblo, near Mesilla, three miles down the road from Las Cruces. They pointed out various remarkable happenings that widened my nine-year-old hazel eyes. There were men in white shooting off rifles to scare away evil from a procession of villagers, while men in black with huge hats played remarkable, enthusiastic music on tambourines, guitars and drums as dancers stepped the Matachine dance in honor of *La Virgen*, who was present as a tiny girlchild in a white dress.

We stay until after dark. Many villagers have gone up the tortoise-shaped mountain, they have walked among the cactus and the sharp rocks barefoot. They come down at night, still barefoot, and their firelit torches make a stunning S shape as they wind down the trail. Kay's tall father bends to point out the fiery zigzag sign in the night, which leaves me thunderstruck. December air in the high desert is so clear the stars are nearby, sharp as ice crystals in the cold full sky. The sight of the S drawn in fire against the black of night has branded my memory with the vision of another entire way of being, with the earth, with other people, with one's body, and with divinity. There are values greater than comfort or discomfort, actions that look like pain and are not pain, paths one can pick through with bare toes and in the dark, bound together by a common, purposeful story. For the first time I have encountered the sacred, the embodied sacred, embraced by an entire community.

My nine-year-old Anglo Protestant mind is altered by this scene, jangled and rearranged. I go to school with some of these pilgrims; round-faced, black-haired José will sleep deeply with his head on his desk and the teacher will explain to us, "It's okay. He danced all night."

Not much my parents or the books at school tell me about the nature of reality will ring completely true against this new measure. Not much will live up to that breathtaking realization, that sheer experiential expression, sanctioned by the adults of Tortugas Pueblo, an entire community solidly behind the deeds: he walked barefoot up the mountain, he walked down in torchlight, he danced all night. And like me, he was nine years old.

To walk barefooted up and down a mountain on sharp rocks, among the spiny cactus plants—that I could not imagine doing. Later, I would learn that some pilgrims made the three-mile walk from the village to Tortugas Mountain on their knees. And, much later in life I would learn that Turtle Island is the earth itself for many indigenous peoples. While the offering on Tortugas is to La Virgen de Guadalupe, it is too close to December solstice not to be a renewal of earth and sun.

Instincts of a Hunter

What my father most wanted to do was go hunting. He would often talk about his boyhood memories of providing food for his mother's perpetually boiling kitchen pots, shooting squirrels and rabbits with his brother Bob in the fields of southern Illinois. He loved guns, loved them down to the screws that held the parts together, stock and magazine, barrel and sight.

He had managed to skip both of the world wars that had decimated and glorified his generation, yet he spoke about the wars, and war in general, as though it all belonged to him. His magazines were men's adventure magazines with stories about hunting and fishing, but also about prisoners on Guam, forced marches, sinking navy ships and men on fire in the sea, Dresden destroyed in a firestorm from Allied bombing. Ever the tomboy, I read the adventure stories as if the wars were mine too; and when he was at work I played with his rifles and pistols with fantasies of growing into a man, being a pirate, a lumberjack, a soldier. He would talk about his love of sailing ships, old galleons, two-masted schooners, the sloops and ketches; he taught me the names and the parts: decks and hatches, halyards and belaying pins, anchors and ratlins. We often spoke in the archaic language of this fantasy—and in my imagination, and perhaps his too, I was a son and we lived on the ocean, not in the high desert without so much as a scuzzy little lake.

But this camaraderie would come later, after he had fully landed his psyche in New Mexico and had recovered from his occupational shock of not being hired for a white-collar job. He became a fry cook, then a short order cook, then he worked his way up to restaurant jobs, then back down to short order cook, providing 1950s versions of fast food—cheeseburgers and fries, onion rings, pancakes with square pats of butter and watered down syrup served in little white jugs.

He worked for one family-owned place that failed after trying for six months to survive, and when the doors closed he, loyal and foolish, was owed six months' wages. From other jobs, he would come home "fired." For periods of time he would sit on the edge of his bed, whistling, drinking coffee, and reading or whittling or rubbing his rifle stock with a soft cloth. This is when I knew and loved him best.

As the daughter who, all by herself, lived with them, I had never felt shame about my parents. They were what is, they were unpredictable and interesting, and life was an adventure. In the fifth and sixth grades, though, my schoolyard friends were the poorest of the children. I did not think of myself as poor like them. Didn't our street have sidewalks? Charlotte lived in one room with a dirt floor with her Anglo mother, a migrant worker. I knew this because I had gone over to her house one day, had seen her deeply depressed mother sitting on a bare mattress. Charlotte's elbows were dirty and as rough as the "poor sores" caused by malnutrition on her legs.

Thinking Charlotte looked hungry, I had brought her home for lunch, following which my mother said, "You are never to bring her here again." This shocked me, though I continued to hang out with her in the schoolyard, along with Julia, whose clothes had holes and who was a Tortugas Indian like José, who had by now dropped out of school. I had not yet consciously noticed that my own clothes had holes where the safety pins split the fabric. Wild-looking Louise seemed never to have had her hair combed. She stood in line at the little burger shack a block from school, treasuring the sheen of grease across the bun of the hot hamburger, and the vinegar pickle smell. Standing in this line was the special privilege of working-class kids whose moms did not have the inclination or time to make them lunch. Every once in a while when my mom had a quarter, that was me too in the line, proudly eating the delicious greasy meat sandwich.

One day on the playground Charlotte and Louise were telling a funny story to amuse me—it was about a cook who had worked at a burger shack and had been fired. "He was so drunk," they laughed, "so drunk he sent a hamburger

order out and there was no meat!" They roared. I laughed too. They bent over. Charlotte's stringy blonde hair flew around.

"No meat on the bun!" She laughed. She whirled to one side, still bent over.

"Elmer was so drunk," they repeated, ready to squeeze out another round of laughter, and then they looked at my face, which must have collapsed. They stopped talking and moving around.

"That's your father, isn't it?" Charlotte said after a pause. I looked at the ground. I had laughed at my own father, they had laughed at my own father.

"We didn't know that was your father," Charlotte said, by way of apology. I could tell she really felt bad. But the shame had come in, sharp as Chicago wind.

My parents, like me, were having a hard time socially. My mother, at age forty-six, had from pressing necessity gotten her first job, working for a photographer, touching up photos, putting a bit of blush on the cheeks of images of high school graduates and brides. This job was a wonderful turn in her life. She was finding the shops around town, which had a fine Main Street, with the Main Café and sweet little clothing shops, a bakery. On her lunch hour she sometimes went from the photographer's shop to Main Street on errands, overcoming her extreme shyness. One day she came home crying.

I was very distressed—what could be the matter? "It's Linda," she said. I remembered who that was, the mother in the family we had visited during our first days of arrival in Las Cruces. The sons were excited, took me to their bedroom to show me the skull they had found in a cave at the foot of the Organ Mountains, a shocking thing to see perched on their bookcase. They exuberantly fed us enchiladas, which were so strange we couldn't eat them, though the family pointed out in delight that even their cat liked enchiladas. "Linda and I were friends in Chicago, and we were always going to be best friends in New Mexico. But today when she saw me on the street, she crossed to the other side so she wouldn't have to say hello."

I had no idea why Linda would have ignored my mother, I only knew my mother was devastated. Her sorrow, and their isolation, were certainly evident. At age ten I began to notice that the police regularly brought Elmer home, and I thought how nice that they must be such good friends to give him a ride like that, although he always called them po'*lice*, not poleece. It did not occur to me that he had spent the night, or longer, in jail. He fell asleep in his chair at night, cigarette in one hand, beer can in the other. He fell asleep in the doorway leading to the kitchen, which was enraging, as I could not get by him to get to the bathroom. He fell asleep outside against the front door in the middle of the night, after loudly singing, "I'll Take You Home Again, Kathleen." His behavior was obviously deeply disturbing, frightening, to Vera, and so it became that for me as well. I began to feel paralyzed in the trap of their rising tension.

One day, that second summer, my mother said, "Help me gather up all the knives." What? She was putting all the sharp instruments in the house into a cardboard box. Why? "Your father is talking about committing suicide. You and I are going to stay at Miss Welsheimer's while she is on vacation." So for two weeks my mother and I moved next door into the basement apartment with the floral upholstery and the huge furry cat, Max, Miss Welsheimer's twenty-four pound Manx. My child's mind could not stay focused on my father's potential for suicide, and evidently neither could his, as shortly after something settled inside my father. He seemed to find himself in the new setting, and some of his anger dropped away.

He landed a job at the Main Café, the big tourist restaurant in the middle of town. He was promoted to "chef," and he wore a tall white cotton hat to prove it. He even gave me advice related to the occupation, "Never work on a concrete floor, it will ruin your feet. Get one of those wooden pallets and stand on that." That's what he did, at work, walked back and forth all day on a three-yard long, double layered pinewood pallet stained matte brown and scuffed black from his greasy footprints as he bent over the six-burner, black cast-iron gas stove or the grease-shimmering flat steel grill or the scarred maple-colored wooden cutting table. He began to talk enthusiastically about his occupation, taking the worker's pride in the details and exactitude of what he did. Descriptions of number ten tins of tomatoes and the precise dimensions of standing rib roasts began to populate his evening narratives. He was ordering supplies for the whole restaurant. He was doing the week's menus.

This job became the occasion for the single time that our little family "ate out" at a restaurant (or anywhere). One evening, my mother and I walked down to the Main Café. We walked past the curio counter at the front, past the garish bronze and silver cash register atop the glass case with the bronze-cast horses and the silver spurs, the Indian dolls and turquoise rings, past the postcard display rack that spun on demand, to the rear of the restaurant, the very last booth next to the kitchen door. We sat in the dark wooden booth facing each other in our modest clothing, heads down, not looking at the other customers. After a while my father came out of the kitchen in his white hat, the middle of his body wrapped in an apron besmirched with the detritus of cooking. He gave us menus and told us we could have anything we wanted. His eyes were round and bright and his head looked small under the hat. His gestures were thickly intoxicated.

My mother had become withdrawn, and could barely speak, her lips pale.

"What would you like, Vera?" He had slung a dishtowel over his arm like a European waiter. His wife lowered her head and mumbled.

"What was that?"

She cleared her throat and read directly from the menu. "I'll have fried chicken with green beans and mashed potatoes, and a wedge of iceberg lettuce."

"Judy," he said, "lookee here on the menu. We have frogs' legs with onion rings." His round brown eyes twinkled at me. I jumped at the chance to please him, and my father was delighted. An adventurous child! He praised my choice. A hunter's daughter! He himself served the heavy white restaurant plates to us, with obvious pride, a steep contrast to my mother's equally powerful shame—about what, I wondered. That he didn't sit with us? That he was the cook? That he was drunk? That he brought the plates himself and so the waitress did not serve us? Or was it herself she thought about, her faded dress? Having to walk past all the other people to the very back booth? Whatever her reasons, we ate in silence, and the adventure was never repeated.

Although he drank all day at work, and then again all evening 'til he fell asleep in his chair, Elmer still had excellent instincts. One day he told Vera he had quit his fine job from the Main Café. My mother's face showed heavy disappointment.

"Why?" she demanded, her voice in the whine zone.

"I didn't like the working conditions," he said. "The oven is bad. I told them over and over, 'get it fixed,' but they wouldn't do anything about it." She persisted in questioning him.

"I didn't like how they treated me." Still my mother was puzzled, nervously disturbed. His best job since we had arrived. Security in paying the rent.

A week afterwards the decrepit oven in the Main Café kitchen blew up. The new cook was thrown through the wall and killed. My parents were horrified and upset for several weeks.

"I knew that was going to happen," my father said. "Poor bastard." He pulled his moustache with the sorrowful gratitude of the living.

Norman

The wind in New Mexico is an entirely different beast than the icicle bayonet of Chicago winter. The winds that blow through the warm Mesilla Valley at that juncture of the Rio Grande River and the tall spine of craggy mountains running for a hundred and fifty miles north and south, those spring winds begin in the plains of western New Mexico, near Lordsburg. The winds spin the dust around and around on those plains other times of the year and then, sometimes as early as February, they whirl up off the earth, join with the wind rivers in the sky and head east, pouring down the lava mesa into the river valley floodplain of the Rio Grande. These winds are fat, swelling themselves with dust particles. From flat ground they rise up out of the western mesa, spreading over the horizon and then filling the sky overhead, earth-lungs blowing enormous bags of wind-borne particles whose minuscule, sharp glass edges are sanding the world clean.

I wasn't afraid of this wind, though it was magnificent in its capacity to hold us indoors and stop traffic in all directions. I could imitate quite well its song, as it howled around our front door, blasting shrapnel up our steps and through the cracks in our walls, especially through our badly caulked window frames. Twice, it came inside and blew the flames away from the little ceramic gas heater as my mother exclaimed in alarm at the dangerous smell and my father rushed to turn off the gas. Then he pulled his moustache and looked at me with his shiny eyes. He reassured me that our cinderblock shack was so badly built and so well ventilated we would never be in danger of gas poisoning.

The first couple of years I would go outside to bend against the phenomenal force of the storm just to see the wonder of such a high wall of traveling dust, blotting the sun to a vague round glow and painting the sky brown. In some years, the storms go continuously for days, the highways are closed, and drivers report their windshields pitted. In those early dry years, I howled with the wind, feeling it all as both adventuresome and interminable.

All the creatures of the high desert caught my attention, the tarantula in the swimming pool, the shiny, six-inch centipede who climbed up the drain into our bathtub, the lovely praying mantises and singing cicadas with their filmy green wings, the endless supply of juniper-colored bright-eyed grasshoppers, and an array of horses, runaway cows, donkeys, burros, roadrunners, hawks, songbirds, vultures, pigeons, mountain lions, bobcats, antelope, toads, crayfish, snakes, lizards, scorpions, beetles, fire ants, and so on, that clomped and crawled and brayed and stung and warbled and hissed and raised dust in the distance, through the precincts we also inhabited.

Except for certain large insects of which all the women in the Roberts' Apartments were deathly afraid—Miss Welsheimer having famously sat up all night in a chair when one mother of all centipedes entered her domain—I took it for granted that we all co-existed together. Then, one day all of us in the fourth grade class, which was made up predominately of kids from Tortugas pueblo and Chicanos, with about twenty-five percent of us Anglos, crowded to the window, watching as our principal, a thin, determined, white man, bent in his pinstripe suit beating, beating, at something on the ground. What ghastly being threatened us so? Finally he held up his triumph over evil, as a palpable communal gasp ran through us. A slender, foot-long green garter snake dangled from his cane, its delicate innards vulnerably showing. A deathly silence permeated us. Grim-faced, we all returned to our lines of seats, turned our less-innocent faces to the front of the room. Grief saturated the air.

Thus we lived in a southwestern state during its drought years, and I learned to love its seamless waves of mountains, deserts and river valley. Malvina's bronze sculptures continued to speak to me throughout my childhood as I asked for dolls that included a Pueblo Indian wrapped in a plaid blanket, and Jackie Robinson, the first black baseball player, as well as two blue-eyed dolls. Rubber, flexible Bozo the clown was pals with Injun Joe, a puppet I made myself with long black hair and a red outfit. When I was eleven I sat at the kitchen table laboriously making four-inch high "early humans" from clay. They were busts of Cro Magnon, Neanderthal, and Java Man, from a picture in one of our school texts. I wanted to ask, "What was life like for you?" and "Did you really have such scraggeldy hair?"

But to know my own family, my real-life aunts and uncles and cousins of Illinois—the connections were slipping away in distance and silence. At first it seemed the bonds with the big Chicago family would continue after a box arrived with second-hand clothing, and I joyfully selected a jacket that had belonged to my cousin Rollo or maybe Steve. It was reversible, khaki on one side, green corduroy on the other. Nice deep pockets for your hands on a chilly day. At nine, with the sleeves rolled up, I wore it as a green coat; at ten it was an adventurous-looking khaki jacket; at eleven the sleeves were halfway up my arm, and the green corduroy was on the outside again because it hid the dirt and raggediness better. At twelve my parents bought me a new coat, thin red corduroy, then the next year a splendid leather jacket with fringe, really fine-looking.

Some time during those disconnecting years, my brother came for a three-day visit and left an Army-issue sweater—a thick-knit coarse-ribbed, olive pullover with a collar and two buttons. I adopted the sweater, naming it "Norman" and playing with it—not so much wearing it, just pretending that I could—or playing with it as though it was a character in the fantasy stories I made up all day whenever I was alone, which was almost every day. Norman, like the Normans my father said had come from Normandy on the coast of France in 1066 and invaded England, "your mother's people" my dad said; Normans, short for "Norsemen," people of medieval Scandinavia, so my father's people too.

I leaped around the living room with my self-made wooden sword and pretend shield, quoting Shakespeare or inventing a story of my own. The Norman sweater, laid upon the chair, became a stand-in for my entire lost family and all their prior generations, in the form of a thin olive green character with hollow sleeves and a very flat chest, presumably giving me advice through the dramas of my imaginary life. I loved Norman, but of my extended family, and even of my brother and sister, I knew almost nothing. I was about to get another jolt of separation.

A TERMINAL VISIT TO CHICAGO

My family had been living in Las Cruces for four years, and I was twelve, when my mother took me back to Chicago to visit the extended family we had left behind. We rode on the train for three days, enjoying the Midwestern landscapes and the starched white tablecloths in the dining car. In Chicago I spent a wonderful, warm afternoon sitting on a porch talking with several cousins on my father's side, of whom I was the youngest, and for a few hours had a sense of belonging somewhere outside my parents' narrow purview, of being part of a family. We visited my sister, who was nervous, as she always was around my mother, who later confessed to me that she and my father had been "too strict" with her. (I can only imagine.)

Then, just before we left Chicago, one of my uncles loaded my mom and me into the back seat of his car, "to show you something you need to see." The back seats of cars in that era were cloth-covered and shaped like couches, offering a lulling sense of security, a sense of the car as a little traveling house. We drove through neighborhoods of comfortable single-family brick homes like my uncle's, and neighborhoods of four-story brick apartments like the one in which I had lived in my early life. Perhaps he was going to show us a new park. I peered with curious child eyes, following my uncle's sweeping arm, the thick cigar in his fingers trailing smoke in its own language.

"Look." He had stopped the car, he was out of the front seat, his face was triumphant. We were staring at a long, low building, wood panels painted forest green, lots of paned windows, a brown sloping roof. The building was appealing, like a giant version of the little green building where we put our ice skates on in Palmer Park, when I was six. But this building's roof had a gaping, charred hole, and windows were broken. Using crude vernacular my uncle explained that African-American families had moved in to "our" neighborhood. A single engine piper cub had flown over at night, and dropped a bomb.

"That got 'em out," he exulted. At first I was just stunned, trying to understand. I imagined little children's faces in the windows. Fire raining down in the middle of the night, people in pajamas running. I turned to my mother for guidance. Her usual shyness had become near-paralysis. She was huddled in the far corner, white as new snow, her face turned away, her demeanor terrified, silent as the deep stillness of endless space. A sense of appalled rage settled on me like a mantle of adulthood. As we drove away, my uncle continued his braggadocio, ignoring our muteness. I felt protective toward my childlike mother. Toward my uncle I felt only rage, and toward the entire family I now felt wariness, fear. In that moment doors in my heart snapped shut.

A few days later, as my mother and I traveled home to Las Cruces, we changed from a train to a bus in Albuquerque, two hundred miles north of Las Cruces. A potbellied man in the bus station, sitting on a bench opposite ours and smoking a cigar, kept pointing to his penis bulging in his pants and gesturing for me to go outside with him. Oddly, he reminded me of my uncle, and my rage rose high in my throat. I formulated a strategy to go outside with him and punch him on the chin for being so disgusting and disreputable. Before I could carry out my delusional plan, my mother noticed and moved us to a safer place.

It would be another thirty-five years before my subconscious would surface with a memory of my uncle molesting me when I was six or so. But what if things had been different? What if he had not molested me, what if he had been intelligent, caring, and respectful, had reached out to my lonely self, had seen me for myself in some way? Would I have imprinted that horrendous white supremacist bombing in the same way? Surely something always dies inside children who witness such violent hatred.

Much later, I saw my uncle's abuse as a grotesque, nonverbal gift, a red flag of warning that hastened my understanding of the problems, racism among them, within my family, and allowed me to realize the use of racism as a kind of emotional construct within my family. A pathology of violent separation from "others." Without consciousness, I had eaten and breathed the poison of this pathology, and have since spent my life locating it in myself and doing whatever possible to comprehend it, neutralize it, transform it in ways that seem beneficial to me, to the people I have loved, and to the people I would love to know.

JOY OF STORIES

My world was nearly entirely my parents, my father in his cups, my mother mostly distracted by her disturbing inner voices. Someone asked me once if I had gotten enough to eat, and I said, "Oh of course," remembering steaks on Saturday nights and white beans or tuna fish on toast on Fridays. But now I am not so sure—I ate a great deal of notebook paper, rubber erasers, raw macaroni, Wonder Bread with mayonnaise, or margarine and sugar. I craved fresh fruit and butter, settled for orange popsicles and all-day suckers of caramelized sugar. Years of horrific nosebleeds were finally solved by Dr. Jones, "the poor people's doctor," advising the addition of raw cabbage to my diet, as my mother's industrial-age idea of vegetables was cans of overcooked green beans. I was sick a great many times—all the usual childhood illnesses, plus multiple episodes of strep throat, sometimes requiring hospitalization. Every kind of flu and bronchial thing; threat of rabies, requiring fourteen burning shots. Ringworm from some puppies, and all manner of rashes. Heat stroke that keeled me over on the playgrounds. Allergies, miserable eye, nose, and throat torments. I had a mild form of polio during the 1952 epidemic, then a wasting thyroid condition, a badly injured knee that went untreated. I began to languish with a cough and tested positive for tuberculosis at sixteen, scaring everyone. I was deeply afraid that I would not live to grow up. But I never, ever, thought of myself as a weak or sickly person, rather one who overcame challenges that made her extraordinarily strong.

The self-discipline that came from living in such close quarters was a tangible asset to my ability to focus. I was up before seven with my bedding folded and stored in the living room closet, where, that first year, a white cylindrical washing machine with fascinating finger-threatening rollers was stored when it wasn't holding court in the kitchen once a week. One day it just quit working, and from then on, my mother and I washed all the laundry in the bathtub with a corrugated washboard. I remember how heavy the basket filled with wet khaki shirts and pants was, and how proud I was that I could balance it down the stairs and out to the clothesline. My mother and I also carried the groceries a mile home, or I put sacks in the basket of my bicycle. I could calculate to the penny what the checker was going to charge me. I was genuinely useful to my family, and thought of myself as having enormous hands, as being extraordinarily strong, fast, and agile.

I could mount the seven-foot adobe wall linking the Roberts' apartments in one grand stride, from a running start past the round "Indian bread oven," bare foot raised to the plastered white wall, and then up to the top in a whirl. There I surveyed my world like Gene Autry on the tallest of palominos. I longed to be a pole-vaulter, rode my bicycle everywhere around town and out of it, my rifle across the handlebars, and went to the rifle range near Tortugas Mountain where my father had taught me to kneel in the sand and shoot flashlight batteries off the fence posts.

He had given me the .22 long rifle for my twelfth birthday, along with shooting and rifle care lessons from him. "Now you can always take care of yourself," he said. "You can protect yourself, and when you run out of food, you can go hunting." He also said, "Never point the rifle at anything you do not intend to kill." And so, though my life would take a totally different course than anything this rifle implied, I did learn to take dead aim, that valuable gift of hunters.

I read voraciously from the library, developed a habit of writing, and, equally importantly, a posture of thinking of myself as a writer, a teller of stories. For years I played storytelling with the marvelous toy my father brought home for me when I was ten. It was the design of a dollhouse, with walls open in the back so you could move figures in and out. But instead of a dollhouse, it was an entire block of businesses in a western town. The main piece was metal with details painted on the interior walls, and about twenty plastic people, and plastic furniture inside. Two stories high, the little town featured a jail, a general store, a bar, and best of all, a newspaper office. The editor was molded to sit in his chair with one leg up on the desk. Whenever I took him out of his office he had to hop on one leg, a feature that did not stop me from making him the central figure in most of the stories—a fearless teller of truth and fighter for justice. I painted his pants and shirt in two shades of blue.

There were other characters, lots of cowboys, a sheriff, and an upright older man who might have been a judge. There were only two women. I embellished the furnishings, making tiny sacks of flour for the general store, a gallows, and a crudely constructed train engine with one open car for hauling stuff (more tiny sacks of grain) in and out of town. In the editor's office, I added a minuscule pot that was supposed to be the spittoon for the bar. Instead, I glued it to the floor next to the editor's desk. I placed the pot on its side, and used black paint to make it appear that a puddle of ink had spilled out on the floor; a bit of newspaper was caught in the ink. The scene looked as though the editor had carelessly knocked the ink pot off the desk as he concentrated on more important things like writing a hot story, or maybe he'd had a vehement argument since he was a controversial town figure, and someone else had torn up his office. Not everyone agreed with him. Truth-telling would always be accompanied by tumult. Even at this young age I knew myself as a writer and that writing is about justice. Writers, no matter what their station in life, had stature, they had a voice. People listened. Writers had the power of persuasion. This was a gift, a responsibility, and a danger.

My Father Talked to the Air

My parents shaped me in generally positive ways, even with their disabilities. My father's drunken ramblings of an evening, as I sat a few feet away, taught me exquisite focus. I could read a book through any interruption or disaster; I acquired a laser concentration that was nearly unbreakable. My mother's shyness and deafness gave me immeasurable patience, and a penetrating, amplified voice. She would attend my performances at school, coming in late with one hand clutching the front of her light brown coat, sitting in the last seat of the last row, near the door, so she could run out should she become overwhelmed. And I, on the stage, made sure she heard every word, every line, every nuance. Later, this would give me a huge advantage as a performance poet in venues that did not have microphones or where I was competing with fire engines, crying babies, jukeboxes, drums, and barking dogs. People might or might not agree with me, but they heard me.

I was (and remain) an open vessel for everyone else's emotions and energies, which floated, or zoomed, or roamed around through my body willy nilly, leaving me in hyper-excited or debilitated states. I was often swept by ecstasy, love of life, and would sob with appreciation over the sight of wild creatures or the night sky. I could not control my own excitements, and so have always dropped stuff all over the kitchen, cut myself paring vegetables, mindlessly put my toothbrush in the refrigerator, and so on. If I cracked a raw egg I could never predict where it might land—on the counter beside the cup, or even dripping like mucousy sunshine onto the floor. Becoming grounded became a lifetime occupation. As a teenager I craved playing sports. I practiced baseball, softball, basketball, and tennis, all by myself, and had pretty good skills. However, on the basketball court at school, I was an overzealous disaster, lunging, driving forward with rubbery legs, my mind so far out in front that my body could not keep up and inevitably went sprawling, sometimes right into other players. My knees were permanently strawberried from floor burns, and the teams on both sides wanted me off the courts. Playing baseball, although I was a pretty steady catcher, I also ran into people, slid past the base without touching it, and slung the ball at some distant star instead of to the players. As bad as this was, swimming was even more difficult; with great desire and certainty I would plunge into the water only to panic and thrash all the way to the bottom. Again, again, again. I was being jerked this way and that in my own rampant energies. This struck me as alternately enraging and hilariously funny.

It seems necessary to explain that there was nothing tragic going on here. My parents were coping with their challenges—schizophrenia, alcoholism, unemployability, oversensitivity—by simplifying their lives, and mostly it worked. If they'd had more of a community or understanding family around them to help, they would have been okay; strange, eccentric, but okay. Ultimately I would come to see them as dignified and successful, once we had sorted through their prejudices and mine. I would have wished them better friendships so they weren't so lonely at times. I would have wished my mother an end to her bottomless terrors and frustrations with herself. I would have wished my child self a real mother, or at least an aunt, who could have protected me, mirrored reality for me, and showed me how to button my clothes and stick up for myself.

At the same time, much of the town was mine to explore however I wished, and because of the tension in the house when my father was home drunk, my mother would let me stay outside at night until eleven or so, long before I was a teenager. There was so little crime in general, we never locked our door. Nobody did. And so the whole world was, somehow, mine. In these warm summer nighttimes, I sat on a tall adobe wall where the croaking reptiles, the abundance of stars, and the shadowy trees were my companions and my confidants. My heart swelled with love for them, and, like my mother, I felt completely understood by beings far outside the ordinary land of human beings. I say "like my mother" a little cautiously, as the reference is to a day that I recall when I was seventeen, when mom came home and announced that she was finally completely understood by someone, and this was beyond mystifying. The someone was a younger woman, a stranger, who passed her in the crosswalk, going across the street. "She looked into my eyes as we passed," my mother said confidently, "and at that moment I realized she knew exactly who I am. She understood me. I have never felt that before."

Not educated enough to recognize receiving silent messages from strangers as a classic symptom of schizophrenia, I felt disappointed when she said this, partly because she had been going through episodes the last couple of years in which she did not seem to recognize either me or my father. And partly because I wanted to be the one who understood her better than anyone, not some stranger.

A being outside the ordinary lived with us, though no one told me its nature so I misunderstood. My father began talking out loud the moment we left him alone in a room, and since there were no doors, we could clearly hear that he was mumbling, apparently to himself. My mother's extreme paranoia about him, which for a couple of years led me to believe he was secretly plotting our murder, misled me about what he was doing. Nevertheless I too talked out loud to myself, or to the air, and to the stars, the trees, various creatures. I talked to myself in the house, riding my bicycle, and walking down the street. Clarity seemed to thrive on this, and a powerful sense of never being alone. The air appeared to give me answers, and a dialogue emerged, in which I remain engaged.

Decades after I left his home, a kind traveler would explain my father to me. She had lived in Sweden about fifty miles from where he was born, in Motala. "The people there are known to be eccentric," she said. "They are woodcarvers, and they inherit a spirit who lives with them all their lives." When I wrote to my father about this, he denied none of it. I also have learned that some Scandinavian people access spirit by talking to the air. And through my father, I am one of them.

My mother was completely encouraging of my writing, and any other ambition, saying "I believe you could do anything you set your mind to." She had visions, she said emphatically, repeated, vivid visions, in which she saw me on stage in front of audiences of people. "How many?" I asked. She always answered the same way: "Lots of people, lots and lots of people."

So there you have it. My parents were not neurotic, not even a little. Some people might say they were both crazy. To me they were completely themselves, honest and true as they could be (which wasn't always all that much). My father talked to a spirit who lives in the air; the walls and total strangers sent messages to my mother. The two of them escaped their families' judgments and the big overpowering city and went to live by themselves where they could just be. Their whimsical humor and love of knowledge emerged unscathed. Their erratic violences settled down in the calmer atmosphere of New Mexico. And I got to live with them. I wasn't taken away, sent to an orphanage or boarding school, or to some cruel religious aunt who would chastise me for my kooky ways. I got to be, free and clear, their daughter.

EXCLUSIONS AND SECRETS

My fantasy of getting to know all the marvelous kinds of people in the world was not coming true. The Chicanas I went to school with, though friendly enough, would not connect with me outside the classroom or gym (where I had already shamed myself as an athlete). Later I would understand the historic power dynamics in this highly diverse state, the colonial separations and injustices. I only knew that exclusion ruled, and it ruled every part of the town. The middle-class family across the street from our cinderblock apartment would not let any of their children play with me. The mother of my working-class friend Marilyn wouldn't allow her anywhere near me after I spit a mouthful of water at her in play. The working-class kids who lived in a set of apartments around the corner from us on Picacho Avenue were neglected and mean. The Spanish family (as differentiated from Chicanos, who lived on the east side of town) would not let their boys play with any of us Anglo kids, and had tied a distressed and irritating dog in their yard who barked day and night.

I was too tough for the girls, and too tender for the boys. I was having real difficulty making friends and knowing my "place" in the scheme of things. After I became an adolescent, the hot spring wind infuriated and insulted me, whirling my skirt up around my thighs. I couldn't bear to turn my back on that wind. I did not want to be shoved, and would turn on the street and scream at the howling maelstrom as if it were a rude but conscious beast, as if it were a god. I would address it as God. As if I were in the dry mouth of the living whale or dragon, protesting the swallowing. Of what in me? My personhood, my childhood autonomy. My genderlessness. The social necessity and vulnerability of wearing a skirt when all I wanted, every day, was to wear pants. The dialogue was perfect, the earth's breath howling all around me, moving me to howl in response. Scouring my ears, eyes, and mouth with sand in answer to my frantic question: "Why?!! Are you pushing me around!! Like this!"

As puberty set in, I was beginning to manifest a transgender sensibility and a lesbian sexual orientation that went beyond being a tomboy. I dreaded having to become a woman. I prayed to be turned into a boy, although nature turned out to be right, I really do swing between the genders in some third place that suits my sensibility quite well. At that vulnerable age though, I could have used some guidance, role models of any kind, but that was impossible in 1953. As I was about to find out, however, even something as simple as learning someone was a lesbian could be a liability to all concerned.

A Room of My Own, Sort Of

My parents, who as I've said had difficulty providing material comforts and frequently seemed to forget that I had a body, had been promising to provide me with an actual bed for months. The rose couch on which I slept in the living room had been given to them at their marriage thirty years before, and it was now six inches shorter than I was. Even they noticed this wretched old couch was affecting my posture.

When our neighbor Jewel offered her spare bedroom to me, the invitation came as a wondrous surprise. I was to move into an area of phenomenal luxury: my own private room, the porch bedroom at Jewel's house. In exchange, the adults informed me, I was expected to be the gardener of the yard around her place.

Jewel, the widow of a cotton farmer from West Texas who now taught junior high school English, had raised her three children in this three-bedroom house. From the time we had moved to New Mexico, Jewel and her family had been my refuge. The son would later get me my first job, making milkshakes, when I was seventeen, ensuring I could go to the local college. Older sister Leela sang marvelously to me as I sat in her kitchen window every morning the year I was nine, and as her babies arrived, nearly one a year, she turned her young boys over to my care for hours on end. Even when she and her husband moved seventy miles east to Alamogordo, various members of the family would drive me over the Organ Mountains and across the Sonora desert to visit for a week at a time.

So at the opening of the summer of this year, Darnelle, Jewel's youngest daughter, who was eighteen, had driven me back from Methodist summer camp near Alamogordo on a long Sunday night. I still recall the mystery of that June night ride between the camp and Las Cruces, crossing the flat sagebrush-smelling land, tall jackrabbits slowly turning their backs away from our deadly headlights as we tore through the tunnel carved by their piercing yellow glow.

Trembling with the intimacy of the experience, I crouched knee to knee in the backseat of Darnelle's car with two other girls my age who had been at camp with me. We were telling stories, secret, never-before shared stories, especially about our fathers. I told about my father's drunkenness, his inability to bring money home. (I did not tell, since I wasn't aware of it, of our family's excruciating isolation, or anything about my mother. We did not speak of our mothers.) Annie Ruth told a worse story, about her father breaking horses by beating them with chains. We felt united in our mutual horror at this bad behavior.

Alone in the front seat, Darnelle covered our whispers with clear Country Western, song after poignant song delivered in her generous, bold voice. Though I loved the entire family, I felt especially privileged to be in Darnelle's company. A redhead with freckles, she was athletic and interesting and going to college. She had always kept a distance from me, but this nighttime over the desert car ride told me that she would be someone I could confide in, a longed-for older sister type. A guide of some sort through the increasing mysteries of adult life.

Jewel's narrow porch bedroom became a place of unbordered erotic and autonomous dreams, as it held my first real bed, my own private lamp, and a little blue record player my father got me at the end of July when I turned thirteen. My first album, Harry Belafonte singing folk songs, was joyfully played over and over, especially a song called "The Fox," about an independent character who lived in the wild and went on midnight runs under the stars to the "town-o."

At night my pulse quickened as I watched the blood red moon out of my new room's window, repeating lines of English romantic poetry about a highwayman in black who was riding riding riding to the door of a lass with a white bosom, "Bess, the landlord's daughter," whose bosom had leapt into my imagination as the most luscious of all possible fruits. My idea of what to do with billowy bosoms was to attempt to lay my head on them. I did not yet dare to notice that it was the highwayman, and not buxom Bess, whose image caught in the mirror of my identification.

In exchange for all this richness, all I had to do was "be the gardener" and "keep the yard." That sounded easy enough, though I had witnessed none of this activity in my parents' rented lives. Jewel provided me with some tools and general instructions. Unable to imagine what gardeners, exactly, *do*, I stood for long minutes with indecisive shears drooping at my side, ready to weep over the very thorny bristles and runaway dandelions that the family expected me to decimate. I had no idea which were the "plants" and which the "weeds," as I loved them all equally. Everything in the yards in Las Cruces had thorns—the delicate mimosa tree and the rose bush no less than the tall thistles and spreading goathead grasses that filled my bicycle tires with hundreds of stop signals. In this land of sparsity, the lovely, spikey yellow flowers of the dandelions were surely a beautiful lushness, surely as desirable as the thin wisps of bluegrass that struggled so incompetently against the dryness of the light brown adobe dust. With growing consternation I realized that gardening was escaping me, as was keeping up my end of the bargain that had been struck between the families.

But now with summer vacation Darnelle was home from her first year at college, and had brought a sturdy-looking friend with her. A slow July pace had settled in. Flies buzzed around slowly, precursors of a polio epidemic that would hit in September. Her being home gave me hope that I still could hold up my end. I remembered how friendly Darnelle had been, driving the car that night—competent, present, protective, accessible. Next time I saw her I would ask her how to keep the yard, how to have the proper discernment, and how to dispose of the bodies of the unwanted weeds.

Late one hot Saturday afternoon, in keeping with the intense stillness of the air, I had closed the screen door silently and then, instead of going into my narrow bedroom sanctuary to listen fifty more times to Harry Belafonte, I unexpectedly turned right and padded on my bare feet across the kitchen linoleum. I was six steps into the living room before even seeing them. They were lying together on the couch.

They had half risen up, their trunks twisted like young athletic trees that had grown together, and as if only one face, their two faces stared at me with identical blankness. Darnelle's friend, stockier, had been on her back, and Darnelle had been lying on her side and half on top of her. They were wearing white blouses and shorts like the phys ed teachers they intended to become. I was struck by how clean they looked, and how frozen in place—an ice sculpture puts out more resonance than they did.

No one was breathing. Our stillness created negative space, which drew our attention into a monstrous force field.

They both seemed to be in a deep meditative state, long rays emanating from their intertwined lower bodies to the iris of my eye, along which their feelings ran back and forth in miniature, like panicky young horses. We held ourselves within the glacier painting while my girl-self, suddenly overly important, figured out what to do with the silence in the room.

The mortification, I saw, was all mine. I had made them insane and paralytic. A thirteen year old had frozen the two eighteen year olds, as a black widow spider might have frozen me but with mysterious potential I had not known I owned. The two did not take charge. No one spoke, the need for air had vanished. We might have hung in space this way until nightfall if some highwayman inside had not ridden me to action. Placing one foot in back and then another, I attempted to erase the scene for their sakes, and in slow motion. Like a movie running in reverse I unraveled the story for them, going backwards into nothingness with intent to leave no shadow of imprint on the floor of their fears. Screen door did not creak or slam, floorboards did not interact with each other. No one's breath got hot or sweated, no voice croaked any passionate outbreak across the slate-gray sea that suddenly united us. Screen door did not creak or slam and I was gone with never a peep to anyone, until this telling.

Grief married silence the next day when I arrived at the family lawn chair gathering and saw her. I was ready to accept a new status toward adulthood: I can keep secrets even without knowing what or why they are. But Darnelle's eyes flew away; she shifted her gaze and left. Never spoke nor sang nor showed herself to me again.

Following this crushing misunderstanding I began taking off the heavy protective gloves Jewel had loaned me. I became acquainted with a black widow spider who had made her home in a certain section of the porous low wall on the west side of the yard. The nearness of my hand to the beautiful glisten of the spider, whose innocence matched my own, settled an anxiety in me. If I allowed her to bite me, in the aftermath of swollen confusion and concern, would someone explain that all dangers are the same, and of our own doing? I could kill her so easily with my hands and feet, yet she never flinched or ran.

Companionable though this friendship may have become it was broken by my first firing and eviction.

"She isn't doing the job to our satisfaction," Jewel told my mother in an understatement that didn't even flicker my mother's conviction that I could accomplish anything in life I put my mind to. My parents took up again their own mishandled job, buying me finally a splendid metal rollaway bed which, when I lay on my stomach with my chin on the pillow, turned into a downward spiraling World War II twin-engine fighter plane, with me as kamikaze pilot, nightly wiping out all foes in behalf of everyone I loved.

A warrior persona was beginning to develop inside of me.

Joan of Arc Comes to Las Cruces High

As a young girl my most intense and certainly most sexual fantasy was of Joan of Arc. Not as her lover (unimaginable), but rather of my being Joan of Arc. Her combination of power, charisma and vulnerability as a seventeen-year-old French nation-creator personified my desire for heroic martyrdom and revolutionary zeal. That she had followed voices she heard at a magic tree paralleled my mystical interactions with nature. That she put on silvery armor and led an army to success against a foreign invasion matched my desire to champion liberty. That she had then been accused on account of her gender, imprisoned, stripped, tortured, interrogated, and then burned publicly aroused my prescient fears of myself as a sexual outlaw. Hers was the ultimate expression of sacrifice.

Drifting off at school I stared out the windows and imagined. The junior high school had been taken over by Nazi storm troopers. The only person who could save everyone was me, and the only way I could do this was to stand on the stage of the auditorium packed with people forced to watch my bravery and grand humiliation. Knowing it was all in their behalf. My sentence: I had to strip completely naked except for a small square of cloth, the size of a bandana.

The dilemma of the fantasy was the endlessly fascinating question of where to put the cloth. Over my little embarrassing buds of breasts that I hid by wearing a jacket all day in any weather? Or should I drop the cloth down, to cover my shiny emerging crotch fur? Every day the solution differed, and when one day I realized I could put the cloth over my face, the fantasy reached a new height of excitement and delight.

I see in this all the makings of a writer, especially one who came of age in the generation that spilled all the secrets they knew out into the public domain in the most devil-may-care manner. We followed the imperative to "let it all hang out." No personal, family, church, or state secret would be safe with us. Over the course of my life, my growing awareness of my sexuality as "lesbian" was not going to stay silent or simple. Words said about gay people would become my heroic banners. My class complaints, even eventually the deeper reasons for my grief-stricken terrors about my mother, my struggles with menstruation, my love for the planet Venus and for mythology, and now my war stories—all would be revealed, excavated, chewed up to extract every scrap of meaning and thrilling desire.

The Spell of Bugs

In the year 1956, my father had again lost his job, and a severe episode of my mother's mental illness was getting started. Her illness was apparently set in motion at her home birth in Manhattan, Kansas, on February 9, 1903. The doctor who attended had come directly from a smallpox case, and passed the infection to my infant mother. My grandparents, Mabel Rae Hull and Carl Hull, named the sick little baby Vera Doris Hull. Grandmother Mabel's fourth baby, Helen, died in infancy of tuberculosis, which later claimed her husband as well. Carl lay coughing on a cot on the back porch for two years before dying when my mother was four. Mabel put the older girls, Sybil and Vera, into the Masonic Home in Wichita, where they stayed for over two years until she married an Irishman, George O'Dell. George was a plumber by trade, a widower with two children, Blanche and Helen. They made a family of seven and moved to Galesburg, Illinois.

My grandmother Mabel left notes about her own family genealogy, which included that we descended from an English lord and an American couple named William and Mary Bacon, who lived in New Jersey in the early 1800s.

Though Vera quit school before completing the ninth grade, she had ambition, wanted to follow her father's footsteps and become a telegraph operator, an advanced applied technical skill for its day. She went to trade school, was all prepared to take a job in her early twenties. "Then something happened…I don't know what. After that, I couldn't."

"Couldn't?"

"I can't explain it. I just couldn't go out and do it. I became a different person." She looked despairing, flung up her hands in a helpless gesture. "I was always different," she said, "always the runt; and my feet are long and narrow." But those qualities, nor the small number of smallpox pits on her face and arms, are not what made her "different." Rather, her mental qualities, that she stuttered, lost her place in conversations, walked with her head down as though she would lose track of her feet on the earth if she didn't watch every step. She was frequently distracted, extremely frightened of social interactions; she had numinous experiences, of which she did not dare speak. She experienced a different set of realities, heard voices, and constantly struggled to keep her balance with this.

Vera was childlike, elfin. She was deaf, or apparently deaf, or selectively deaf, most of the time. You would say something to her and she would stare in response. Or she would say something utterly inappropriate, out of the blue, as though having an inner dialogue with an entirely different set of references than any we knew, or were. I would go into a kind of startled shock, or turn it into a joke to reassure her. My father would walk out of the room, muttering. Or laugh. He was remarkably patient with her in certain ways, yet often called her stupid. She called herself stupid. "I'm retarded," she would say. Or, "I have the strangest thoughts." But she would not divulge them. She would hold her head and say, "Oh, it's horrible, it's horrible." Her suffering was palpable, sometimes relentless for months. Yet she also had a wonderful, if inexplicable and largely private, sense of humor. And at times she had an incandescent, irresistible glow that was pure delight.

She encouraged me to publish my poetry, borrowing a neighbor's typewriter so I could send in formal submissions to magazines, which inevitably rejected them. She, as well as Miss Welsheimer, encouraged me to enter the annual poetry contests at school. We put the money I won in a special fund my mother kept for my college tuition, stocking it with her extra change, and often my babysitting and allowance money.

Vera had a fascination with science, and spoke of the sky's lights in awe. Her sense of wonder was contagious; I loved to borrow her little Kodak box camera to photograph the stars and moon, thinking I could absorb some knowledge that way. Bits of science I would learn from study, and from scientists I would come to know, but that sense of shining, sterling wonder was my mother's gift. This would take me through many perilous times, as no matter what is happening, there is always something "interesting" about it, some part of me that is awe-struck.

My mother's smells were coffee with milk, talcum powder, potatoes and onions fried together, white beans boiling, and laundry soap. I was suspicious of all those smells. Would they lead to a life of my mother's distress? She had held a job as receptionist at the photographer's for several years, seeming to gain confidence. And then in 1956 she suddenly fell apart.

For the next year, Vera sat in a rocking chair in her own world, or paced the living room on the bias, six little steps one way, six little steps back, her hair disheveled, her eyes lightless and bleak. She was adamant that we were to kill nothing, and the house filled up with cockroaches, so protected they never felt the need to hide. Many, perhaps most, days she stared at husband and daughter without a flicker of recognition, her face sometimes a gaunt contortion of inconsolable anguish, sometimes a blank screen. Elmer would not go against her wishes, especially if it would make her cry, as that always broke our hearts. He would not take her the forty miles to a psychiatrist in El Paso. He had promised never to do that, never to turn her over to hospital authorities. He was totally sober during this era, sober and serious, concerned about his fragile wife and his frightened daughter.

During the worst year of her breakdown the restless cockroaches were like living extensions of my mother's mind, her secrets, the rays of Vera's madness embodied, given permission to run loose through every cranny of the little apartment, sparing no space, no private domain, gleefully swarming the light bulbs and filling the drawers with their egg casings. Not even the toothbrush could escape the influence of her psychosis, which affected me until I was also hallucinating, seeing giant roaches in the grocery store and feeling them in my hair at school. Of course my fear was that I too was crazy, affirmed by my jumpiness and my inability to concentrate at school. I was losing my grip on understanding.

At school I could see the letters on the blackboard, knew they were "language" and that this was a language I was supposed to know. Yet nothing connected, I could not read the sentences and the letters were meaningless marks. I developed a nervous tic, and out of the corner of my eye, large shiny creatures with antennae sporadically climbed over the edge of my desk, so I looked straight ahead trying to see as little as possible. I had begun to stutter. "Aphasic," one of my teachers explained, although that is a term used for language loss resulting from brain damage. *That* condition I would actually have in my twenties, but for now, whatever I had, it was disastrous, was flunking me out of high school.

Our neighbor Miss Welsheimer, who was now my Latin teacher, a quite imposing figure, stepped in to help me, forcing me to take a flunked test again, and scolding me into redoing homework. "You can do this, I know you can," she'd say, glowering at her troubled neighbor's troubled daughter as though without compassion. Shamed, but also brought into consciousness by the scolding, I disciplined my mind, did the work over, and managed to squeak past my junior year and go on to finish high school.

Then one day my mother recovered. She lifted the "no kill" ban. She began to eat with us and talk again. Gleefully, my father and I aimed spray at the insects and swept up their bodies. We were free of the spell of my mother's withdrawal.

But now my parents wanted to tear me loose from high school. They themselves had quit prior to finishing the ninth grade, taking jobs to help their families. I suppose they just expected the same of me. Or, perhaps, they could see the horizon of living together, and could not bear to let me go. First came the shock of learning that the patiently gathered college fund, which had reached the unimaginable sum of $250, had been spent. "We needed it for the rent," my mother said, her palms turned up toward me in her "I can't help anything" gesture.

Next came an overt plea for me to support them. "We would like to talk to you." My mother's serious voice. They sat together, each in the designated chair like Mama and Papa Bear, and very matter-of-factly told me they wanted me to quit school and get a job to help them out. To everyone's astonishment, mine especially, I said no. "No, I am going to go on to college." At sixteen I knew for certain that my destined paths were poetry and philosophy—the subjects of which were yet to be determined, though the gleaming path was perfectly clear in my mind. This was a short time of utter clarity that would sustain me through what were to be several muddled years.

Boxes of Separation

Cultural boxes were rigid. I tried in vain to become friends with Chicanas. The boys could date me, that was acceptable, but it was the dashing, athletic girls I wanted to know. While my parents refused to eat Mexican food, I began to rebel against my father's disparagement of red sauces and secretly ate flat red enchiladas with a gorgeous fried egg on top, sold on a paper plate out of the back door of a house on Brownlee Avenue, and bought the savory steamed tamales peddled by the tamale man from his little white wagon on Picacho

Avenue, for a nickel each. I went with neighbors to the "Enchilada Suppers" at the Catholic church on Main Street, where people ate communally at long wooden tables, with a choice of red or green sauce. I could not know the people, but eating their food brought me a sense of companionship.

My ecumenical nature was encouraged by the Methodist church taking us children on a field trip to El Paso, where we received a tour of the Jewish synagogue, and were shown a mezuzah. Afterwards, in Sunday School, we made little sample mezuzahs and took them home, a step toward breaking down the various segregations in our society.

I was considered the religious child of my family, and was given a large bible with illustrations and a red ribbon to hold the page place. After I grew up, I inherited the family bible, in Swedish, that had belonged to my paternal grandmother Frida. I struggled without success to understand and claim in some personal way the words, the paternal genealogies and stories of this book. Poetry was easier.

Neighbors and family alike called me a poet from the age of ten. My childhood poetry traveled through my girl scout troop (they performed the ballad I'd written, no doubt a celebration of New Mexico) and then I was thrilled that the Sunday School teacher at the Methodist church read my poem, a prayer exalting life, out loud to everyone. I was understanding the social cohesion manifest in art, and its capacity to express the spiritual.

During my twelfth year I made crosses as gifts for the neighbors, using my father's little metal files, while sitting in the nonfunctional car he had bought for $50. Using the car as my private room, I would file large nails down into square bars, and tie the crosspiece to the main bar with thin wire. I filed a groove around the top so a string could hold the piece, and then made presents of them to the soldiers and their wives, renters in the Roberts' apartments. I insisted that everyone call me "Jody" because at any moment God was going to answer my prayers and turn me into a boy. That nothing of the sort happened, and that I was left to set my own course through the sharp teeth of adolescent gender sortings, gave my life a navigational setting at the borders of social "reality" and the solidity of inner necessary meanings. Within that tension I would eventually set my art, and voice, and mind.

Gender was an agonizing box. At age sixteen I looked up the word "lesbian" in the dictionary. No one I knew used that word, nor the word gay, or dyke or transgender. Or even gender. There were boys and girls, blue and pink, take your pick. There were queers, whatever that was, and always said with extreme disapproval by the other adolescents. Everyone got married and had children, like it or not. Miss Welsheimer was in some ways a great model of a single woman—self-employed, independent, keeping a great cat. But she had to repress her lesbian sexuality and live unpartnered. I didn't want that kind of spinster life, I wanted to engage my whole heart and share all of my being, I wanted to be totally in love, and totally in the world. I wanted to be free to pursue whatever I had come here to accomplish, and learn.

The gender box was closing in. At thirteen when I got crushes on girls and women teachers I became alarmed that I wasn't developing correctly, and brought psychology books home from the library to help me understand what was happening. My crushes were just a phase, the books said, I would recover. I hoped so, because the gender box felt to be a very dangerous one to fall out of, and land...where?

One day my schoolmates, a group who were ordinarily my friends, were talking about queers. Not seeing the trap, I said, "I'm a queer." The silence that followed settled on me like a cape of separation. I would not remain friends with any of them, and felt the loneliness keenly. I was less and less interested in becoming a woman, and didn't want to be a man either. My body—or something—was leading me down some unknown path.

Then at fifteen I had a glimmer of possibility. Our neighbor Jewel took me to San Diego to visit her oldest daughter for a few days, and we all went to see a play, Shakespeare's *A Midsummer Night's Dream*. There on stage, in that perfectly balanced, androgynous character of Puck, I saw myself reflected. And with a role to play, a guiding role. Puck is in the play, yet not in the play, guiding people into and out of the drama. The actor who performed this part was luminous in that in-between space of masculine and feminine, with a particularly joyful, whimsical glow. I recognized this while having no name for it. When I came back home I was still excited about my inner identity that was suddenly real, and felt very grown up, secretive, and rebellious. I didn't need to choose between Adam and Eve, neither of whom I liked anyhow. I wasn't the prom queen or her date, nor was I any of the people who allegedly envied them. I was something else entirely. I might even get to keep a short haircut. I might get away with feeling like myself.

BEAUTY OF THE EARTH NAKED UNTO HERSELF

First, though, I had to live to grow up, and some days that seemed not in my stars. One night I woke with a particularly dramatic nosebleed. When both my pillow and a towel were soaked through, my mother went out into the dark to the nearest telephone, six blocks away. She called Dr. Jones, who stuffed gauze into my flooding nasal channels and told my parents to feed me vegetables with vitamin K in them. He said that I had bled to the point of near hospitalization. While Vera was gone, I had a vision. I had been frightened and so decided to see if I could call up Jesus to help me. And, I did. Perhaps visions ride on the horses of powerful emotion, guided by the strength of our minds. At any rate, there was the form or apparition, looking like the picture of him that I had brought home from Woolworth's one day to hang on the living room wall. I could see that this was not right for me, this was not going to help, this was not even particularly real. I would have to wait. I was disappointed yet oddly settled. I thanked him for coming, and sent him away, aware that I had called the vision up.

My spirituality would now center on nature, and I would try to understand creatures as well as understanding humans. The rest of the country may be industrialized, dug up, stripped, malled, drenched with petroleum, and layered over into a comatose state. In much of New Mexico and certain other areas of the Southwest, a sensitive person can experience the rocks as still present and talkative. No machines or superstitious people have told them to shut up. Creatures sing with you and deliver messages. Portals are open to other worlds, and spirits flit in and out of their multiple levels of reality.

The earth is naked in these parts, she is not wearing her matted trunks or dense green mosses and lace flowers; even most of her flesh has blown away, so her bare bones are singing to you directly. For mineral people, this is exhilarating. She is multicolored chert, white and red shale, schist and granite, she is lava and obsidian black, and green turquoise, she is slate and basalt grey and every shade of sandstone tan and, at times, underground, the quartz is ice blue and so resonant you could faint. You could lose your balance in a long jump and twist your ankle as I did once in an abandoned mine in Tortugas Mountain, and have to be carried out by the tall, kind, taciturn engineer who had pressed his flashlight against the side of the tunnel and said to me, "Look." My breath stopped, suddenly being in a glowing blue gut of a place. And like me you wouldn't care that you fell, because that heart-stopping blue glow of the internal flesh of the mountain would stay with you all your life as a glimpse of another way of being a body, of having an inner radiance, while the hurt of the twisted ankle was gone in a matter of days.

But for plant-loving people, this nakedness of rock can be disturbing. When my mother arrived in New Mexico, she was very upset about the aridness of the land. The topsoil was a thin layer of sandy crust and the trees, like the elms transplanted from the east coast, were skinny, tentative and brave. Everything was dead, she thought. This was frightening and made her angry. My mother stared out the windows at the blazingly bleak landscape that I already adored and she felt the place heating up to blast furnace intensity in the May and then June heat, as my father struggled to fix the big, musty, straw-filled air conditioner. Water would gurgle through the straw and the fan would blow coolish air through the maze. The motor was amazingly noisy. She became angrier and angrier. Since he insisted on meat every day, she took the little food budget and bought cans of Spam. Every day we ate Spam. Now, Spam is an okay food; you can live on Spam with eggs for quite a while. But every day and every day and every day, and always with so much anger. This rage got into the Spam, like mold, and spoiled it.

After a while my mother began to see with mineral eyes; she appreciated for their survival the creosote mesquite bushes and skinny mimosa and transplanted elm trees. She admired the spiky century plants and thorn-armed prickly pear for their defensive adaptation. She really began to see the stunning, raw beauty of the land itself, the play of lights and shadows, the dramatic interactions of earth with wind and rain, the awe inspiring upward stature of the mountains. She saw what a living painting it is, everything interacting. Many days at sunset the three of us were compelled with one impulse to go to the western window together (the other window was rattling under the strain of bearing up the air conditioner). We must look at the sky over the west mesa as it dissolved into colors, and we must exclaim about this out loud. We must watch for a long time. This became the only prayer we ever did together, though we never called it that.

BEST FRIEND

The postwar economy had been booming across the country, and especially in New Mexico. Anglos were building suburbs and moving into them. It was damn near impossible to be white and poor at this time, a family had to put some effort into this, had to have fragilities out of the reach of bank loan privileges. My father's fatal flaw of taking his paychecks to the poker table or buying drinks for all his bar buddies, and my mother's incapacity to grapple with the world—despite holding her low-paying job—left them in their isolation. And they made do.

Meanwhile in the mid 1950s, the makeup of Las Cruces was changing, especially because of its relation to White Sands Proving Ground (now called White Sands Missile Range), Army property on the other side of the Organ Mountains. What was being proved? That rockets could fly farther and more accurately than they had in World War II. Or that a man could ride a rail so fast he would break the sound barrier. And that the U.S. could make more atomic bombs than could the Russians.

White Sands Proving Ground had been established in 1945, a 3,200 square mile area encompassing the Tularosa Valley, a broad basin that stretched from the eastern side of the Organ Mountains to the piney Sacramento mountains above Alamogordo. The range went north up the state to parts of the Jornada del Muerto. People took us as kids to the White Sands National Monument, an ecologically fascinating playground of sixty miles of snow-white gypsum in high dunes, populated with white jumping mice and white foxes, and tiny little gray shrubs that grew in the murky desert floor between the dunes, where, amazingly, if you dug a two-foot hole, water seeped in.

The road across the mountains and the Tularosa Basin to Alamogordo was frequently closed for hours while the Air Force tested rockets and planes. The Fourth of July parade in Las Cruces, in addition to school bands and people on horseback in fancy Western garb, featured long, sleek rockets and the new Nike antiaircraft nuclear missile on truck beds, passing one after another in a show of the country's growing long-range force.

New people were moving into the Mesilla Valley, sidewalks and asphalt roads were everywhere, and housing developments as well, replacing chicken farms and corn fields with rows of suburban houses held together by sweeping blacktop roads.

Technicians at White Sands Proving Grounds, among other middle-class folks, lived in brand new, three-bedroom stucco houses each edged with a new architectural feature—a carport—and painted one of three colors: yellow, green, or sand. In one of the green ones my friend Francine lived with her parents and a pair of huge silver Weimaraners, whose long tongues hung from the sides of their mouths. Francine was the child of Syrian Christians whose families had immigrated to Boston; after her father's death her mother had remarried and they moved to Las Cruces. Lucky, lucky me.

Everyone needs a best friend, and I had been trying for years to acquire one, especially as I slid increasingly into a scary and puzzling gender limbo while my peers paired off into idyllic heterosexual couples, and the girls discussed their appearances and the personalities of their boyfriends to the exclusion of nearly any other subject. Then along came Francine, who must have felt like an outsider because her family was Middle Eastern, and also because she was way too smart to be like the other girls.

We would walk each other home, chattering all the way, halfway the one or two miles to her house, then halfway back, then halfway toward her house, and so on. Francine was just enough of an outsider, and an intellectual, and an open-hearted person to find me interesting. Her love and acceptance of me was enough to get me through the social perils of high school. Her parents were fascinating; both of them worked at the White Sands base, as technicians, and seemed really smart. Francine herself was the smartest person I had ever met, a whiz at math and science, serious and conservative, but witty and fun as well.

We congregated with a small group of misfit kids, several of whom I believe would discover themselves as gay later in life. Francine and I especially had fun with Lee, whose sarcastic wit matched ours.

I hoped we could stay this close forever, but when we turned sixteen she started going steady with a tall, handsome guy named Skip. The night she showed me his ring around her neck, I drank six vodka gimlets (which her mother was mixing in a pitcher) and staggered home, falling down in my old fourth-grade schoolyard on the way, right on the spot where the little green snake had been killed. I lay on my back trying to see straight, staring at a big double moon.

Francine would marry Skip, though first they would both go to college in Boston. I would go out into the world looking for love, for a wonderful woman to love. I would do this secretly, without telling even Francine, who was clearly not going to marry me. And she was entirely too normal anyhow, I needed another outlaw like myself.

Adolescents in the absence of adult-sponsored initiations into adulthood initiate themselves, and each other. So I drank liquor, beginning at puberty age when my uncle in Iowa gave me my first swig of whiskey. At thirteen, my school chum Sharon took me to the music store where we stole records, a thrilling skill I wouldn't repeat until later when I was starving. By the age of sixteen I was smoking and coming home blind drunk; the wondrously destructive habits of my father and his whole generation were now mine.

I turned seventeen and still had no vocabulary for who I was. Puck was not a name. By then I knew that the word "lesbian" described me, and was thrilled that the word came from the place of a poet who loved women. But the library did not have Sappho's poetry. I spoke to no one about any of this, as my experience of walking in on Darnelle and her lover had taught me well to be quiet, walk softly, carry a big secret.

I could do that. But. Who would I love, then? Other kids were dating, some were getting married or wrecking their reputations by turning up pregnant without being married. Francine was going steady with Skipper, hooking me up with boys for a double date, "So we can still stay together," she said. We could still be best friends even though almost all her attention now went to him. But how was I going to meet someone my attention could go to? How would I even recognize that she wanted my attention?

KILLING THE OLD ROOSTER

"To a real nice girl," Lee wrote across his picture in my 1956 high school annual. He was already good-looking, though his smile wavered just a bit, and the inscription was a triteness that belied the witty and lively conversations we had riding together on the bus from school. The series I remember best surrounded the cat we had to cut up in biology class. To cover our horror we had recreated the cat as Minerva, goddess of wisdom, giggling and seeing who could make the most outrageous puns whenever we saw a dead cat along the road.

Lee and I complemented each other in ways different from other boys and girls. For instance, I knew how to shoot a rifle whereas he had won a 4-H blue ribbon at the County Fair for his baking soda biscuits.

Lee's round, flared nostrils and narrow nose bridge, along with his highly arched and very expressive eyebrows gave me the impression of a working pair of scissors. And as his wit sharpened, so did his facial expressions. As high school proceeded, he lost his baby face and increasingly gained his arched, scissors look, and his sweet smile had to be earned.

One day he was very agitated. "You have to do something for me. I'd do it myself but I just don't have the heart. But you could do it, I know you could."

"What's that?"

"I have this rooster I raised for 4-H, and now that he's old, *mumble mumble*," Lee had turned his face away for the last part.

"What is it? What do you want?"

"I want you to kill the rooster."

"What? What for?" I knew Lee's family lived on a farm outside of town, and that was why he continued on the bus for a full half-hour after I got off.

"He's old, he's no good for fertilizing eggs. But he doesn't know that. Lately he's gotten more and more aggressive, he keeps chasing them around, and, and, he keeps *raping* the hens!" I must have looked skeptical, as he continued.

"Yes, it's true—he's raping them, and he chases them all the time, which isn't good for them, they're always so tired, those poor chickens, he even chases them out into the road. He chases *me* when I try to feed him." He paused, "I just don't know what to do."

"Why don't you just—" I ended with a gesture of slitting my throat.

"He's my rooster. I raised him when I was a little kid, and my parents say I have to be the one to kill him and I just can't. I can't do it. I'm just too tender-hearted." He started to snort at himself, and the sound turned into a high whinny of a self-deprecating laugh instead.

"I could do it," I say, feeling heroic, thinking I could rescue the chickens. I could impress Lee. I always wanted more attention from him than he gave me, not that I wanted a boyfriend, but something else unexplainable.

"Oh, I know you could do it."

Our eyes met. It's as though we were coming out to each other in this admission of the reversal of roles. That was the closest we came to acknowledging our mutual gayness, to naming the mysterious link that held us together. "Gay" was a word we did not yet know but that hung in the air between us like a net.

"My grandmother killed her own chickens," I bragged. "She grabbed them by the neck and went flip! Like *that*, and they were dead." I didn't tell him that this was an anecdote of my mother's and nothing I had ever witnessed.

He looked horrified. "We use an ax and a chopping block," he said, and here came the widened nostrils and the scissors effect. "It's more civilized."

"Civilized or not, I'll come help you," I retorted.

Deciding the last thing I should do was tell my mother, I made up a plausible alibi and rode my bicycle the four miles out to Lee's house that Saturday for the Big Rooster Kill. I had never been out there before, and though the ride through the green fields and cottonwood groves might have been pretty I didn't notice, I spent the time trying to assure myself that *the act* would be easy and I could handle it. Hadn't I chopped up an entire tree with a small hatchet the summer I was eleven?

With a shocking crown and cape of long, steely, jet black feathers and ominous spikes on the backs of both ankles, the rooster, a Rhode Island Red, was quite a bit bigger and badder than Lee had described, and the creature realized early on that he must never get caught. I saw Lee's rather remote and tired-looking mother look up to watch us chase the rooster while she did yard chores. This doubled the humiliation of our not making a smooth job of it.

We went round and round and round that big flat yard for at least an hour. We were dusty and raggedy-assed and nervous and pissed off. He was just as determined, and fast. Finally, Lee got a cardboard box and threw it at him a few times until it landed open side down on top of him. It was Lee who reached inside and grabbed his feet. I was scared to death to touch him, with his big old spurs and fierce beak.

"You hang them upside down for a while," he said, "and they sort of go to sleep. See how he is now? Hardly struggling. They go into a kind of trance." He grinned without mirth and I could see from the sardonic lines on his face how much he hated rural life. "And then you lay them on the block and *whang*! Chop ther head off."

To my great relief, though I was "chicken" at the catching, I was fearless at the chopping. The chopping block was a large stump that received the rooster's entranced head and half his big body as well. My first chop was preceded by an enormous back swing, and missed the bird entirely. Fortunately, the ax came down on another part of the chopping block and not my own leg. The second try was sickening, just a bit of neck. The third try was in a hurry but got the head off. The body rose up at once and whirled in a ballet, drenching us in a spiral of blood, then went off on a dreadful dying chicken dance that made me queasy and guilty despite Lee's insistence that they don't feel a thing when this happens.

I stayed through the rest of it too, figuring that when you kill something you have to go all the way through the process with them or it cheapens the event. Lee's mother took charge of the de-feathering, which stank and took forever, and when the innards at last spilled out we had the amazing find of seventeen whole pecans that the rooster had stored in his craw instead of the usual stones. I thought that was an interesting collection for him to have undertaken. I put his spurs in my pocket for sentimental value.

Lee walked me out to the road where I mounted my bicycle. Already we were both nonchalant; we weren't going to talk about this adventure or how we had exchanged roles. We weren't really going to come out to each other for a long, long time.

RESOLVE

At seventeen the Organ Mountains began to call me to them.

I had a series of dreams about the mountains. I had tried to write a poem about them but, unlike one I had written about the main irrigation canal, the "mother ditch," as a place of life and death, this one just couldn't come together. I wanted to express the mountains' complexity, their beauty, and their danger. Soon I was looking at them constantly, and my desire to climb them was stronger than any other urge. I told Francine about this, and to my surprise Skip said he had climbed them, knew the way, and would take me up there. I only knew him as Francine's boyfriend and the captain of the football team. He didn't talk much. Always class-conscious, I knew he lived in a huge house with several vehicles out front, and that he was very smart; he wanted to be a geologist and later, would go to the Massachusetts Institute of Technology in Cambridge.

One brightly lit January day we—Skip and Jill, another working-class schoolmate, and me—drove out the road that circumvents Tortugas Mountain (now it was called "A" Mountain by students at the Aggie school), whose low flanks I had climbed in the ninth grade with two of my teachers and a schoolmate. Years prior to that, those same flanks had gripped the stunning S shape of flames as Tortugas people paid homage to the Mother, Guadalupe. About six miles east along this road we came to what Skip called the "Cox Ranch," and he parked his truck near the outcropping of wedge-shaped, sand-colored rocks below the tallest peak, Organ Needle. I was surprised to see a grove of trees, oaks as I recall, though maybe they were junipers, and they were hostessing a large family of talkative mockingbirds in the bright morning light. Skip, who knew the terrain, said there was a spring and a cave nearby. I knew that place, and thought it was the one within which my father's friend's sons had found a skull after digging a hole in the floor of the cave, La Cueva.

Two dusty-brown does looked up as we walked around the rocks and started up the slopes whose composition changed from sand with boulders and brush to ankle-threatening loose boulders, and then very hazardous slate-like shale, quite loose and bad for the nerves. At one point I was sliding up a steep and sideways incline, while peering with some alarm down about a five-hundred-foot deep canyon rim only two or three feet to my right. Like a comic book character—roadrunner or one of those other chase cartoons—I scrambled faster, using my hands to increase speed, a kind of skittering motion to get through the loose stones. And then we were high and mighty, at the foot of the fluted granite spires, the Needles.

We stopped to eat lunch, privileged to witness five blue mountain ranges to the west and south. And to the north, the long plain of Jornada del Muerto, where Trinity Site had exploded with the first atomic bomb just a little over a decade before, a national journey of death. But I wasn't thinking about that. Instead, my petty class jealousy kicked in as I saw that while my sandwich was peanut butter, Skip's mom had made him fried chicken.

I'm not sure if Skip then took us up to the needle called Little Square Top on the left with its several small peaks or if he took us through the rim walls past the Dark Saddle notch, or even—which would have suited his nature—up Organ Needle itself, the highest, at just over nine thousand feet. The usable air had noticeably thinned as we puffed our way up solid granite, using hands, knees, elbows, and reached what turned out to be layers of toothy spires near the top, stopping to rest in a wash of sand and brush nestled between the bare spikes. Jill sprawled exhausted on the ground. Skip went on ahead without us. In the time he was gone I realized that Jill was sexually attractive, lying on the ground with her muscled, working-class body and short dark hair. Plus, she was breathing heavily in the oxygen-starved air. My rush of feeling shocked me, since I didn't have a crush on her, had not so much as kissed any woman, and I had to look away.

Skip returned, his long legs angular as he balanced in the narrow terrain.

"You should come on up—it's only eighty feet, it's not hard. And at the top, the stone is so thin and pointed you can practically throw your arm over it, and see the whole Tularosa Plain. You can see into Mexico."

We were surrounded by the teeth of the dragon mountain, standing in the open maw, and she held her great breath. I looked at him, looked at the spire of greyblue mountaintop not very far above us, and looked at Jill seeming suddenly frail with her eyes closed on the ground. And I said no. If she couldn't go, I wouldn't go either. Skip, watching me shake my head, was dumbfounded, repeated his entreaty. I looked at my feet as I shook my head, feeling both strong in my decision and disappointed that I wouldn't get to see the other side, wouldn't get to think of myself as a "get to the top" sort of person. Yet here in this grand moment, witnessed by the ever-changing Organ Mountains, I sealed my pact with women. "Whither thou goest, I will go." And the inverse, "I will not go anywhere without taking you with me."

After a while, Jill regained her strength, and we started down, sliding and bent at the knees. So that was my initiation. You climb a mountain to find out something about yourself, which you can only learn from that journey.

Goodbye Cinderblock

Now it was time to escape the confines of my parents' apartment, and time for them to let me go. I would have become a waitress after high school except that Miss Welsheimer and her teacher friends interceded, getting me a fifty dollar scholarship to the college just outside town, on the way to little Tortugas Mountain. And, equally necessary to my forward motion, Jewel's son (Darnelle's brother) had gotten me a job as a soda jerk and fry cook at the canteen on campus for the summer. I was set.

I packed a suitcase dating from Chicago days. My father had gone out to the pay phone and called a cab to take me the three miles to school. The apartment still smelled like the bacon and eggs he had fixed for us earlier. He was nervous, upset—did I have everything, did I have a toothbrush, did I need to take one of their (skinny, ragged) towels. I was crazed as freedom lagged, arriving in the carriage that would release me at last from the spring-wound tension of growing up under that roof. He talked in spurts, sitting in his chair, wanting to hold on to me a moment longer; I paced, staring out the window trying to conjure the cab, trying not to show my smoldering desire to flee.

My mother was nowhere to be seen. A few days before she had said, "After you leave, you cannot come back." I felt shocked and must have looked it, as she continued with great earnestness, and in her most formal manner. "This is our house now, Elmer's and mine. You can come back to visit for three days at a time, but not to live here again." This was her version of goodbye. No matter how the world beat me up, not to come home again, not to have "home" except what I forged for myself, out there. I felt a trapdoor opening beneath my feet.

And, I thought I deserved better from her, but there was no negotiating. I would just have to make sure to never need to return.

So here I was setting out, seventeen years old, a young woman from a very small town with a fairly high IQ but who was overly self-conscious (and badly dressed) and so not suitable for a white-collar job (information compliments of the local employment agency); a young woman accompanied by a spirit guide straight from Motala, Sweden, never discussed in the family; an emotionally led, compassionate young woman with the seemingly unrealistic ambition to become a poet-philosopher and impact the world, but with no connections, no extended family, and few job qualifications—though I did know what it took to be a fry cook.

Instead of a rich internal treasure to locate myself in the whirl of chaotic cosmos and challenging human interaction, I had one stupid, divisive phrase with which to describe myself and where I was going: "free, white, and twenty-one." I had my father's mystifying advice, "Remember who you are," and my mother's equally mystifying, "I see you on a stage in front of hundreds of people…" For social skills, I had my father's wretched bar jokes and my mother's abysmal shyness. I had my own crooked teeth and extreme body shame; the sense that no matter what I did I was the wrong sex, and loved the wrong sex, and was the wrong class, was giving the wrong responses, and had so much the wrong haircut. My attention drifted easily, and so did my reflexes. Mostly I felt like an animal (a friendly animal) who lived in a lively but wild forest of my own invention, and I was going to feel like that for a very very long time. The cab to take me out into the world didn't have time to honk impatiently; I fled from the little cinderblock box with its delicious food and accepting love. And its mysteries.

THE BODY AND ITS DISCONTENTS

One night I was in the basement of the barracks that housed us, ironing my uniform. It was about midnight, the time I had been told to use the ironing room when I wouldn't run into anyone else. And taint them.

The light overhead made the room bare—bright and yellow, except for the stairwell, cast in black shadow. Slow careful footsteps. Someone came down, then stopped.

I looked up. Silence. I set the iron on its base. She stood a couple of steps from the bottom, bent over, deliberately in shadow. She was slender. She was careful. She spoke in a low voice.

"We're afraid to show who we are, so I can't come down any farther. But we wanted you to know." She spoke to me, against the danger that she would be charged with "guilt by association" and dismissed in disgrace. She spoke the subversive message.

"Some of us are with you."

I don't know if I replied, or thanked her.

I don't know if I stared into the dark at her feet, in polished black lace-up boots, and said "What?" She spoke again.

"Some of us are with you." I know she skittered back up the steps as fast as she could. I know the gift of her words, fifty years later, still gives me shivers.

A GAMBLE ON LOVE

Yvonne Mary Robinson and I always joked that we had won each other in a card game. We met during a Christmas break that I was spending with a schoolmate who was from the same town as her. I was eighteen, Von was nineteen. The first day I caught sight of her she was on her way to the Catholic church with her mother. The next night we met for a game of cards.

The small northern New Mexico town of Springer was having one of its coldest winters, but the heat our threesome put out in that little country outbuilding, playing poker at a tiny table under a bare bulb, could have overcome glaciers. Von was wearing a black cowboy hat, white shirt, pressed Levis. I too had pressed Levis, a snap-button shirt, and the beautifully tooled black cowboy boots that my brother had left behind in my mother's closet. These boots were the subject of some amount of derisive fun, and possible envy, as they were old-fashioned, high-heeled riding boots. I was just trying to fit in with these rural, and therefore more authentic, New Mexicans, but they of course knew I had never spent more than two hours on the back of a horse.

I learned that night that Yvonne Mary Robinson was a real cowboy who had raised her own horses and competed in rodeos. Her mother was Polish, from Cleveland, and her father was Scots-Irish; she had dark features and complexion. She was a child of New Mexico village life, delivered in a home birth by a Chicana midwife. She spoke with a Spanish accent, and said "Híjole!" as an expression of amazement, like the Chicanas I went to school with, and, as I would learn, she was often taken for a woman of color. Her friend told me Von had been elected Rodeo Queen, and no wonder, with her radiant smile and black curly hair. My attraction was instantaneous, and also alarming. Was she—like me? Was she a lesbian? How could I tell? I couldn't just ask her, so how would I know how she felt toward me?

Fortunately, Von took the lead. "There are always a couple of jokers in the deck," she said. My ears paid attention suddenly, as there was only one joker in the deck we were playing with.

"I'm a joker myself," she said, dealing cards.

As we sat across from each other at the little table, her friend's expression grew puzzled when we continued joking over the cards, each clutching five of them.

"Joker is wild," I said, watching Von's face, gratified when she guffawed, because we weren't playing with the joker card.

"Two of a kind is what I'm looking for," she ventured, scrutinizing her cards. We smoked skinny little cigars and played for a while.

Then she eyed me and threw two cards down, face up. "Pair of queens!" Her dark eyes asked a question, and her rosebud mouth seemed ready to turn this into a meaningless joke if needed. She was asking me to dance with her, in the air.

"Pair of queens wins every time," I rejoined.

"*Aces* are the highest card," the friend protested.

Von, sensing a bond forming, laughed nervously, too hard, choked out, "Pair of queens beats a straight flush." (Which of course, it doesn't.) I didn't understand all of her jokes, but there was no mistaking the erotic mischief in her eyes, that these jokes had to do with being lesbians, and that her attention was fixed on me and I was reciprocating. My eighteen-year-old heart thundering under my snap-button cowboy shirt.

The last night of my visit, Von managed to get away from her family and take me for a ride in a pickup truck. Driving down a back road under a brilliant December moon, she cut off the headlights. The cab filled with the misty, altered state of falling in love. I had always wondered what that was like and here it was, we were floating down a ribbon of road in some other world. When she stopped the truck for our first kiss I knew I would do anything to be with her.

Within three weeks I had abandoned New Mexico State University at Las Cruces, where I had been living in the dormitory, working in the canteen as a fry cook, drinking myself silly, and only more or less showing up for classes. Miss Welsheimer had made sure I had a scholarship, fifty dollars from the American Association of University Women. However, my longing for love trumped everything, and as soon as I met Von I moved to Portales, on the eastern side of the state, where she was going to school to become a teacher.

But whatever the dreamy exhilarated state of "in love" was telling me about how life would go was completely undone by the reality that Von had no way to come out, and no intention of threatening the fragile connection she had with her parents, who were paying for her education by selling off the family cows. She was dependent on them, and this was not a benign dependency. When Von was fourteen she had fallen in love with her teacher, a woman, which caused a great scandal. Her father had told her that if he ever found out that she was a lesbian, he would kill her. This was my first shock: we were not acceptable anywhere, least of all among her family. So, Von would not be moving off campus to be with me. I really was a wild joker, and I was on my own.

Shock number two arrived when I took a job in a meat-packing plant and was fired for being too slow at slicing and wrapping the meats. Then I took another job as a motel maid, and was fired for not being able to make the bed right or clean the mirrors properly. My third job was waiting tables. This came more easily, just memorize the orders when you can't read your own scribbling, and stack the heavy plates up to your armpits along your skinny arms. Increasingly skinny arms. The big drawback was that the pay was so small it paid for only some of what I needed, no matter how many hours I worked. Fifty cents an hour and no tips. I could rent rooms to get a roof over my head, but I couldn't also pay for heat, electricity, or food. The job gave me one meal a day; I had to steal everything else, snatching crackers and cream off the tables, stuffing blocks of cheese and salami under my shirt.

I tried for a year to live with Von in Portales. She had so many qualities that I loved—everything about her was gorgeously charming. She was smart, intellectual, funny, yet also down to earth. She was an athlete, a competitive gymnast. She had the strong hands of someone with a craft, the skill of leatherworking, and she showed me the box of precious tools she had saved for, collecting them one by one over the years, the hole punches and bevellers, the small selection of stamps, the set of Exacto knives just like mine, the calipers reminding me of my dad. She had the sensibility that accompanies hand crafts, the meticulous patience and capacity to take measured steps.

Von was exactly the degree of butch I was looking for. She had integrity, and seemed committed to contributing to social change. All these qualities, plus her physical beauty, flowed into my heightened state of desire. Because of her upbringing, however, she was sexually repressed, a huge disappointment. She was romantic but not really sexual. And given the confines of her dormitory room, shared with three roommates, and the discomfort of my dark, unheated rented rooms, there was no place for us to spend time together in a bed.

Now for shock number three: my weight dropping away alarmingly, to ninety-two pounds, so that the hot spring wind pushed my bicycle over with me on it. Shortly after this happened, I decided to join the military service. My brother had served in the Air Force (where he acquired the sweater I called "Norman") and he had become a sergeant, so that road seemed possible. My instincts said "no" but they didn't present an alternative. My stomach said, "It's just like any job, only with a guarantee of three meals a day." The recruiter told me the Air Force would continue my education, and to eat a lot of bananas so I could get my weight up and could get in.

Von agreed that I should go, perhaps was even relieved that I would be off her plate. We tenderly held each other, grieved the loss of each other, our failure, our weakness somehow. Our love wasn't strong enough to "conquer all." Wasn't that it? I continued wearing the silver ring with a green turquoise stone she had bought for me, and her Guadalupe medal with "I love you" scratched into it.

Site of the Crime

In a few weeks I was at an Air Force base in Texas going through basic training, and then through medics' training. What on earth did triage and carrying guys on stretchers have to do with poetry, I wondered, feeling off course with my life purpose as I understood it.

The military in 1960 was well thought of. Its reputation as the army that had rescued Europe and Asia from fascism had continued into the Cold War. They were honest, upright, courageous, sensible—like the Boy Scouts. Right?

The military was also ahead of the nation's other institutions when it came to integration, directly after World War II. I had black sergeants, one man and one woman. The woman reminded me of Miss Welsheimer, dignified, even-handed, and holding her boundaries. The man, Sergeant Washington, was warmly engaged, so that young recruits confided in him. One day he said to me, "Men have no idea about the lives of women. Men have troubles, but the things women tell me are so much harder."

These two were good role models; however, the rest of my experience was disturbing to my sense of right and wrong. Women were second class, frequently scolded by the male officers or given more arduous trials, like three times the normal dose of tear gas in the gas mask testing chamber. We had to guard the barracks at night, ostensibly from Russian "enemies" who were of course nine thousand miles away. In reality we women guarded the barracks from male soldiers who tried to break in and rape us. How crazy was this? Most of the GIs were good guys, by the way, but why did the military tolerate rapists? Anyhow, we were instructed to yell "Man in the barracks!" when a workman entered our spare precincts.

The aesthetic of barracks life was spare to the extreme and, at night, holding down a two-hour shift of "barrack's guard" felt like being in a movie, eerily moving through the sparsely furnished building, entering each room without regard for the privacy of its occupants, shining a flashlight at each window to check for broken locks or intruders.

After training as a medic, I was assigned to a hospital job at Andrews Air Force Base in Washington, D.C. Sometimes I was washing patients, carrying bedpans. Sometimes I was in the ER, strong enough to help carry three-hundred-pound patients. Sometimes I worked in the nursery, where only two of us cared for thirty babies. We swabbed their bellybuttons with iodine, changed them, carried some of them to their mothers, bottle-fed the remainder, rocked them when they shrieked.

Our schedule at the hospital was supposed to be ten days on, three days off. But it was designed to make us work extra shifts—we'd work midnight to 8 A.M., and then come back for a 4 P.M. to midnight shift, then back again at 8 A.M., and so on. In a ten-day period, we'd actually work fourteen shifts. For this we received room, board, and $80 a month. I was sending $50 a month to my parents, who were coming apart in my absence and couldn't pay their rent.

The doctors gave out lots of speed, ostensibly to help chubby women take off weight, and they freely passed the Dexedrine caps out to the rest of us too, which is how we got through our swing shifts. Shifty. Sleazy, actually. Now, I was young and heroic, so I didn't mind all this. What did upset me was the gay hypocrisy, in which I was participating. Homosexuality was not tolerated, we were told, instructed to turn people in who lingered in each other's rooms, hugged, or held hands. We were told to stay away from gay bars in the city. Some noncommissioned officers would even offer drinks and a night in their apartment, then turn the woman in if she accepted. The officer did this treachery in exchange for immunity from a disgraced discharge herself.

At the same time, the place was running over with men and women who seemed to me, even in my near-ignorance, very gay, very very very gay. Especially the sergeants.

A group of women who were being processed out for homosexuality was declared off-limits; we were not to associate with them in any way. The term for this was "guilt by association," an interesting method of isolation.

Incensed that someone was telling me who I could and could not know, could and could not befriend, I immediately broke the rule. When I was called in for a warning I told the captain in charge that I too was a lesbian and didn't see anything wrong with that.

Naively I imagined—what? A slap on the wrist? "Gee, we are so sorry, we have to let you go?" Instead, men in trench coats marched me into an interrogation room after searching my belongings, seizing letters, addresses. They would notify everyone whose name they had acquired, to drive them away from me. In the interrogation room they intimidated and deprived. I was vulnerable and alone; it only took three days for me to come apart. The room was bare, lit by naked bulbs. We sat at a table, me on one side, two investigators on the other. They wanted me to confess to particular crimes of lesbianism, they wanted details. I cannot tell you how humiliating this was, what a strip-searching of the soul, what a betrayal of love and relationship. And to my shame, I gave in.

I was criminalized, that's what it means to be arrested and interrogated and confined to barracks. I became a nonperson. And my crime was…what was my crime? Not lesbianism, obviously, though everyone was pretending that's what it was. My crime was *saying it out loud*. My crime was authenticity. Honesty. Honesty, that obligation of poets and writers.

I would spend a couple of years puzzling through the first layers of the morality of what had happened, and the shame heaped upon me. Ostracism is a profound experience, something my parents must have felt often enough. This form of it was concentrated and totally overt. The women in the barracks were told not to speak to me under any circumstances, not to visit me, not to sit with me while I ate, not to make eye contact. My roommate and others were charged with reporting on me.

This cloak of untouchability was humiliating, yet it was something more as well. The dayroom would be full of chatter until I walked in, and then silence. Eyes staring, then looking down. Eyes riveted, and then pushed away. Even in my bubble of isolation and confusion, I sensed that I had a kind of power to cause this deep silence, a silence full of lies, and they were not my lies. A silence full of potential speaking.

Even though I had been placed under barracks arrest, I had gone on acting as a lesbian, seducing a woman who lived across the hall from me. Doing a painting in my room of a woman whose eyes stung out at the viewer, whose hair was long and green, and whose fingers were flames. So when the anonymous woman came down the stairs to deliver her message of solidarity, I took this to mean that some of the other lesbians approved of my refusal to be cowed, to stop being who I was. And from the hastily delivered message of support for me, I understood that "some of us" meant that at least a few lesbians were talking to each other, were "with" each other too.

Faust and Me

I had two captains in charge of me, one male and one female. The woman was harsh in her criticism. The man was fatherly, sympathetic, kindly. A couple of times, he drove me around the base, a welcome outing from my jail of loneliness.

While we rode he told me, discreetly, that the other captain, the woman, and a female first sergeant were long-term lovers. I had no way to comprehend that kind of hypocrisy, so it made me feel crazy. Later, after I had studied, joined and founded political movements, I would understand the phenomenon of oppressed people collaborating with the system by turning against the people like them, rather than joining in common struggle against the oppression. People take the path of least resistance. I would also understand that while lesbians had been welcome in the armed services during World War II, Dwight Eisenhower had sent a negative message through the military after the war. McCarthyism had silenced American dissent. Many people on the Left and in Hollywood, not only gays and lesbians, were closeted and blacklisted during this repressive period.

After my discharge, however, my struggle was just to find solid ground and a direction for my life. The captain, Captain D., kindly drove me into Washington DC, helping me locate a room at 11th Street, N.W. Now I could find work and start over. The room had windows and its own bathroom. I quickly added a hotplate. I owned nothing except a few items of clothing and a blanket that a sympathetic woman who worked in stores on the base had stolen for me. (Ironically, her sympathy came from the fact that she was slated to be discharged herself. For stealing.) Regardless of my barebones circumstances, I felt optimistic.

A few days after I had settled in, someone knocked on my door and I opened it to Captain D. He had come, he said, to bring me a present. He was carrying a record player and handed me a thick black cardboard-cased album: Gounod's *Faust*. I had never heard of it.

"An opera," he said, as he set up the player and started the record.

I was flattered that anyone would think to bring me an *opera*, noticed already the sweetness of the music, the seriousness of the theme taken on by Gounod. Mostly I was flattered that the captain thought so much of me as to bring his record player and the album to my modest one room. Naively I believed at first that he appreciated my mind and sensibility.

He described the story of the opera to me. Faust is a scientist who has sold his soul to the devil, Mephistopheles, in exchange for youth, virility, and love. Specifically the old scientist wishes to sexually possess a young working-class maiden, Marguerite, who sits sweetly spinning at her wheel, in the vision Mephistopheles uses to entice the old man. Faust seduces and impregnates her, then drops her. Shunned by society and her friends and family, she goes mad, kills her baby, then dies of grief while awaiting trial. Just a perfect gift to bring a young working-class woman whom life has just crushed. So much more interesting (to say nothing of revealing) than, say, flowers or chocolates, or *La Boheme,* an opera about starving young artists who love each other. Even at the time I wondered why he had brought me such a morbid old man's story, and why he himself carried a tragic look on his face.

I thought that perhaps the captain would contribute to my meager existence; I had heard that older men sometimes gave money to young women, though had no idea how anyone arranged this. I had gotten a job as a barmaid, which sounded romantic enough at the time. Unfortunately, this bar was a dim den of self-annihilation primarily serving desperately alcoholic people not quite poor enough to live on the street drinking wine as the bowery bums in New York so famously did. The bar was a seedy establishment not far from my room. I was appalled by the condition of the customers—poised on the precipice while I shoved them closer and closer with each drink. I wasn't cut out to be the barmaid who leads people into their self-imposed hell; the role made me unhappy. I wanted to be an artist, not an executioner. One man in particular stayed on my mind, his face mottled with sores, his complexion the heavy yellow of late cirrhosis. Every day his poor mother came to sit beside him while he drank, seeing him through his terrible demise. After a week I couldn't bring myself to return to that despairing place, not even for my paycheck.

But despite my obvious needs, the captain had not brought practical gifts, not wine or food, not new sheets or money for rent. Rather, he brought an album by a French composer, along with a little record player, and insisted we listen to it together while he told me its strange and drastic story. I noticed that he seemed to relish the bare mattress aspect of the scene and I was not flattered when he attempted to have sex with me. I was fortunate that he accepted my "no" and did not force me. So I did not become pregnant and even further disgraced, isolated, and impoverished, at risk for becoming the opera character who harms her own child, his semen the poisonous elixir that finally destroyed my life.

Later, listening alone to the opera, I saw that he thought of me, imagined me, as Marguerite, the tragic and sexualized victim and he the hopelessly enamored older man. He had a daughter my same age, twenty. Captain D. must have wanted, in some impossible way, to understand himself, to collude with my innocence to do something he knew was wrong. Fortunately he went away, leaving me to ponder the mystery of a person seemingly conscious of the tragedy he desired to visit upon me. Perhaps because his perversity was wrapped in a blanket of "opera" he was less aware that it was a murderous impulse.

A long time later I would realize the real and priceless gift given and received that day—the Faust story, which is interwoven with the ancient Greek story of Helen of Troy. This experience, including the captain's objectification of me (and me of him) helped feed my later infatuation with Queen Helen, she of the ever-returning stories. I had been cast in the myth. Let life be as nasty as it please, myth changes everything! Myth puts us on a path of meaning. Was my character that of Marguerite, the seduced working-class woman, or Helen, the sexual outlaw? At the very least, I was the Helen who chooses her own loves, no matter what the consequences.

Myth and Reality

I wasn't living in any beauteous state of heart in those first two years after my discharge from the military and disgrace with friends, family, and Von. I was close to committing crimes of utter alienation, of carrying out a robbery just to express that I felt cast outside by everyone, that something precious in me had been pilfered. My sense of belonging to humanity had been stolen. So why not become a thief myself? Alarmed at what was happening inside me, I decided to get some training and a better job. The one I had managed to land, making subways of shrimp salad or salami at Eddie Leonard's sandwich shop, allowed me to work the night shift so I could attend school during the day.

Medicine had not lost its appeal just because at age thirteen I had traded in the idea of becoming a doctor for the headier ambition of writer, poet, philosopher. Now, since the military had gotten me started down this practical path, why not continue, I thought, and signed up for a year's training as a medical laboratory technician. I loved the table of elements, learning about the pattern of atomic numbers. I loved the term "valence" and its meaning—the electrons most likely to be found in chemical interactions and bonding. I loved nature being so orderly-seeming, the molecules lining up according to balances of matter and energy, the elements around us combining to create the precious gasses that enable our lives and deaths.

Learning to handle a hypodermic needle, how to find a vein and draw blood, then measuring, testing, spinning, and spreading the red life soup thinly on a glass slide to examine the cells and lively microbes. Learning words like "calibration" and "hematology." Getting the chance to look into a delicate waving forest of mold in the magnification of an electron microscope. All of this was thrilling.

Before the year was up I had a job in a doctor's office as his general assistant and laboratory technician. I traded in the embarrassingly short blue nylon uniform from Eddie Leonard's for a white nylon "nurse's" uniform and white shoes.

I had also decided to undergo psychoanalysis and "straighten myself out." I had been interested in psychology as a kid, having brought those books home from the library to try to understand the crushes I was having on other girls. Now I was reading everything I could find, which wasn't much, like *The Homosexual in America*, but there was hardly any information about women.

The psychiatrist was Frank Caprio, a Freudian, and he was willing to treat me for very little money. I realized later that this was because he was writing a book, *Female Homosexuality,* and needed me as a case study. Lying on his brown leather couch, I felt his voyeurism acutely. However well-meaning, he made me angry when he used ethnic categories to assign personality types—being northern European meant I was "anal," he told me, which made me furious, especially as he seemed to brag in telling me how "oral" he himself was, as an Italian. I thought, as a lesbian who loved cunnilingus, wasn't I entitled to be "oral"? What I heard him say was that Judy was an asshole, Frank a big fat generous mouth. Of course I did not tell him this. After all, I was anal. His implication was that he enjoyed life, ate it to the full, while I did not. Inherently incapable of joy.

But my life's adventures had me so scared that I thought trying heterosexuality couldn't be worse than what loomed so near—addictions, crazed companions, and a walk on the violent side of life. I hadn't yet noticed that beautiful, successful-appearing women were in more trouble than it might seem.

Dr. Caprio told me my main problem was my body, I needed bigger breasts. Marilyn Monroe's size 36 the ideal, I suppose. Wear falsies, he said, and men would find me attractive. This was a typical unquestioned attitude at that time, that women were responsible for everything that did and did not happen to us, and the solution to all our problems was to become more pleasing to men. Never mind what we ourselves found attractive.

Women are masochists by nature, he said; you should find the masochist inside you and embrace her. On another occasion he exclaimed over a story I told of being with a lover in a hotel room. "All those lonely men wandering the streets, any one of whom would have liked to spend the night with you—what a waste!"

The commodity aspect of the expected female role of sexual service to men, usually accomplished through marriage, was not lost on me in this one-sided dialogue, which lasted nearly a year before I kicked open the door of goodbye, and fled toward, if not joy, at least passion. At least love. I had a new thought: Why couldn't society change? Why was his "treatment" for me to destroy who I was—his advice for me to wear false breasts, then learn to entice and manipulate. He imagined I couldn't get a man, it never occurred to him that I dressed to keep them at bay and even that didn't work. The arrogance of his position, that lesbians are unattractive, boiled my blood, boiled it into the thought, why did *I* have to change? The ball of sullen resentment in me began to solidify into something resembling a warrior creature, with teeth beginning to click together.

Marilyn, Oh Marilyn

Before I left Caprio's care, he told me a professional secret: he had a friend who practiced in New York City and L.A., whose patient was Marilyn Monroe. It was against the rules of psychiatry to tell me about her, he said, and then immediately told me she had been extremely depressed for months, had been casting about for some other way to be, to find her place in the world, or who she really was… and so, he said, in her desperation (that was his term), she had gone to Fire Island. My ears perked up. I had heard of Fire Island, though only in hushed tones. Fire Island was some kind of Gay Mecca, and not just anyone could go there. I certainly couldn't imagine going. It was like Avalon, or any fairy underworld, you had to know who to ask, you had to know the code.

This was like my inability to become a beatnik; you had to have the correct slouchy posture, and costume, and cocky attitude. You couldn't just walk into the smoky café or bar with the black painted walls and try to take a place among the transgressive bearded and disheveled male poets, you couldn't just transcend that liminal threshold in any dumb outfit, not the short overly-sexy nylon (spill proof) blue Eddie Leonard's Sandwich Shop uniform I wore all night or, later that year, the white polyester nurse's uniform with the mandatory beige stockings and white shoes with the long grey raincoat or the plain brown pocketless, shapeless pants and tucked in long-sleeved decidedly unpoetic cotton blouse and nondescript shortish but not really butch hair, or the brown loafers with thin white socks folded over once like an obedient schoolgirl's. No, I would never make it as a beatnik. But that wasn't my goal. I was trying to get *into* the working class, not out of the middle class. They were trying to go wild, I was trying to come in out of the woods. To still my crashing heart. To find a way to wear a decently androgynous haircut and still put food on the table.

Yes, to go to Fire or any other underground Island, you had to know someone, and you had to really be prepared to find out what you were made of. You had to have some kind of ticket, some confidence. You had to have the right aesthetic. Marilyn Monroe always had the right aesthetic, with her combination of childish pout and size 36 breasts, she *was* the national aesthetic, and she had used the luminosity of her photogenic gifts to maneuver into the highest echelons of society. She also had talent and ambition.

That Marilyn Monroe had imagined for a moment that she might be a lesbian, this was an amazing thought for the twenty-two-year-old social outcast who worked nights making sandwiches and slicked her hair back to go to the gay bar on weekends. Who was now on a Fire Island of her own, in Frank Caprio's office, asking whether she might be "curable" of a life that seemed only an affliction. And here was the doctor's revelation that she, Marilyn, the greatest beauty of the US of A, the great Monroe wanted to see *this life*, my scummy little life, this outlaw lesbian life, *as if it might be a better choice*. Better than her ex-husband Joe DiMaggio, the great first baseman of the Yankees. Or her ex-husband Arthur Miller, the great playwright of Broadway. Or her alleged loves Robert Kennedy, the great attorney general, and John Kennedy, the revered president.

Not long after this visit to Fire Island, on August 5, 1962, Monroe died. The coroner called it an overdose, and suicide was the first national assumption (though conspiracy theories abound, especially as she was linked with the Kennedy brothers). I was devastated by her death, that an artist, a talented, ambitious working-class woman could climb so high and not make it very far into her thirties without crashing.

Sometime later that year I abandoned Caprio and any more notions of trying to become heterosexual. If he was sanity I would choose psychosis. I would gleefully, gratefully, and hopefully gracefully waste my life doing what I craved most: loving women. In celebration of my freedom from normality I went to the men's side of a shoe store and bought black loafers. Now here was outfit and attitude: black Levis, white long-sleeved shirts, white socks, hair slicked with men's hair pomade, cigarette dangling, its thin white paper tearing off a small sample of that sweet rose lip. Maybe I couldn't be a beatnik but I sure as hell could be a dyke.

Still, because I had no confidence to go into the beatnik coffeehouse near Dupont Circle, I couldn't know that poets Audre Lorde and her pal Diane DiPrima were in the beat world of New York City during that era. They were older, I was barely getting started, my notebook still stuttered. I was so hungry for them that meeting them would have made me stumble and flail. Their big city sophistication and boldness of speech would have intimidated me then, as it did also later, but later I would know better how to hide this, and how to see their vulnerabilities as well. Later, we would become important in each other's lives.

PEACHES

I was twenty-two and looking for a door to anywhere else. Love, adventure, self-ness. I crossed over into another world then, finding a bar full of dykes who were dental assistants during the day, and flaming queens coaxing sailors into the marijuana-smoked bathroom for trade. The walls were painted black, and nothing literary went on—that would have to wait. But the beautiful language of the queens and longtime lesbians was rich with humor, pun, innuendo and double entendre, the sexy code language of secretspeak and crossover. No one used real names, lest they end up jobless after being cited in a newspaper article. I took the name "Sonny." Denizens of the bar included outrageously courageous sequined queens in long gloves and false eyelashes declaring themselves "on the rag," and somewhat stiff lesbians protesting that I shouldn't have my thigh touching theirs while we danced drunkenly to "Moon River."

At first I knew only the bar scenes, which did not lead to friendships. I did learn some things though. A long-time lesbian of middle-age named Peaches had suddenly changed her situation: on the spur of the moment, over a drunken weekend, she had married a man who was a drinking buddy.

"Married? Peaches?" the dykes who knew her said.

"This isn't right."

"Peaches would never do this."

"She's been depressed."

"He must have persuaded her while she was drunk."

"We have to do something about this."

And so, like a group of Amazon warriors in a B-movie, they decided to retrieve her, to rescue her from a life they were certain she did not want. Surrounding the apartment where her new husband had her holed up, they invaded. They forced the husband, a cab driver, to leave them alone with his new wife. I seem to remember the phrase "hustled him down the steps." Seven or eight of them poured into the apartment and, after talking to her, took their pal Peaches out with them, and back into her former life as a dyke. Hopefully they also dealt successfully with her depression.

What struck me about this dyke story, besides the daring of this group of working-class lesbians to go up against male authority, and besides that as a group, they succeeded (at the very least) in giving their friend a chance to think over her situation, was their overpowering certainty that Peaches was a dyke, and therefore would never have chosen to marry a man of her free will, would have to have been severely drunk and depressed, "not herself." *Herself* was a dyke. This collective statement about dykeness as a state of being worthy of protection, not to be given up lightly, moved me greatly, heartened me. Dykeness, their action said, is an authentic way of being, an affirmation I badly needed in the aftermath of my unbalancing military and psychiatric experiences. My road was increasingly engaging with authenticity, escaping the demons of disapproval and punishment, guided by voices inside of me which had begun whispering the chorus, "some of us are with you."

Since the interrogation, I had seen all authority in a new light. I was totally disgusted that my country, which I loved, wouldn't spend five thousand dollars to educate me, yet could spend tens of thousands to harass me, my friends, my lovers, and my family. The Air Force paid thirty-five thousand 1960 dollars just to teach me to make a bed, brush my teeth, and hate the Russians. Then, countless more dollars to interrogate me, to send two investigators from DC to New Mexico to terrorize my girlfriend and attempt to take her teaching career from her, to confine me to barracks for three months, receive reports from my snitch of a roommate, to make certain no one at all was talking to me or slipping me notes of encouragement.

Perhaps seventy-five to a hundred thousand national dollars was invested in criminalizing me, and giving me an incredibly important counter-education in the process. I learned a great deal about lesbianism as a threat to the social order. My eyes were opened to the social order itself, and I did not like what I saw. Again and again I would be brought to a place of understanding that something was terribly wrong—and it wasn't me or my love for women.

WOULD YVONNE COME BACK TO ME?

The winds in Washington always felt pointlessly erratic or slack, the air limp. Soggy gray winter abruptly turned into stifling summer, an atmosphere I found intractable and sullen. My own internal compass jerked and stumbled, as though whisked every which way by tiny meaningless breezes. My warrior self was humiliated in the military; my healer self would soon become cynical in the medical industry; my poet self felt excluded and irrelevant in the beat scene. And my journey through a year of psychotherapy left me willing to be labeled "insane" rather than try any longer to "go straight." I wallowed in the purposeless, mindless wind in which I seemed forever caught. Unlike the strong spring winds of New Mexico, this one whirled here and there, then grew flaccid, without fire, oxygen or direction. I felt I was dying.

Love wasn't working out either.

Von had written shortly after my discharge that she needed to stay away from me, perhaps forever. My understanding that I had betrayed Von was a continual leak in my heart. I had nearly caused her to be kicked out of school, to lose any chance of gaining a teacher's certificate, of being able to fulfill her highest dreams. I was devastated that my love for her could bring her such pain. Of course she was right to never see me again, to stay away from the blight that was me.

I had, after all, nearly ruined Von's young life. Only the intervention of a (closeted) lesbian teacher advocating on her behalf and blaming everything on that wild one, me, had kept her in school. Yvonne had nearly lost her precious teacher credential because I had "confessed" to our love. Military men in beige raincoats from the Office of Special Investigation traveled two thousand miles to Portales, New Mexico, just to accuse her of being a lesbian. Then they went a few hundred more miles to Las Cruces to make my parents miserable with the news that their daughter was a sexual outlaw, rejected by the entire United States of America. My father now refused to speak to me. He took it all personally, my mother said. He felt *I* had rejected *him*. Rather than that the government had rejected me. Later I would look back and realize that parents had no support in those days to help them understand what might be happening with their lesbian and gay kids.

We struggled to understand ourselves. What was a dyke, anyhow? Yvonne had known a few lesbians from West Texas and East New Mexico, and they all occasionally drank together or drove hundreds of miles to the same Dallas drive-in. But they weren't protective of each other, and from Von's experience they were rivals much of the time, even mean. She had big radar about meanness.

Yvonne stayed out of touch with me for two years.

One night in bleakness I asked myself, what if I had only one year to live. What would I do with it? want most? And the answer was immediate, it was bright-faced Yvonne, she of the flashing smile, black curly hair and muscled hands, she of the infinite integrity and desire to be a useful servant to the world. If only I could be with her again. So I wrote to Yvonne in Waukegan where she was teaching and I told her I knew she had every reason to never talk to me in her life. I knew what I had done to her. I told her something like this: "But I have looked everywhere to find someone like you. It's you I want to be with, you I miss every day. I cannot find anyone I would even begin to love as much as you. No one else measures up, no one else has your love of life, your love of people, your desire to help the world. No one else has your love of literature, your love of knowledge, your sweet smile…" I included gas money in case she agreed to visit, and so she would know I was 100 % serious.

To my astonishment, she arrived within weeks, grinning and gunning the motor of a little spiffy, saucy, bright-red Triumph two-seater. Despite how terrified she had been at almost losing her college degree, she was no longer dependent on her parents, she was far away from the small Catholic town, and she had her own money. She was also forgiving, willing to take another risk with me. She thought I was worth taking a chance on. She loved me. She applied for a teaching job, got it, moved to DC, and we rented an apartment together. I was ecstatic, and my life seemed to be moving forward again.

Yvonne had a well-developed social conscience. She had been teaching upper-middle-class children at Waukegan and was eager to teach students who were less privileged. Washington's northwest district (full of people, especially black people, fresh off the tenant farms of the south) seemed a perfect match for her. Being black haired and dark-complexioned, and very down-home country, she always felt more at ease in this community around people who resembled her.

We were so much more grown up now, we each had jobs, and we were far from the strictness of her parents and the lasting threat her father had hung over her head. We were also far from the paternalism of her college, which fed its students milk clotted with saltpeter to keep their sexual impulses to a minimum. I no longer needed to hide in a laundry bag for fear of her dorm supervisor, or eat leftover meat and cake from the paper plates her roommates sneaked in from the cafeteria. We had salaries, we had our own apartment in a big city.

Now we had liberty, right? Well, not really. As a teacher, she could not come out, so I could not write anything gay or lesbian under my own name. I think she knew that this restriction was intolerable to me, and she reacted by making fun of my writing. Why couldn't I write *real* poetry, she asked? But how could I write real poetry if I couldn't use my real life? My real love? My sense of truth began to fester. As a result, my poetry was faltering—what was I writing about? I seemed to have no subjects, no depth, no real connection to place, or people, or myself.

I found much beauty in the arts of Washington, the free operas and plays. Jean Genet's *The Blacks*, and Benjamin Britten's *War Requiem* moved me beyond words. I wept over the plight of the artists in *La Boheme* and returned seven times to see the Swedish film *The Seventh Seal*. Yet despite the uncanny pink of city light cast on the low-hanging clouds, and the brilliant, slow autumns, the expected majesty of the Capitol and Senate seemed instead ominous, unwelcoming, needlessly authoritarian. Riding my bicycle among those shroudlike buildings early in the morning, my eyes and ears were on the upper tiers near the roof where thousands of starlings treated the buildings like a set of seaside cliffs and built their own apartments. I cherished them and their outrageous noise as something the authorities could not control.

By the summer Yvonne moved to D.C., I had completed a junior college program and was looking for a four-year school so I could get a B.A. degree. Education had meant the world to me since I first began saving for college at the age of nine. For the past two years I'd been going to Montgomery College in a nearby Maryland suburb, commuting directly from work for night classes. I had enough exposure to life to know I wanted to study people rather than literature. I already knew how to write poetry fairly well, but write poetry about what? Surely I needed to know more about humanity. The elite white colleges of the East Coast were completely beyond my modest means (three thousand dollars compared to two hundred dollars). I had applied to the University of Arizona at Tempe to study anthropology, and had been turned down. Now I searched for an affordable school. Antioch University in Ohio had a work-study program that seemed perfect for working-class people, but they also turned me down. I had screwed up my grades too badly in my faltering start at New Mexico State, during my love fervor.

There was one school in town that understood how a person could get off to a false start, could maybe be the first generation of the family to set foot in their doors. That was Howard University, which had been established in 1867 to serve African Americans. Fortunately for me, Howard accepted people of other races as well, though in the early sixties they had few such applications.

I anticipated that my doctor boss, the internist, who seemed to want me to succeed in life, would be excited that I had decided to attend Howard. I don't know why I expected this from a man who, six months after I started working for him, requested that I segregate the office, as though we were going to continue Jim Crow.

"Why would we do that?" I had asked, astonished that integration could be a problem for him. "It's not about me," he responded. "It's some of the white patients. They don't want to sit in the same room with blacks." I was silent. "So I want you to separate the patients, blacks in the morning, whites in the afternoon. Or do it by days of the week."

"I want to think about this," my fear feelings screaming, "Fool! He's going to fire you!" My righteous feelings equally vehement, "But this is so wrong!"

Next day, "No, I can't do this, I just won't do it." Waited for the other shoe to drop. Instead, he went around the moral dilemma, kept me on, and opened another office in Virginia, which he offered to his white patients in Washington who wanted segregation.

Now, a year later, we were standing in the lobby outside my little cubicle talking about Howard University. He was flipping through the pages of *Life Magazine* under yellow lamp light, at the table where I laid out the magazines to distract patients while they waited hours for him to arrive.

"Not a good idea."

"Why not? Why shouldn't I go?" I persisted. "It's affordable, they accepted me."

"You won't like it," he said. His mouth was grimly set, as it was over our increasingly contentious discussions about the Vietnam War. "It isn't appropriate for you to go there."

The postman was more blatant. "Aunt Jemima is going to take over the White House!" he shouted three or four times at me one day, a reference to the fact that Martin Luther King had given his world-shaking speech on the steps of the Lincoln Memorial.

On my first day of class, the white taxi driver was the most explicit of all, and I suppose he spoke for what was really on the minds of the others. "You'll be raped the minute you step foot on campus," he insisted, while I gaped at him from the back seat. "I really should refuse to take you there."

"Then I'll just walk," I rejoined.

I might have fallen for all this paternalistic, false protectiveness if I had not experienced being an open lesbian, if I hadn't been interrogated. If I hadn't been untouchable, no one allowed to sit with me while I ate. If I hadn't seen how terrified other women had been made of women like me, by men like this.

Once again, Malvina Hoffman's sculptures were talking among themselves inside me, reminding me that it was possible to know all kinds of different people. In some world I hadn't found yet.

At this time, I started to meet a circle of gay and lesbian African Americans that Von knew through her work in education. I especially loved getting to know one couple with whom Von and I spent a lot of time, including a two-day trip to Harlem. One of them was a literature teacher, who asked to see some of my poems, and praised them lavishly, the first person to do this since my high school days. She had been a pioneer, the first black cable car operator in San Francisco in her youth, she told me.

At times I found myself badly equipped to know them, to engage with their same level of sophistication and generosity. My attitudes were ignorant, the jokes I told (learned from my father) were deeply offensive, my responses to their real-life stories were emotionally inadequate. I was constantly having to readjust, face my shortcomings, turn them into insight. I was like a crippled insect trying to climb a wall, never having looked at myself, never having noticed that a leg or two of my soul was missing, the wings were stunted, the feet had no flexibility. But I was eager to learn, and found that what I was learning filled my lungs with new air that I did not yet recognize as a spirit of liberation that was not just about black people, it was about me as well.

THE POLITICALIZATION

When Yvonne had come back to me, I was thrilled. She was still mostly a stone butch, but I realized that sex is not primary in life compared to real companionship and shared values. However, I also was not going to be chained to some notion of fidelity just because of her sexual limitations. I had affairs now, just as I had when we were first together, and even more guiltily, because now we were living together and I had to sneak out. But at least I had love, and some kind of sex life.

Now, as a team, as a couple, we delved into Washington's underground gay and lesbian scenes, and learned as much as we could about power, sexuality, race, and class. What creates change? As the Civil Rights movement swelled, and Lyndon Baines Johnson took on a War on Poverty at home and an escalation of war overseas, the heart of Washington was embroiled in contradictory forces. Through the Howard University work-study program, I worked with African-American children around 14th Street NW, whose families were fresh up from the south and the grinding grip of tenant farming, while Von worked in the mostly black school system, and bitterly experienced the entrenched corruption, bribery, absence of caring that characterized the paternalism of Washington. A physical education teacher in a district stripped of resources, Von visited several elementary schools in the course of a week's work. She would rage when she arrived home in the evening, rage at coming upon two administrators asleep on tables rather than working, rage at the school principal who locked all the athletic equipment away so the yearly inspections would show how neat and clean she kept everything. She would rage at how little was expected of black students.

We kept up with national events. We felt that a revolution greater than the civil rights movement was needed, and was coming, but from which direction? Yvonne, who read everything, couldn't say, so we put our ears to the ground. We became attracted to the teachings of the Black Muslims. Elijah Muhammad blasted from our radio, messages completely critical of white America. Black people were supreme, he taught, and white people were "the devil." While this nationalism was alarming to hear, we also saw plenty of reasons why such a critique would be heartening to a frustrated group of people. Side by side with their fiery rhetoric, the Black Muslims seemed to be accomplishing material gains for their people: schools, farmlands, businesses, banks. They were walking around sober, well-dressed, and self-confident. Whenever I walked in the neighborhood on my way to coach girls' softball, I passed the Black Muslim bakery, saw the women sitting within, calm, self-contained. They dressed in long-sleeved dresses, which in a way was like the way we dyke lesbians dressed, in that their bodies were not on display for men's eyes, their sexual charms were not used to entice attention. They did not smile or ingratiate themselves in any way when I went in to buy some bread, good bread, whole grain bread, the first I had ever encountered. They did not smile, nor were they hostile. They were indifferent to me and the power of my color. They didn't care a thing about my becoming a customer. Or not. They seemed, at least from my outsider's view, to have found a way out of at least some of the oppression, the bruising turmoil of ghetto that surrounded them. They had found a way to be *unto themselves.*

It was not lost on Yvonne and me, at least subconsciously, that we had *not* found such a way out. That while we were doing okay for the moment, we felt desperately trapped for the long haul of our futures. Our occupations were at odds in the stifling atmosphere of closeted gay life. For her to be a teacher, I must not be a writer, must be silent (dead) or so subtle in my writing as to say nothing at all from my authentic being. We smoked too much, went to lesbian and gay parties where the middle-class mostly closeted black professionals, drank too much. The teachers were not out to their families, and did not live together. I went to Baltimore, to a segregated white lesbian bar where the women seemed stilted, tiny in what they allowed themselves to express. Working as a nurse in a doctor's office, I saw gay patients, young guys who were semi-public with their orientation yet were killing themselves with hepatitis, turning tricks in the city parks, the "P Street Beach." I saw despair behind the eyes of closeted lesbians I knew, and felt keenly the smallness, the petty jealousies that threatened all friendships, and the ultimate insanity of our lives. Lives pretending we did not live together, did not love. What we had all sold for a tiny bit of security. We knew the cost, had heard the high shrieking, like a tornado hidden in the laughter of the drag queens who did not hide their love for men, who expressed endlessly in every grand-glorious gesture, and who risked injury or death every day they went out on the streets. We, however, were not yet ready to pay that price.

So Von and I, eyes locked in unspoken understanding, listened to Elijah Muhammad rant at the white devils, and then a new voice came in: Malcolm X. He was electrifying. At first he sounded like Elijah Muhammad, but we listened anyway, we had no other models for change. He was beautiful in his photographs, charismatic in his speeches; we followed his travels in the news. He traveled, and came back with a revolutionary new message. There were light-skinned Muslims. There could be a world-wide movement, one that even included the "white devils." We felt hope, very personal hope that we had not felt from any other leaders, not John Kennedy, certainly not Johnson, who we considered a corrupt hypocrite. We had not felt this kind of hope from Martin Luther King either, though we admired him and believed in what he was doing. We were helping to integrate the country as fast as we could, though we didn't think integration would make enough difference to us, as lesbians, or even enough difference to the impoverished black children with whom we worked. We felt that a harder shell, something bigger, needed to crack open. Malcolm X struck a note that reverberated in our heartstrings. Maybe because he spoke to both community-building and movement-building. And he was breathtakingly honest. Where King was inclusive and always led from a place of love and nonviolence, Malcolm said that violence in the form of self-defense was every human's right; he was the author of the phrase "by any means necessary" that would later become a rallying cry of the Black Panther Party, calling for self-defense in black communities.

Howard University

My eighteen months, from June of 1964 through December of 1965, as a student at Howard University were life-changing. In the many years since, I have met black women who would have given anything to have been a nurse or medical technician, who wanted to go to Howard University and could not. I know what a privilege it was for me, a white working-class woman, to attend. At that time Howard did not encourage or recruit for an increase in integration, and this would become a contentious issue a bit later. In 1964, when I entered, the school had nine thousand students, of whom one hundred were white. (I wonder how many of us one hundred were lesbian or gay, and felt out of place wherever we were.)

The first thing I learned was my own whiteness. Though extremely self-conscious about my body, I had rarely given skin color a thought. I didn't have to, in the white-dominated world in which I lived, so I forgot about it, and when Yvonne and I spent time with the African American community on 9th Street, where the kids played and danced at block parties til one in the morning, my whole world seemed dark-skinned, and I just placed myself in it. Only when an on old black woman spat at me one day on the street did my whiteness suddenly jump into view.

But my whiteness came into focus every day at Howard University, not from open hostility, but rather, curiosity. The physical education teacher at Howard required us to take a shower before and after class—as though responding to old stereotypes about cleanliness. The shower was a group arrangement, a set of overhead water-spraying spouts in a large open space. Twenty women crowded together under the water. Excruciatingly shy about showing my body to anyone except a lover, I made myself as uninteresting as possible, folding arms in close to my ribs and keeping my head down.

Nevertheless I began to feel that hair-raising sensation of eyes upon me.

Lots of eyes. When I glanced out of my bubble of self-protection it seemed that *every* eye was upon me, seemed that every darker-than-mine face was turning, surreptitiously, to view me, and I realized I was the stranger here. I saw that these women were curiously inspecting my body, as a *white* body, a white female body. Perhaps these young women in the midst of their peoples' great liberation movement were enthralled by my naked vulnerability, or were looking for signs of alleged superlative attractiveness, or were asking, are white women really flat-assed as everyone said?

Perhaps they were underwhelmed by the smallness of my breasts. Perhaps they noticed I had muscles and was not plushly invitational. Perhaps one or two harbored lesbian desire, who knows?

Perhaps I hallucinated the whole thing, but I don't think so.

Through those eighteen months at Howard I experienced what it means to be an outsider due to race; to be exotic, mistrusted, despised, ingratiated, envied, objectified, and on the other side of a lonely wall. I longed to call out, "I am not interested in black men!" In my fantasy this would lead to friendship, or at least relaxation of tension, with straight black women. But what would I follow my noble admission with? "I *am* interested in women?" This would surely cause a rush of women through the nearest door away from me.

At Howard I learned several important things. First, white people, including myself, knew next to nothing about the lives and histories of black peoples. That U.S. slaves had rebelled long before the Civil War, Haitians had won independence from France, and thousands of Blacks from the U.S. had populated Liberia. That after the Civil War, freed slaves had operated farms under the tenant farm system and held office. That Marcus Garvey had led a Back to Africa movement. That the white Protestant slave owners were often the worst, not because they were terrible people, but because of their religious philosophy. At least the Catholics believed everyone had a soul, and was a human being, was one of God's children. For Protestants in the 18th and 19th centuries, Blacks and Native peoples were considered animals, and animals were to be owned and exploited. (3/5 of a person.) I learned about the pushback to Reconstruction, as white supremacists began lynching and jailing, and police began terrorizing to reestablish white-only rule. The history and situation of the mass of black people was very different from that of gay people, clearly.

So where on earth did gayness fit in any of this? A police detective in New York City was quoted in a *Life Magazine* article on lesbians and gays, that we were "germs" who should be cleaned off the city streets. Wasn't that dehumanizing also? What was "human" then, if various groups of us were not included in that definition? Some of the deepest philosophical questions were surfacing through my life experiences.

To the police we were the lowest of criminals, to the Marxists we were decadent, a selfish side effect of capitalist excess. To religious people we were sinners who needed to give up who we were ("become a Lutheran," my sister had said when I wrote her about being kicked out of the service for lesbianism). And to the psychologists we were to be cured, turned into heterosexuals even if that meant electric shock or "aversion" therapy. The walls around us seemed insurmountable, as Von and I gazed at each other, seeing in our bright eyes not only desperation, but also courage. We believed in our right to exist, and to love. We would not give up looking for a doorway to another way of living as who we were.

My enthusiastic, radical, sociology teacher, Dr. Nathan Hare, provided me the first key to that door when he brought a small magazine to his sociology class, waved it in the air. "Here is another oppressed group," he said. "You should all read this." The magazine was *The Ladder*, the country's only lesbian magazine, which advocated for gay rights. From then on I bought it, a fragile little rectangle of resistance, wrapped in brown paper as if it were heavy-duty pornography, from the newsstand near Dupont Circle that Dr. Hare told me about. I noticed the stand carried *Sexology*, another magazine with articles seriously exploring issues of sexuality, and took that one home too.

From *The Ladder* I learned about Mattachine Society, which had a Washington branch. I joined the Mattachine Society and to my surprise, Yvonne, caught between bravery and fear, joined with me. She could not come to the bars that had police raids, following which school teachers and other professionals found their names on the front pages of newspapers and lost their jobs, licenses, credentials, reputations, but many of the gay people in Mattachine were professionals, so it felt safer. And still Yvonne was incredibly brave to join. Maybe we could change the world in time to have a life together.

Through Mattachine planning meetings we had met Barbara Gittings, editor of *The Ladder* (assisted by her longtime lover, Kay Tobin Lahusen). Barbara, along with gay activist Frank Kameny, planned a picket of the White House for gay rights, specifically for government employment. The picket, held in the spring of 1965, was the first such demonstration by gay people. Nervously, Von and I took part—two of a dozen or so people. The women were strictly instructed to wear skirts, the men suits. We were to look straight, "normal"—not culturally "ourselves." We were to resemble government workers. My ill-fitting women's shoes scraped my feet raw as we walked and walked. Seen through the iron fence, the White House looked remote, not imposing but inaccessible, cold. I felt exceedingly strange and self-conscious, nakedly so, and also angry that I couldn't wear pants, still wasn't "myself."

As I would find out much much later, "looking straight" was not what Mattachine's founder Harry Hay had in mind in the forties, as he himself had pranced around in dresses. But the continuing repressive atmosphere created by the McCarthy era had put a steel clamp on cultural activism or anything that could remotely be considered "communist" or "different." And Harry Hay had been a communist. Communists became "untouchable" during McCarthyism; people avoided anyone labeled a "Red" because of guilt by association; everyone feared reprisals. Yvonne and I didn't know anything about Harry, but we had come out into one of the most restrictive periods for gay people in the nation's history, though we didn't know that either. We just lived it.

APPLYING METHOD TO THE MADNESS

Another important part of my Howard education was a research method that Dr. Hare introduced us to, called "Participant Observation" (later called *observant participation* by LGBT researchers embedded in their "own" communities), which involves informal interviews, participation in the group, making and recording observations, taking part in collective discussions, examining personal documents, and paying attention to people's life histories and mythologies that give their lives meaning. Participant observation provided me with invaluable methods I would later use in both poetry and prose.

I was exposed to perspectives I had never heard before and was learning histories I would never have learned at a white college. The lessons were clear: stories, even broadly accepted "true" stories, are interpreted from particular points of view. And so they can change. They can hold contradiction. At the same time, I saw the class system through the mirror of blackness, witnessing the indifference of privileged Howard students toward the new immigrants moving into Washington from Southern tenant farms. I also clearly saw the stingy, cruel deprivation of (white) landlords toward these same people, shutting off their yard water faucets, refusing to eradicate rats and giant insects, allowing rotten steps and dysfunctional windows. I recognized that my parents lived in similar deprivation for years, with a leaking roof and inadequate heat. I was learning that what makes people powerless is having no voice or organization to advocate for them.

I was beginning to get that "my" powerless community was gay and lesbian, and its issues were different from those brought about through race or class. I was excited about having a method. That I could put my own observations to work and learn something about gay people. That just by living consciously, I could become knowledgeable. I began to make notes about people I knew. Von and I often talked about the few characteristics of gayness we knew about. "My mares were lesbians. I'm sure of it," she would say. "They mounted each other, they acted like they were in love."

Why hadn't someone studied animal behavior, to subvert the idea that we were "unnatural"? What if gay people could study themselves in some scientific way, to see where we might come from? What did we have in common with each other? What was this with butch/femme? Why were we so despised when we experienced ourselves as perfectly okay people, as so did everyone else up to the moment they learned of our sexual orientation? Doing any kind of research on lesbian themes seemed dangerous, however, perhaps because of the military and my humiliation from that entire experience. Though we had no idea yet why this was true, times were scary.

During this period, I felt brave enough to write an article for *Sexology Magazine*. My article, which the editors called "A Lesbian Speaks Her Mind," asked for a change of social attitudes toward lesbians, and specifically criticized the psychological approach of the times:

> One psychiatrist, at least, has even suggested doing away with the word "lesbian" entirely, on the grounds that no differences exist between male and female homosexuals. The lesbian, who may have discarded the standard feminine role primarily because she thought it involved becoming merely a sexual object, must surely be repelled by a dogma which attempts to explain her entire existence in sexual terms.

> Some lesbians become so dismayed by psychological diagnoses of their sexual and affectional preferences as narcissistic or as symptomatic of "arrested development" and so incensed at having their strongest romantic attachments dismissed as a search for another mother or as merely "mutual masturbation," that they decide not to read any more about lesbianism. How ironic that efforts to understand the lesbian scientifically should in reality only contribute to the already unflattering self-image society has given her!

I used a pseudonym on my article out of concern for Yvonne's very real fears that she could lose her hard-earned teacher's credential, so italics at the bottom of the first page read, "Christine Cummings is the pen name of a 26-year-old sociology student." The article's tagline was: "An inside account of the feminine side of the female homosexual." "Christine" was what my parents had almost named me; "Cummings" was for the poet ee cummings. When writing

Another Mother Tongue in 1983, I tried to remember "Christine Cummings," but erroneously came up with the pen name Carol Silver, which I had used in *The Ladder* possibly, or even as a child.

The Psychoanalysis of Who the Dyke?

"Dammit Dammit Dammit!" Blue jays outside my open French doors were getting an earful. "You rotten sonufabitch!"

It was late 1965, and I was living in the upstairs rooms of an old parsonage with Yvonne and my former lover Pat. Elated by the acceptance of my article in a nationally distributed magazine, and bolstered by the feminist ideas beginning to surface in the country and by discussions at Mattachine and in *The Ladder* about gay rights, I was again turning to writing poetry, my first love. I was trying to write a satire about my experience with psychoanalysis. I wanted to be political, yet also funny, and I wanted the humor to bite. But I couldn't get the piece to work, the humor just wouldn't take shape. I wanted something that would be a sharp critique of everything wrong with the psychoanalytic approach to homosexuality of the times, but a satire of just the doctor didn't seem complete, something was missing, and I struggled day upon day of my precious time. I was sick to death of my writing not coming into focus.

Finally, a massive rage overtook me. Ripping the pages in half, I threw them on the floor, and jumped up and down on them, screaming. Fortunately, no one was home to witness this. At the end of the dramatic fit, a marvelous clarity fell over me. I knew what was needed: I had to make fun of the dyke figure as well as the doctor. Because both of these characters were in the story together, her naive romanticism was equally contributory, alongside his paternalistic and self-serving pontifications of normality. Showing her complicity somehow gave her/me a kind of power, the possibility of change, *because every part of the story needed to change.* I decided to give her a name I had never heard any dyke give herself, a name that seemed absurd, "Edward." Now I no longer felt trapped in the story, because I knew that I could change the character of Edward within myself, and that somehow this could change the entire situation. The result was the satisfyingly satirical piece, "The Psychoanalysis of Edward the Dyke."

A Change of Tactics

At Howard, one of my black friends was Larry Jones. We sat in the back row of Dr. Lorraine William's class, whispering and critiquing with acid tongues. Larry was years younger than me. He had a long optimistic stride, an engaging, expressive face with intense eyes and one missing front tooth, which gave him a vulnerable look and a very slight, intriguing lisp. I wondered sometimes if he wasn't, perhaps, lovers with one of his friends. "I like to lick and suck," he'd said once. His friends were intellectuals who kept a distance from me. Larry always reached across to me, and I reached back.

"Where are you from?"

"Gary, Indiana." I thought this was funny, Larry from Gary.

We questioned and criticized all authorities. I said, "They control so much of what we think."

He said, "Even what we consider monstrous."

I said, "What?" not quite understanding. He said, "Even what we consider monstrous, they have taught us to consider monstrous."

We were sitting in a place we called the "Chicken Shack," one of the very few eateries near the college. I went there every day that I could afford for two pieces of chicken in a basket with French fries and plenty of Louisiana hot sauce. Larry often joined me. I loved his vivacity and intellect, his blazing desire for social revolution. I was certain he would be a fabulous writer. In class we sat in the back and imagined ourselves to be great rebels and critics.

Dr. Williams was inviting a select group of women students, she announced in class, to meet for intellectual discourse. I was very excited about this, and went up to her after class.

"May I join?"

"No, this is for black women only," she said. At my downcast face she added, "They need it more than you do."

I had so much respect for her, yet through my initial hurt feelings some other wisdom gleamed. Separatism was a tactic. I had already seen this in the black neighborhoods, passing Black Muslim bakeries and meeting places. Separatism is a way of establishing a viable life even in the face of unbearable and unrelenting oppression. A way of gathering one's self to one's self, in community.

The war continued to heat up as we rolled through 1965. Young people were becoming suspicious of the motives of their government. For one of my classes I checked Machiavelli out of the Library of Congress. The last person before me to have checked the book out was Lyndon Baines Johnson, when he was a senator.

Yvonne and I attended a huge antiwar rally, and listened to a riveting speech by the president of a new organization, Students for a Democratic Society. The tall, blond young white activist was Carl Oglesby, and the speech was so real, so right, and so stirring that I never forgot his name. We were thrilled to have this kind of leadership coming from the white peace movement, to give us hope that we could have an impact on the direction our country was turning, and to help offset the gaping hole of radical leadership we felt after the assassination of Malcolm X.

The two teachers who so impressed me at Howard, Dr. Williams and Dr. Hare, who would one day be associated with Africanism and Ethnic Studies, were not integrationists. Rather, they advocated self-authorization of black people, and Black Power.

My last memory of Nathan Hare is from early fall of 1965, sitting in a semi-circle of students in his living room on a straight backed chair with Yvonne, Larry, and his girlfriend Rose. Yvonne and I were privileged to have been invited to a discussion of the meaning of the Watts riots. Nathan, his gracious wife, Dr. Julia Hare, and other black intellectuals praised the actions of the people of Watts, who had rioted in Los Angeles for five days, drawing national attention to the dire conditions of black people in inner cities. The fiery scenes were a stark contrast in method to the peaceful marches and sit-ins Dr. Martin Luther King had been leading.

"They took power into their own hands!" Nathan said. He was very enthusiastic, and clearly saw the riots as a move forward for black rights. Larry was excited by this as well.

"But they burned their own neighborhoods!" I exclaimed, trying to understand how this was an act of power. I could have understood perfectly if they had set fire to white neighborhoods. Only years later, after I read Toni Morrison's novel *Sula,* did I understand: Sula stops a group of aggressive young men from hurting her by cutting her own hand. "If I would do this to myself," she said, "think what I would do to you." And yet, the Watts neighborhood never recovered.

Yvonne and I went home from the meeting shaken, not sure what we had learned. We were also somewhat alarmed that Blacks in Watts had attacked white motorists and burned white businesses. Were we going to be caught up in a civil war?

During lunch at the Chicken Shack, Larry pointed out a "crazy guy" who was, all by himself, picketing the college, walking up and down in front of the main entrance. He was extremely militant, Larry said, and believed that Blacks should move to seize power without any input from whites. His name was Stokely Carmichael, the man who would go on to make "Black Power" the slogan for a new movement. He was Dr. Hare's student.

One day soon afterwards, Larry left me on the street as he was going to a meeting with other militant-minded young black men.

"Can I come with you to the meetings?"

"No, this is not for you." This was no longer an integrated movement. Dr. King's nonviolence had gone as far as it could, according to Larry. Now it was time to move into a new militancy, *to make something happen* rather than asking for it from the white establishment. Even the heavy Washington air seemed to have shifted as I absorbed this new imperative for action. But before I would get anywhere near "action," I would go to a place of utter stillness. I would nearly die, and then return.

Falling Into a Place of Transformation

Fall of 1965 was my last term at Howard University. For a variety of reasons I had decided to quit even though I still needed several units of credit to graduate. Then, early in 1966 I began to act strangely, bumping into walls, then lurching off-balance headlong down the steps of our house. In February, I went to see a doctor, but he missed my symptoms even though I fainted in his office. He told me later that he'd thought I was a "hysterical female." The next day, I fell over on the couch and began to shake in a convulsion. Pat and Von rushed me to the nearest hospital, with Yvonne's fingers holding my tongue so I wouldn't choke on it. There they were told I had fallen into a coma and would probably not live, and would almost certainly never recover. I had encephalitis, an inflammation of the brain which causes seizures and neurological damage, assuming the person lives.

And I did, awakening after three days. I had lost memory and vocabulary, didn't recognize anyone at first, and had an enormous headache. Friends came to visit, Larry Jones one day, and on another day B. and L., our closeted lesbian friends who were Von's fellow-teachers. I was emotionally volatile, which shocked them, but I was just riding a beam of energy that at first was like a broad ill-mannered wave. For weeks I struggled to regain focus, and when I finally did, it came in like a laser beam pointing me in a brand new direction.

What happened during those three unconscious days I will probably never remember, but I had returned from the three days of coma with a ferocious courage, and where I had been trying to fit in, trying to "be of use" in conventional terms, I was now a fire set free, and focused.

I had awakened in love with the world, an intense, daily feeling of optimistic joy that would sustain me for a decade of forward rush. The coma, the swelling of my brain, and the fits had wiped away my fears. I was flooded with the courage that love of life brings. I was full of joy. Perhaps this was something like the off and on beam of my mother's love for everything, a generalized, slightly giddy gratitude toward the net of life itself. My near-death had left me awakened on a path that felt like one that had always been mine; my heart rushed to embrace the journey.

Meanwhile, Rose contacted me to say that Larry had gotten his induction notice from the army, and had lost his mind. He was in St. Elizabeth's hospital. I gathered myself together and took a bus to see him.

St. Elizabeth's was a cavernous, brick citadel of a hospital that had once housed the poet Ezra Pound. Larry was sitting on a wooden chair in the middle of a large, high-ceilinged room, clothed only in a hospital gown. Our voices echoed and the lighting was eerie, sort of gold and red with deep black shadows, like a nineteenth-century set. I pulled up another chair and he told me about his breakdown, how he had panicked over his draft notice.

"I opened the envelope and I freaked. I know I scared Rose to death."

"What did you do?"

"I remember screaming a lot, and how I pulled the phone out of the wall and swung it around the room. The cord kept hitting all the furniture as I went round and round. She couldn't stop me. I think that really scared her." Larry and Rose had been married only a few months. I could certainly imagine doing something like that, given enough pressure. But while we were hearing that more thousands of young men were being inducted, it seemed that only a few were actually going to the war zones of Vietnam.

I mentioned this. "Why are you so freaked out?" I hoped not to sound too naive.

He was emphatic. "I know what they're going to do. They're going to send me over there and put me on the front lines and kill me." I was silent. "Because I'm black," he added, as though I didn't get it. And I didn't yet get it that a disproportionate number of black men were going to the heavy combat areas, were sent on the most dangerous missions.

"Can't you go to Canada? I've heard a lot of guys are going up there for sanctuary."

Sadly, he shook his head. "No, that's not for me." We talked a little more and he said again, "They're going to send me over there and kill me, I know it." To my ears, this sounded paranoid. To the me of that time, the military was like a big dumb animal, not a deliberate, dark-person eating machine. But I felt very bad for him that he was so scared. After a while I stood up to say goodbye. Our eyes held each other.

That was the last time I saw him, though for years I would imagine I saw him on the street, bounding toward me on the balls of his feet, his white and black striped shirttail blowing casually behind him, his eager smile with one tooth missing making him look vulnerable and sweet.

Awakened on a New Path

In June of 1966 Yvonne moved us to Albuquerque so I could recover in a place she considered "home"—New Mexico. She moved us into an apartment, I got a job as a car hop, she got a job teaching English in a middle school. And we hardly knew anyone.

Von, always protective toward me, called me a couple of tender names. One was "Jusie." Another was "Babby," her own version of "Baby." We had been close in Washington, but once we were in Albuquerque as I continued to recover, we grew apart. I had come out of my coma a different person, but she was also different. We were playing with a restlessness between us. She would remain a responsible person, a good citizen, a loyal lover. And though she could be gruff and emotionally withdrawn, she was looking out for me. For example, years afterwards she would tell me that she had paid off my entire hospital bill, some five thousand dollars, an enormous sum at the time, requiring monthly payments from her modest paychecks, payments that went for years.

I, on the other hand, was flying high on a new joy and a reckless sense of possibility. I wanted to roam, to see what was outside the confines of our narrow lives. In the aftermath of my illness, I keenly felt the smallness and isolation of my life with Yvonne. We were trapped in a tiny box, a "closet" as it would come to be known, and we knew it though we didn't say this to each other. But I was searching for whoever might be searching for me, longing for me, out there in the wide world. Somebody who was an artist, who had a ticket to a bigger life, who wanted change, big change. I wanted someone with a key to unlock this terrible tiny life I was trapped in.

Then one day Von and I were invited by a neighbor to go into the Sandia Mountains looking for red maple leaves, and I saw her. A small, determined-looking woman with a handsome profile and a strongly set mouth. She had a butch way of walking. The moment I laid eyes on her, I wanted her. Wanted to know her, and very quickly wanted to keep her in my life, to be with her. Wendy's expression and posture caught my attention across a meadow length of territory. She was striding up a path toward the top of a hill, and her face was thrust forward. The set of her mouth was courageous and her gait was firmly stepped and confident, self-assured and strident at the same time. I couldn't stop looking. Although I would become enamored by her lively spirit and laughing eyes, that initial impression of the lift of her chin and set of her lips into a sensuous muscle of will was what first drew me.

Later, I was thrilled with her competent hands and long, guitar-playing nails. Not only did she play steel-string guitar and sing, she carried a camera everywhere. Talked about painting. Here at last was a woman who wanted to go somewhere and who was not going to be stopped from getting there, who wasn't going to settle for a boxed-in life. I was ready for a woman like Wendy, ever since the encephalitis had enveloped my brain and stripped it of all belief that following rules was going to take me where I needed to go.

Who was this mysterious, completely confident, twenty-one-year-old New York woman? Yvonne was just as smitten as me, and almost as hungry. We both wanted her, it turned out; we flirted and talked to her, became rivals for her attention.

"She wants to be an artist," I said.

"She wants to be a teacher," Von said.

We invited her over for dinner, took her to a bar in Santa Fe, danced with her. I stole a drunken kiss on the way home. We both expressed adoration for her, her confidence, her promise of real life. Then she left, went back to Antioch College.

Our life went on, plodded on. I worked in the County Welfare Hospital, gradually recovering my speech. Yvonne taught school in Belen, south of Albuquerque. Both of us were straining at inner chains, smoking more intensely, waiting for something.

One night Wendy came back without any notice, just climbed in our living room window in the middle of the night. That night she and Yvonne left me alone as they hung out nakedly in bed, smoking and talking all night about teaching. I was relegated to the living room couch to sleep. In my abandoned grief I stabbed my foot with broken glass and bled on the rug. They were not impressed with this dramatic bid for attention. After a while they announced they were going to New Orleans for a few days. Wendy had awakened a new sexuality in Von.

"It's just this one trip," Von said. "Let me have a few precious days with her, and then it will never happen again."

While the two of them were in New Orleans, Wendy, realizing how thoroughly Von was trapped in her life in New Mexico, tried to rescue her. "Come to Chicago with me," she offered. "It's a great city, and nobody really cares what anyone else does. It's not like New Mexico where practically everyone you run into during the day knows your business." But Von couldn't imagine that life, or maybe she worried that she couldn't easily get a job in the Windy City.

Von came back, expecting to take up her life with me. She thought that I would wait for her, would tolerate her intimate adventure with the woman we were both in love with, who talked confidently about social change as an inevitable part of life. Yvonne thought I would choose the security of staying with her. And I could have. But she hadn't seen the new fire in my eyes, how it created a deep hunger for a freedom of being, to explore who I might be. There was no explanation for who lesbians were, no way for Von and me to understand ourselves, and no way to find out, to ask the world for answers, to make changes.

Living with Yvonne and her fears was trapping my voice, the artist in me, and the rebel who wanted to help the world to change. Her truncated walk was like a metaphor for our inability to stride forth into life. I saw an open gate now, as Von's affair with Wendy gave me a moral, or at least righteous, emotional leverage to leave her, and I took it, moving out by December of 1966, that momentous year in which I had died as a good girl, and had been reborn as an artist, lover, and rebel.

FREE TO BE THE POET OF MY DREAMS

After leaving Von, and moving into an apartment on Silver Avenue in Albuquerque, the quick discovery came of how disorderly I was as a housekeeper. Nothing would stay in a stack or category, everything I owned, open books, notebook, laundry, plates, ashtray, swirled into a chaotic landscape on the floor. I was embarrassed by this. But now I was free! Free! With no more cautionary restrictions, I was now a lone operator; I could define myself however I chose. I could even call myself a poet, and write about anything at all. I saw a poster of Lawrence Ferlinghetti, a poet from San Francisco, wearing a sea cap; immediately I bought one and went to Smoky Joe's, an off-campus bar on the main drag. I sat at the bar holding a little notebook and told anyone who asked that I was a poet. (Of course I knew I wasn't yet a poet). From here I met an artist, and went to his studio. Rick was painting a portrait of his girlfriend, who had gone to West Texas for a week of work. When he told me her occupation my attention was immediately riveted. Her name was Ruthie.

Ruthie had been forced out of her parent's home in Oklahoma at the age of thirteen, to go work on her own. Imagine this, living on the street, selling your body to sometimes crazy-fanatic strangers, trusting night after night that when you walk upstairs with your customer, he won't call you a filthy Jezebel, beat you or cut your throat. Then you give him the gift of your beautiful young body, your intimacy, your personal attention. When I met her, Ruthie was hooking to support Rick. She too had wanted to be an artist, a painter. In one of his paintings Rick had portrayed her as a nun, and perhaps this was his way of complimenting, of honoring her essential being. I was outraged that she sold her lovely body to support him. Why didn't they take turns working, and both paint?

My poem "Asking for Ruthie" was meant to be a cloak of protection, an amulet for her, by saying the realities (as I saw them) of her fragility within her occupation, "cut / by broken nickels in / hotel rooms and by razors of / summer lightning on the road." At the same time asking for some greater force or being to protect her, "sun cover her, earth / make love to Ruthie / stake her to hot lunches in the wheat fields." The poem ends, "let her newest lovers / be gentle as women / and longer lasting." Asking for a greater love, an expansive love blessed by nature. Asking it for both of us. Both of us sexual outlaws.

Without realizing it, I had adopted what was going to become known as a "dyke uniform." Rather than social rules, I began to follow my own desire to wear pants all the time. I also began to come out to people; when someone told me they thought a particular woman, R., a student on the University of New Mexico campus, was a lesbian I waited for her outside her classroom, went up and introduced myself by name and then, "I have heard that you're a lesbian. I'm a lesbian too, and I would like to know you." To my great relief, she recovered from her initial shock and agreed to get to know me.

One night, at my instigation, R. and I drank some wine and then took a flashlight and some black spray paint and walked around the neighborhood looking for a suitable, smooth-faced wall. I had written a poem about walls breaking down, walls needing to break down, and decided to put the lines on a real wall, to get the poem up off the page and out into the world. I kneeled on her shoulders as she boosted me up while I painted. Very satisfying experience.

The next day I went to see my handiwork and noticed a mob of people, including soldiers out in full regalia. Presence of olive green army trucks. Some soldiers were wielding long-handled brushes, huge buckets. They were whitewashing my poem! To my amazement, the wall on which we had painted my poem about breaking down walls was a national guard armory wall, and the poem was now being treated as an attack. What is it about art and the military, being so at odds? Slinking past, head down, yet once again I had an eerie sense of being powerful, no matter how accidentally, and this time not as a lesbian, as a *poet*.

STRETCHING OUT

From hanging out at Smoky Joe's I became part of a group of semi-artful drop-out people, including Ruthie and Rick. I did not lose track of Von during this time. After I left her she seemed to hold her balance; she took a teaching job with junior-high kids in Belen, south of Albuquerque. But the pain of not getting to be who she really was took a certain quirky turn.

"I've bought a house," she told me. "Come out and see it." The house was isolated from people, surrounded by the incredible beauty of mountains and desert, yet with enough groundwater that cottonwoods grew in the yard. Inside, the rooms were completely empty, just plaster walls, wood floors, linoleum and cupboards in the kitchen, kettle on the stove. But not a single stick of furniture. Not a chair, not a table, not a lamp. No curtains or blinds.

"I've drawn a line at conforming," she responded to my question about why she kept her house so barren. "I will obey their rules, and I will be the best teacher, and the best daughter, that I can be. But I'm keeping something for myself, my protest."

We sat on the floor, backs against the wall. "When my mother and my aunt come out to visit, they are so upset by this. They pressure me, man. They cry." (Von was at the forefront of white people using the new slang word, "man!" This was coming from the Black Movement's getting rid of the old racist diminutive "boy" for black men; "man!" had now become as ordinary an expression as "wow!" or "jeez!") It was her mother and aunt who had given Von her odd, jerky walk, by tying a short rope between her legs to make her walk like a girl. She sucked on a cigarette, her silver rings flashing off her brown fingers. "But I don't care. I tell them, 'This is my house, and I'll keep it the way I want.' What can they do?"

I laughed in appreciation of her rebellion.

Separating from Von emotionally was harder than I had thought. I used poetry to do it: "if you lose your lover / rain hurt you / brown rabbits run under car wheels. Should your / body cry to feel such / blue and empty bed?" The poem resolved with advice to move on, "comb hair. Go here or there. Get / another." I didn't tell her I had written it.

Brazenly, I bought a bright blue motorcycle and rode it to my night shift at the "Indian and Welfare Hospital" in Albuquerque. One night a fellow didn't like how I looked at him and punched me at the counter of a hamburger stand. He was a local pimp who needed to dominate women; when I tried to report the assault the cops just laughed at me, and it was clear to me they did not like dykes. I felt foolish for having gone to the cops, and my face hurt for a long time, but at least I had tried to stand up for myself, I hadn't just run home. I kept riding the bike.

On a cold winter's day of 1967, I opened my door to a Western Union guy with a telegram. My heart beat fast, as a telegram could only mean that my parents were sick, or one of them had died. My hand shook as I tore the envelope. The words were all in caps, with the word "stop" instead of a period. The message was completely incomprehensible. SHUTTERS SHUT AND OPEN SO DO QUEENS STOP CALL ME STOP. There was a phone number at the bottom.

For a couple of hours I studied this cryptic message. Who had sent me this crazy thing? "Shutters shut and open so do queens." Was this a quote from someone? But who writes like that? A flash—Gertrude Stein! I began to laugh, recognizing Wendy's whimsy and cleverness. Shutters are on windows, and also cameras; queens are powerful women. She knew that Von and I had fallen in love over jokes about pairs of queens. The telegram meant she was open to knowing me, not just Yvonne. She was also saying that jealousy didn't need to shut us down.

So I called her, and in week or so she visited. This was not a good visit. I was sick with some long-lasting gastric problem. So unromantic. Wendy was restless, seemed disappointed in me, wanting something from me I felt I did not have, some independent courage or capacity. I took her for a ride on my motorcycle, then when the motor died she seemed disgusted that I couldn't start it again. I had only potential and élan, endless endless willingness to try anything, to fall off the end of my capacities, get up, and run out to the end of them again. But not much stability in this architecture. Perhaps she sensed this. She was still with her man lover, wanted to stay with him. Then why come all the way to see me? Was she wondering if I could be strong enough for what she wanted? What did she want? In perhaps mutual irritation and disappointment we parted once again.

Now another woman came into my life and this one definitely wanted to live with me. We met in Albuquerque's only gay bar at the time; she began flirting immediately and showing me the money in her wallet, which I took as a wonderful, expansive signal that she wanted to take me home and take care of me. I had read this correctly. We got along well in bed and out, so Karla Tonella and I began to live together. She was generous in heart, mind, and body. A native of Albuquerque and a lover of arts and knowledge, she supported my budding poetry with all her heart. Karla, sweet, sincere, and aggressively protective, was exactly what I needed.

By June of 1967 she had moved us to Placitas, twenty-five miles outside Albuquerque in the Sandia Mountains; she rented a house owned by the poet Robert Creeley, who had just gotten a job in upstate New York. At that time Placitas was a little Chicano village that also contained a small Anglo arts community and she thought I might thrive there. "You're better than all these guys," she would say of the loquacious, competitive and gregarious poetry community, which included Larry Goodell (the den mother/father), Stephen Rodefer, and, as a visitor, Gene Frumkin. I wasn't a grown-up poet, not yet, but her words of unconditional support sent a rush of optimism coursing through my skinny veins.

The fellows came over for her good cooking and our warm hospitality; they gave noisy, confident poetry readings of their own work, in which I don't recall participating, though I must have. The women attached to the men mostly sat listening, after the alarming fashion of hippie women. The little community called us "Gertrude and Alice" and waxed nostalgic about the salon in Paris, as well as the one that Robert Creeley and his wife Bobbie had facilitated out of the very same big rambling house in Placitas.

I showed my work to a few people, hid out in the glorious little dark wood back room Creeley had built as a "poetry studio." Imagine that! A whole little room just to write poetry! I locked myself in there, day after day, hoping for a miracle, going outside at night to humbly praise the sky full of brilliant stars, then back into the magic wooden room. Was my trust in myself misplaced? Would my poetry have meaning to anyone besides me?

My own poems came with difficulty, small, not adding up to anything much in my critical mind. One for Karla, "in the place where," about our love-making. One for black women in Detroit following a civil rights riot. One for women of Vietnam in the rape of war. Another for Larry Goodell who taught me to dance to the thirteen-minute Doors song, "Light My Fire." Larry Goodell, my angel (or someone similar, Steve Rodefer maybe) arranged a poetry reading for me at the University, to which an astonishing number of supportive people came. Evidently they saw me as a promising poet. Funny that I had no sense of this myself, felt I had a really long way to go to learn my "craft or sullen art," as Dylan Thomas had put it.

After a while Karla began sleeping with one of the fellows in the community and I realized our relationship had run its course. I would have left but didn't really have a place to go. One night I dreamed of looking up to a cobalt sky. A huge frigate bird with a six-foot wingspan was flying past, black-bodied but with a stark white head. Suddenly the head turned and gazed intently at me, and I saw it was a skull. I awoke soaked in sweat, deeply disturbed. Some kind of massive change was calling my name. My restless hunger increased, but for what?

December floated toward its crispy mesquite-smoke end of 1967. Just before New Year's, Karla answered a knock at the front door and suddenly there was Wendy Cadden. She had arrived out of the blue in a second-hand white Volvo, of which she was very proud, "my first car," came into the house, said her hellos, and promptly announced that she had dropped acid. Pupils enormous, face pale, she spent the afternoon and evening wandering among the venerable old rooms, saying incomprehensible fragments of sentences, not coming near me, muttering, taking pictures now and then. I felt very sad, disgusted even, and went to bed. Our friendship had seemed so full of promise, already I had changed much about my life because of knowing her. I had left Yvonne and the chains of stability, had declared myself a poet and a lesbian, had been punched out for riding a motorcycle, had scrawled poetry on a wall in the middle of the night, had even gone to Mexico for an adventure. Through this she had remained mysteriously, recurrently, present in my life. And I had expected to know so much more about her by now.

About ten o'clock the next morning she got in her car. What on earth had this visit been about? Why were we disappointing each other again, why couldn't our connection fall into place? I stood outside in the cold December air, saying goodbye, holding myself aloof.

She started the motor, then leaned toward me, cocked her head with a little impish smile.

"Why don't you come with me?"

My studied indifference dissolved.

"To Antioch? To Ohio?"

"Sure, come for a visit."

Feeling stunned but acting like a released spring, I said, "Wait a minute!" Dashed inside the house, took thirty-five dollars (my savings), a notebook, my blue denim jacket, a second pair of Levis, told Karla I was going on an adventure.

I wonder if Wendy was surprised when I climbed into her Volvo. Or had she known she would acquire my company ever since she had composed the cryptic telegram about shutters, queens, and opening? We stopped up the rough road in Placitas to pick up a fellow who wanted a ride to Columbus; he fell asleep in the back seat for the duration. New Year's Eve came and went, the black razor of highway up the Midwest to Yellow Springs cut the past to pieces. Wendy stared ahead, driving through ice. I sat in the front seat in an altered state, putting out so much heat it didn't matter that the window on her side did not go up, or that the Texas panhandle was particularly bitter cold that winter. Every once in a while she looked over and locked eyes with me, burning a hole through to the back of my skull and down my spine. Not touching except to hold hands, blazing with possibility, we drove like an arrow of flame through the frozen air into our astonishing new life.

1968: Jewish Radical Students

My background as a working-class Protestant woman did not prepare me to understand the world I entered when Wendy settled me into her basement apartment in a collective radical household. I could barely understand what people were talking about, or why they were so impassioned. Was Wendy going to be too much for me? I frequently fingered the thirty-five-dollar security money in my pocket. The night we arrived from Albuquerque she led me down the steps to her basement rooms, a narrow mattress against one wall, small lamp on the floor casting warm light over it. The adjacent room was larger, featured an easel with her painting, strong earth and kerosene smell of acrylic paints, paintbrush cleaner, and marijuana smoke.

I was still a total innocent to the world of younger people. For instance, I got my period soon after our arrival, and lay groaning in pain on the living room couch. Wendy brought me a two-inch ball of something earth-brown wrapped in tinfoil, a medicine obviously.

She came back about fifteen minutes later. "Where is it?" looking at the empty tinfoil.

"I ate it."

"*All* of it?" Her face registered astonishment.

"Wasn't I supposed to?" Then she bent over laughing, holding her stomach. I had consumed the household's entire month's supply of hashish. Which had no apparent effect on me.

The household was a political collective, whose focus was analyzing the appropriate role of radicals in a revolutionary movement. They had anticipated Wendy participating in activism that semester, but she brought me home instead and we holed up in her basement, making love nonstop on the narrow mattress next to the larger room, where she was painting a replica of the well-known photograph of Black Panther leader Huey Newton, seated in his wicker chair. She also did an abstract painting of various mechanical shapes. What is that? I finally had to ask, and she connected the pieces for me—a pistol.

Wendy and I continued our delicious entanglement unabated. I wanted nothing except to melt together with her like two spoons of butter in a frying pan. As our sex-saturated days and nights in the basement surged on, January became February. Our next-door neighbor, Beth, who was married to Carl Oglesby, remembers coming down to our den, finding us coiled asleep, cheek to cheek; she was transfixed with a tender feeling. And who had ever seen such a thing as two women tangled together in rapture? Lesbianism was not an open subject on the campus, yet people noticed us. We began coming up for air, moving past our encapsulated sex-dripping privacy and the late nights of unwrapping our sticky bodies from each other long enough to sneak upstairs to the kitchen to make a single heaping plate of hot dogs and eggs scrambled with onions and cheddar cheese.

There was no rule she seemed unwilling to break, even driving her white Volvo brazenly up onto the sidewalk, and this thrilled me. I was more than ready to break out of all the rules that had ever confined me, and my lovers, until now. I wanted to stride out and run. I wanted to be a tornado causing oppressive walls to collapse. A breath of Freedom had burst into my life and I was transfixed, trying to gulp it all down, learning fast. My father's fiercely independent spirit reared its head within my head, its face became my face. But while my father had earned his freedom at the price of loss of status and social power, these people claimed it as a part of their class and age privilege; they were young, gifted, white, outraged, and supported in various measures by their families. They also had courage, conviction, and determination to make social change. They were wrapping their minds around theories of how to have an impact. They roused up hope I had never felt before.

After Wendy and I surfaced, we began to go to the movies on campus. Wendy had worked as cashier and so knew the side door that allowed free access. We saw Charlie Chaplin becoming a machine in a statement about the alienation of factory work and the role of speedups in production. We watched Wendy's personal favorite several times: the French film *Jules et Jim*. Gradually I absorbed the culture of Antioch, understood that there were two distinct camps, the hippies and the politicos. They were at odds, though overlapping in their alienation with mainstream culture, and their reliance on drugs for entertainment. Music, oddly, was not a big part of this experience; films were. There was much talk of how and whom to organize. The workers, of course, the proletariat, of which evidently I was a prime example. I was a "*real* American," as Wendy's friend Vicky Jacobs said, shaking her long curls, holding her curled fingers to her lips, giggling and saying, "Where did you find her! She's so beautiful!"

We engaged with the idea of fighting back, of resistance, more than academically. Wendy, and probably others, were supportive of the gradually developing Black Power movement, whose energies had first stirred me on the campus of Howard University two years before, sitting with Larry Jones in the Chicken Shack. People could resist oppression and could force necessary changes, and black people were already engaged in this. And as, a generation before, my father had helped establish the labor movement, I too could participate in a great movement. But what did that mean?

Rules of all kinds were made to be broken, this group's actions seemed to say. Almost entirely Jewish, mostly from New York City, these students had been born just as World War II ended and the impact of the Holocaust hit the world full force. They were driven by the reality that silence and trust and keeping the rules were the sure way to lose one's life, family, and people. They questioned everything all the time, and tested every boundary. Discussions were high-pitched, endless. Why hadn't the Jewish people fought back against the Nazis? Why had they lined up? Why had they let themselves be driven onto the trains even after they had to have known where they were going? This seemed to be, that year anyhow, the most pressing question for these young people, a question that surfaced continually.

Films about World War II and the years leading up to it, were coming out, films avidly dissected for their radical content—resistance, where was it, who did it? An early Russian film (*Potemkin* I think, by Eisenstein) with one figure going against the crowd as it surged down the steps away from the guards was wildly cheered, treasured as a spark of hope—someone running against the grain. Turning toward the Russian guards, not away from them.

When a film about the Warsaw Ghetto Uprising came to the Yellow Springs theater, the question of whether the Jews had resisted the Nazis was answered, resoundingly. Yes, people had resisted, even though for arms they had mostly a few pistols and some Molotov cocktails, they had fought with every possible tactic, had won the moral victory. The Antioch students erupted in exclamations and cheers. Now the rousing late-night discussions amped up. What was self-defense, what circumstances demanded the moral obligation to fight back and, here in the U.S., to fight early and hard on behalf of—whom? The most obvious translation of the European/Jewish travail onto American soil was the civil rights struggle. This group wanted to know how to contribute, how to fight back effectively, whether and how to support armed struggle. Some would go in a cultural direction, away from militancy; others would support armed struggle, one or two even participating in Weather Underground activities; one already had a box of greasy bottles stuffed with rags in her possession, held on behalf of the militant black students at the nearby black college campus, who weren't arguing anymore about whether to engage in armed struggle, but rather were preparing for that certainty.

The radical movement coming from the white privileged colleges was mostly populated with young people who had never worked or brushed shoulders with workers. They were conscientiously interested in "workers" but had no idea who they were, only that they were supposed to organize us, and lead us in a revolutionary manner. No one had taught them anything about the realities of gaining input from workers themselves. I was mortified to speak up in their heated debates, as I simply did not know the language, and besides— despite their warm friendliness—there were times when I thought they really disliked working-class people like me because I hadn't done everything "right."

My mind, especially since the encephalitis, wouldn't hold on to abstract principles. I liked concrete examples, and experiential knowledge; hypothetical situations irritated me. Yet there was no doubting their sincerity and their fiery determination to make social change. I wondered how they were going to do this in this country, in this decade, and why it mattered to know the difference between Trotsky and Lenin; why did people need to be called the "proletariat," why did they hate the "bourgeois" so much yet attend an elite school that had rejected me? I felt that I disappointed them; once, M. asked what my opinion was, and everything stopped while I stammered, not having any idea how to engage with their specialized language.

Sometimes they surprised and offended me, like the day K. came back from the grocery store with meat and butter under her odd-looking fur coat. She unloaded herself defiantly. She was practicing, she said, for the time when she would need to steal to get food.

I had stolen food, of course, but I could not fathom anyone doing so out of choice, for practice. I had stolen food because of weighing ninety-five pounds and slipping, with no options except to join the service and get three meals a day. And I did not want to tell that history to these avid radicals, though in retrospect I think I could have trusted them to try really hard to understand me. I was ashamed of everything about myself except for a dawning sense that being a lesbian was my most defiantly courageous stance and needed to be a public statement.

THE CELL

By late April my observations of the factions at Antioch began to form themselves into characters in a play. I called this play *The Cell*. The script was sparse to a fault, and was perhaps not so much a play as instructions for something that could become a play. Yet, shortly after I completed the manuscript, just a few pages long, Wendy showed it around, and pretty much the whole art department of students said they wanted to be in it or otherwise contribute.

A fellow who had been trying unsuccessfully to make a post-apocalyptic film volunteered to direct my play, and we were off and running. *The Cell* was architectural. The setting was a basketball court, without bleachers. Chairs, to be occupied by the audience, were arranged in rows facing out in a square formation, with an empty space in the center. This space, called "the cell," was occupied by a cast member, "the prisoner." The backs of the audience were to the prisoner, who was imprisoned by the arrangement of the chairs. People in the audience were thus characters in the play, known as "persons with seats." There were two identical stage areas, at two opposite points of the square. Each area was occupied by an identical set of characters known as "persons without seats," consisting of a mother, son, and daughter, plus some barnyard chickens. The daughter was nude, encased within an egg-shaped plastic structure, known as "the cell," in which she could only rock back and forth, unable to move. The job of the chickens was to care for her and help her be born. The son was named Jack, and he was trying to climb a beanstalk, or chop it down. Jack spoke only through a musical instrument. There were also four platforms, one on each side of the square, occupied by "prison guards" who wore black suits, black sunglasses, and carried rifles. Their speech consisted of orders to the audience not to move or speak, and under no circumstances to give up their chairs.

Separated by ropes stretched across the other two diagonal corners, neither "family" could cross this barrier. A final character was a black and yellow dragon, who could freely travel all around the gym. The nature of this dragon was not described in the script. The prisoner's goal was to get the people with chairs to get up and move their chairs, allowing the prisoner to escape. Should this happen, the guards were to spray mace (not really of course) upon the escaped prisoner, who was then to fall unconscious on the floor. What happened after that was up to the audience. The whole gym was thus also "the cell."

The art students were marvelous in their enthusiasm to create props and be in the cast, and Wendy's housemates turned out for the cast as well. As I had noticed with the campus overall, two factions surfaced: the hippies and the politicos. The hippies wanted the family to have hookah pipe props, with the chickens taking care of daily life while the family was having fun. The politicos gathered around the character of the dragon, and ingeniously turned it into the media. They wore black and yellow armbands, and rode around in a black and yellow "press car" powered by their members pushing it (the group looked like a big-headed caterpillar). They interviewed members of the audience, asking how the play was going, what did they think it was about, what was going on with the person in the center of their chairs who was beseeching them?

As rehearsals went on I was hoping that person, the prisoner, would be me, that I could make pro-lesbian statements, and describe the isolation and alienation I felt as a woman beyond social definition. I had a strong belief that, despite all nervousness, my tongue would know what to say. Meanwhile, two weeks before the date we had set for two performances, the director quit.

This was a depressing turn for a day or two, then I took a breath and went around to each of the cast and told them I had never directed anything but would show up for however they wanted this to go. So they turned out for it.

Shortly before the big day, members of the Black Student Union approached me and said they had read the script and wanted to be a part of it. Wendy's friend, and quickly mine, Linda Wilson from Harlem, had taken them the script.

So the prisoner became a black man, and the issue became white privilege and Black Power. The first night came. All the costumes were made, the "Jacks" played trumpet and saxophone, and the naked women in the egglike plastic cells were so provocative they had been the illustration for the advertising posters, all of which were stolen within two days of being posted.

The audience was asked to remove their shoes, the pile of shoes adding a shadow of Holocaust imagery, and no doubt adding to their sense of vulnerability once they were inside the ordered chaos we had created. Every chair was filled. The families and chickens had made up a little plot, while the press went about in their black and yellow line with microphones to embellish their rude interrogations. The prisoner yelled for release. I don't think anyone got up voluntarily from a chair at first that night, as the guards paced overhead, telling the audience to stay put no matter what. Then, about halfway through, the prisoner accelerated his pleas, pushing on chairs to make his point, and people got up and out of his way. The guards "maced" him and he fell to the floor. At that moment, a group of black students burst into the gym; they grabbed the prisoner and dragged him out the door. This was not part of the script. Pandemonium reigned in the audience, and the play ended.

The second night, every seat was again filled. This time, a group of white students, all male—as I think the black students had been as well—had decided to pull off a coup of their own.

Hardly had the dual plays gotten going when the white would-be radicals burst into the gym. They ignored the prisoner where he already lay "maced" on the floor, grabbed the nude women, climbed up the guard towers and replaced the guards, down to their black jackets, black sunglasses and, of course, the plastic machine guns. They began shouting orders. Again, pandemonium.

When the milling people had finally gathered their shoes and gone, the cast, somewhat disconsolate, mourned that they hadn't been able to finish the play. I was extremely upset, first with myself, as I hadn't written in a place for me to either stand or sit in the gymnasium, so I had spent the play hidden behind one of the basket posts. I was neither a person with, nor without, a seat. I too felt disappointment that we hadn't gotten to finish the play. More than this, I was upset with the white students for abandoning the prisoner, grabbing the women and, from what I could determine, simply replacing the guards. I picked up one of the guns and bashed it to pieces on the back of a chair.

"What's wrong?" one of them shouted. He looked with pained entreaty into my face. "We thought this was what you *wanted* us to do."

"No, no," I cried. But I couldn't tell him any more than this. I felt placeless and mute.

The play experience had taught me a great deal, about my own sense of being literally nowhere. And about a gaping difference between the white and black men. The black men wanted to claim their own and go somewhere else together. The white men wanted to replace the white guard authoritarian structure with themselves. The white women, meantime, were off in another world, almost unrelated to this one, waiting to be born. The horn players wanted to make a ton of noise, without paying attention to each other.

The play was a marvelous success in terms of turnout, and people at Antioch wanted to engage me about it but I shied away. I was upset that we had nearly destroyed the gym, had stolen stuff for props and, most of all, revealed a deeply disturbing statement about the motives and methods of young radical white men.

The Argument

Wendy and I headed west in her car the next day. She had graduated from Antioch but didn't want to attend the ceremony. Not long after we hit the interstate out of Ohio, directly beneath Michigan, we came to the intersection: turn north for Detroit, or continue straight across the continent to California. She stopped the Volvo in the middle of the crossroads of the two broad highways, turned off the lights, then the motor, and we had an argument. She wanted to settle us in Detroit, where we were to "organize the workers." I thought this sounded like the dullest and most futile of exercises. Possibly even dangerous for lesbians. Autoworkers had been organized in the thirties, and could damn well take care of themselves now. And if they couldn't, what could we possibly tell them? We knew nothing about making automobiles. And I could imagine us in another collective like the one we were leaving, full of argumentative men, only not as jolly, not as artful, just as sexy, maybe even demanding of sex. I shuddered at this. How could I protect my love for Wendy from them? And the weather unbelievably cold, especially for women and gay folks.

My driving desire was to get us to San Francisco, and my motive was love. I adored being with Wendy and did not want to lose her to virile and taciturn blue-collar men in the straightest zone of the country—the auto industry. How in the hell could we possibly live together in that atmosphere? I knew it would be impossible, that I would lose her very quickly. San Francisco, I had heard, would be a place we might make it together; it might be easier to be gay, though I wasn't certain of this. But Wendy's political focus was about organizing people. Whatever was to be organized in San Francisco? I didn't have an answer for that. The workers were in Detroit.

So typical of Wendy to have stopped the car in the middle of the highway, heightening the drama of the decision that we had not discussed: where shall we go? Fortunately the intersection was well lit and very few cars came by; we had started our trip late and it was now about midnight. We steamed up the windows as we argued passionately for two hours. I can't imagine now what kinds of arguments came into my mind; I didn't think "keeping you" would go over so well—would Marx approve? And she was about freedom over anything else. Yet I persisted, and eventually her hand moved to the key, she started the car, moved us forward, past the junction. As we headed west, I nearly fainted with relief and exultation; I had won. Maybe we would get to stay together for a while.

The Arrival

Now she had a new story for what we were doing together. Once in San Francisco, we would go to the docks and find Vicky Jacob's boyfriend Baxter. He had bought a genuine Chinese junk, an ancient sailboat design still in use, and he needed a crew to sail around the world. Although most water, especially the ocean, was frightening to me, and I considered Baxter truly strange, so that this prospect filled me with horror, I didn't let on. Let stoicism prevail. Let the moment fall where it would, like a handful of divinatory sticks, at least we would be in San Francisco, and we would be together.

I loved the city on sight, the interesting neighborhoods, the playfulness and sometimes elegance of the paint jobs, the variety of detail on the houses, the ghostly fog traipsing in through the up-and-down streets. We stayed with Beth and other friends from college while deciding what to do next. Almost immediately my lover drove us to the marina. Oh damn.

Wendy was persisting in the Baxter quest. A remote young white man, he was extremely tall, slender, and unpredictable. A child of the excessively wealthy upperclass, he seldom spoke, and was questing after meaning long after the beatnik era was gone. He and Vicky had gone to Amsterdam, where nothing would do but to act out a scene from the French movie she and Wendy both loved so much, *Jules et Jim*. A woman has two lovers, marries one, desires them both. The two men are friends who fought on different sides during the Great War. They all attempt unsuccessfully to live together but her inability to choose continues until she drives a car with herself and Jim into a lake, while Jules watches from the shore.

In Amsterdam, Baxter set out to replicate the final scene of the film with himself driving, Vicky as passenger. He rented or bought a car, a classic of similar vintage to the one in the film. They sat in it, aimed it, their nihilistic weapon of choice. But Vicky leapt out of the passenger's side the second before he plunged it into one of Amsterdam's canals, and she held her breath as the vehicle vanished. Minutes passed while her heart trembled, and then his head bubbled up to the surface.

Now we proposed to be, just the two of us, on the high seas with him. Whatever was Wendy thinking? I had no idea. She loved sailing, had crewed on sailboats on the Atlantic coast. But that was for a day's sport; that wasn't "around the world." I solaced my anxious self by imagining that the boat would be a vivid green, friendly lizard of a thing, with two or even three masts, red and gold trim, like something—though in miniature—I might have painted under my father's crafty roof. We wandered the maze of docks until my feet hurt and the sea wind cut me in half. That Vicky must have made the whole thing up. But then, there the boat was, a very faded, uncared for, venerably old, gray dead-dragon-looking Chinese junk.

"This is it!" Wendy was excited. She went below to find Baxter while I paced the unpainted, splintery deck, noticing how chilly San Francisco was actually, and vowing to acquire a warm coat. (I did after a while, a gorgeous dark blue, nearly black, Navy surplus peacoat, which served to keep me through several San Francisco seasons. These well-made wool coats have the advantage that you can button the double row of buttons up under your neck and the coat flap comes up another scratchy inch or two so you can duck your teeth behind a fabric shield in a chill wind.)

Never well-acclimated to weather, hot or cold, I was shaking when Wendy came up from below deck. The afternoon wind was well up. She looked very disappointed.

"Let's go." As we trudged up the dock she explained the situation. "We can't sail around the world with him. He has decided to live on fifty cents a month."

Trudge trudge. "How does he do that?"

"He eats nothing except oatmeal." We walked on as I assimilated this information. A yellow-beaked gull on the rail let out a squawk. The sea breath invaded my nostrils, and now smelled deliciously of liberty. The wind in the Bay Area cleanses the whole place for a couple of hours every day, making way for endless possibility.

"That might not be such a problem…" she paused. I pondered living on only oatmeal, bobbing across the Pacific. We walked a few more yards. "It wouldn't be a problem, except he has epoxied his hands together." To get the picture I had to ask her twice about this last detail. Epoxy is a particularly permanent glue, and Baxter had spread it on his palms, then slapped them together and let it dry. He was studying Buddhism, American style.

Within a year or two we ran into him again, on Telegraph Avenue in Berkeley, wearing a thin orange dress, chanting Hare Krishna with the other devotees. His hands were blissfully free, his long fingers slapping a tambourine, his eyes fixed on peace. I was extremely grateful to the Krishnavites and their bhakti devotion for saving me from having to sail around the world in order to keep my love. Instead, we found something else to do. We joined the revolutionary movement.

WE SAW EACH OTHER

"Go upstairs," we were told. Wendy and I had gone to a party in the Haight. "They're watching films." Upstairs was an attic room, stuffed with women lying on cushions, draped on each other and riveted to the screen. Oh, it must be some imported lesbian sex stuff, I thought, a little lasciviously. Instead, the film was a sort of National Geographic special, on the lives of African army ants. What? But yes. The ants, shown in close-up, marched in columns all day, eating their way across the landscape, carrying their queen and her eggs with them. At night they had no den, no quarters of any kind, no opportunity to make a structure of straw or mud. So they made it of themselves, using their own bodies. A number of the females locked their legs, horizontally and vertically, constructing a many-storied living hotel. The others climbed into the protective pockets created by the geometry of strong-armed sisters and slept.

I was just as gripped by this scene as the other women, who kept saying, "Wow, look at that!" We 1970s dykes were nomads making "place" like those ants—without homes or family, except what we could make for each other. A dyke song lyric I heard recently says it this way: "I like girls who are freaks and have no place / so I make the place, I make the place in my arms." (Animal Prufrock, 2010)

ENGAGING WITH THE LEFT

"Goddammit! What do you think you're doing!" I was storming through the upper rooms of the house on Portrero Hill. We were having a party, so the downstairs was crammed with people, mostly leftists and some musicians, including the big bearded barefoot guy in a long raggedy-assed black coat, who swayed up and down as he played electric guitar with Wendy every week, showing her new licks, new chords. Tonight Black Panther Party Minister of Culture Eldridge Cleaver had just walked in with a tall, blonde, and self-conscious girlfriend. Some instinct suddenly sent me upstairs to our bedroom where I found my lover with one of our male roommates, in *our* bed. I tore through the upstairs while a naked Wendy raced behind me, seeking instant reconciliation, and the man glared in angry disappointment.

Those Lesbians! So jealous!

Up until now I had fought, sometimes successfully, with my intermittent jealousy of Wendy's sexual connections with other people, my emotional taming greatly aided by the ways she showered me with tender attentions such as I had never experienced. Following that fiery night we negotiated an agreement. She came up with the terms: we would have an open yet committed and loving relationship, within which we could have sex with anyone we wished, so long as we did not bring it home. No names, no faces, no stories. What we were to bring home, she stressed, were the heightened feelings, the electric turn-on acquired from sexual connections, and this would refresh our own sexual magnetism for each other. Could such an arrangement really work, I wondered?

With her radical political sensibility and willingness to engage in all aspects of the movement, Wendy was leading us into the various struggles in the Bay Area. We attended Panther rallies in Oakland parks, and a huge gathering at the Scottish Temple. Between late fall of 1968 and spring of 1969 we participated in the S.F. State strike, which culminated in the establishment of "the first Department of Ethnic Studies," changing academia across the country. Members of the Black Student Union teamed up with the Third World Liberation Front and had support from thousands of students and faculty. Wendy and I operated as "nonstudent organizers," taking photographs while running round and round the 19th Avenue neighborhoods across manicured hedges and lawns chased by club swinging cops on tall horses. To my surprise, the movement for ethnic studies at San Francisco State was spurred in large part by my hero Dr. Nathan Hare, who had relocated to California after being fired from Howard University for opposing the administration's desire to see

Howard become 60% white. Black student activism on the West Coast caught fire in demanding a Black Studies department, to be headed by Dr. Hare, who was pushing "Black Power" forward; he first used the term "ethnic studies" to replace "minority studies." The Black Studies Department he headed in 1969 is now called "Africana Studies."

Wendy and I had also joined the radical filmmaking group Newsreel, covering events exploding in Northern California, especially as the Black Panther Party took moral and political leadership, with free breakfast for children programs and confrontations with police over their harassment of people in black neighborhoods. Wendy had been distributing the party's paper, *The Black Panther*, and was one of two white women occasionally invited to help with layout. She was also loaning her car, the faithful old white Volvo, to party members. The Newsreel group consisted mainly of white middle-class men and the women attached to them—a typical Left arrangement at that time. Wendy and I were not close to anyone, had little access to actual filmmaking, but were just accepted as "the girls." As with other political enterprises that survived the era, this group changed over time, becoming much more inclusive long after we were gone.

One week at a rare Newsreel party (the Left was very work-oriented) a straight-looking woman with a lush body and an attitude full of verve leaned in to try to kiss me—my breath caught in anticipation of the first acceptance I had felt from the San Francisco Left, which seemed adamantly heterosexual. Her long hair swept down between us, stopping the moment of flirtation, yet the intriguing possibility of the Left accepting lesbianism, despite Marx, hung in the air. This was Marilyn Buck, who was about twenty at the time.

Sometime later, the organization sent Marilyn and me on a mission to post flyers on Telegraph Avenue, announcing a talk by Eldridge Cleaver at UC Berkeley. I carried the posters and stapler, while she looked for appropriate spots. After about the third success, two young uniformed cops approached us: "No posting." I was strategically acquiescing when Marilyn began to scream at them, calling them everything she could think of, a tactic that made no sense given the power differential. They looked at the flyer and promptly arrested me, since I had been the one committing the illegal act. My arrest was politically motivated on their part, as the phone poles were so coated with staples from posters that had gone before ours that all the wood could have rotted and the poles would still be standing.

At the station they put me in a small holding cell. Worry arrived as I went through the pockets of my peacoat, finding a tiny stub of joint that Wendy or our friend Tommie had left there when one of them borrowed the coat. I dropped this dangerous item, which could have gotten me a jail sentence, onto the floor. Sweat. Surely they would search the spotless cell. Two cops, a man and a woman, took me into another room and strip-searched me, a humiliating experience that had nothing to do with the unfound joint or the misdemeanor charge of "posting," and everything to do with the name "Eldridge Cleaver"—a name which evaporated my white privilege, not that I had this insight at the time. I had few insights at the time, everything in my life was forward motion and emotion. Being in the cell gave me a panicky feeling of claustrophobia; then someone from Newsreel quickly bought my way out and I kept quiet about the strip-search, which had shamed me.

Newsreel was doing important work, but Wendy and I weren't getting anywhere in the organization with the editing or filming that interested us. I went to work at the *San Francisco Express Times* newspaper as a typesetter, absorbing through my fingers the various leftist factional positions. After a while the position of poetry editor opened up and I asked for it, was immediately told "No." I was getting tired of hearing this word. We were beginning to see the first stirrings of women organizing for themselves in the marches. Among the signs advocating no more war and support for various issues was a new one, a startling one: Women's Liberation! I was skeptical. Weren't we in enough trouble as lesbians? Surely we didn't need to take on any more.

PEOPLE's PARK: MAY INTO JUNE 1969

In January of 1969, Californians were shocked into an awareness of the dangers to nature of our industrial way of life, as a two-month oil spill began poisoning the coast of Santa Barbara. Pictures of oil-soaked birds broke hearts as Californians volunteered for the shoreline clean up. It was in this context of heightened environmental awareness that a group of UC Berkeley architects led a protest that quickly escalated into mass demonstrations to protect an area of land on Telegraph Avenue that became known as "People's Park." The university regents wanted to use the space for dormitories, but the idea of open space with trees had caught the public imagination. Wendy's friend from her Antioch days, Peter Adair, invited us to be part of his film crew, as he was making his own film of the actions, and when we arrived on Telegraph Avenue to reconnoiter with him, handed us large still-frame cameras with protruding lenses.

Having a recording job put us right in the middle of everything. My first day was thrilling, as the large, chanting crowd marched from the campus onto Telegraph Avenue, where they were met with tear gas canisters and helmeted, thuggish policemen. I stood in the middle of the street shooting stills until my face was burning off, and then ran to the nearest spigot where a young man helped me wash the gas out of my eyes. I felt the high emotions of being swept into a mass movement whose purpose, to bring nature to the forefront, seemed so right, so congruent with Berkeley's values.

Peter took beautiful footage of the rebellion, especially of the young men. People's Park actions were exhilarating. A group of about thirty of us would rush to an empty lot and in half an hour plant it into a beautiful mini-park with grass, flowers, small trees, and bushes. A local nursery was supplying the green life in truckloads; people standing in the back of an open truck handed out shovels, rakes, and trowels. We supplied the fast labor, passing along the sod grass from one person to the next, the last one laying the sections down side by side, like hunks of bright green rug, snuggled in as though they had always lived there. When the police arrived with their swinging clubs to tear it all up and ravage us we scattered, with the whispered message, "we're regrouping" at such and such corner. There, another empty lot, another truckload of plants with shovels, and our eagerness, our sense of useful statement. The smell of sod transcended our fears. Our message couldn't be more clear and easy: Green life matters more than corporate profit.

In our daily sojourns into the war zone of Berkeley, Wendy and I split up so we wouldn't be distracted with worry about what was happening to each other. One of the young gay guys who so frequently hung out with us or slept on our floor paired up with Wendy. I wandered around on my own, knocking down police barricades, meeting up with them now and then. When the police beatings escalated, at times Wendy and I were the only women still on the streets, and when we noticed this we would fall back to safety as best we could, though the police would cordon off the area so there was no way to leave until sunset.

Dozens of people were injured, some permanently, by the shotgun pellets used by the police on "Bloody Thursday," May 15, 1969. Sitting as an observer on a Telegraph Avenue rooftop across the street from where Wendy had posted herself, a student named James Rector was shot in the chest and lay dying. Another man nearby was permanently blinded. Other people were wounded in this fray and subsequent ones, when they caught buckshot in the face or chest. One block away on Dana Street, as I sped toward the corner of Dwight Way, I saw a heavy, pink-faced policeman raising a rifle. My quick reflexes spun me into the opposite direction or I would have taken a blast of shot in the face and chest as others did that day. Instead the pellets rattled off the back of my jacket.

People's Park confrontations escalated as the city and the university brought in National Guard troops and surrounded the park area with a chain link fence. A huge march of thirty thousand citizens protested Rector's death and Governor Reagan's shameful use of the National Guard and his obvious support for police use of lethal ammunition.

Eventually the regents and the city reached an agreement to allow a park space that could be shared by all. I loved the positive actions related to the People's Park rebellion. For once we were building something, rather than just being chased around. We were bringing "ecology" and the relation of humans to nature to national attention. Images of the authorities tearing up flowers, uprooting small trees also got some attention.

Following these demonstrations, which continued into June, came news from New York City of the Stonewall uprising. Lesbians, gay men, and transgender people poured out of the Stonewall bar, sick of police harassment, fought with their bare hands against the men in blue with their swinging clubs. We were excited by this news, which would impact our lives by the end of the year.

Capp Street and 'The Common Woman Poems'

My days were taken up with a job at Presbyterian Hospital with a woman boss whose brittle style I did not like. What was I doing that mattered? Earlier, when we were getting to know each other, Wendy had asked me one of the most important questions I'd ever been asked. "Why don't you come with me?" Why didn't I just drop everything and get in the car with her? An invitation to engage with her life, a life utterly different from anything I had ever experienced, a path to the volatile and exhilarating left movement, and a peek at the liberal, literary, successful, confident upper-middle-class. More than this, a path to a love that wanted change, wanted to participate, wanted to be a force in the world, and knew how to connect with like-minded radicals.

Now, as we entered our artistic and political dramas in San Francisco, Wendy asked me the second most important question I'd been asked. She suddenly stopped me in the middle of one of my enthusiastic gushes on the subject of poetry. She got her dark-eyed serious face, tightened the muscles in her cheeks and said: "Just why is it that you write? What is it for?" I was astounded, stopped in my forward rush. A moment of pure consciousness ensued. I realized that poetry could be more than a gift, more than a way to get attention, more than emotional expression to save my life, more than a ride on the breath-horse of the times. Poetry could be directed purposefully. Her question has never left me, though my answers have gotten more complex.

What was poetry for? Wendy's astute and sharply driven question would haunt me, still haunts me. Poetry has a purpose, *is* for something. Art is not simply for its own sake, not even when it is a gift to the cosmos or to one's neighbor. Art is for something, even when it is deeply personal, in service to the poet's own psychology. A poet of the world is of use in the world. An activist poet stirs the world to action. Would the world find a use for me? I hadn't written anything I really liked since "Asking for Ruthie" and that wild play *The Cell*, and now my life did not seem the least bit artful. Wendy, at least, was taking photographs for Leftist organizations, but what was I doing?

Summer brought a terrible shock as the Charles Manson gang exploded onto the national scene with a series of horrific murders in Los Angeles, which they crudely attempted to pin on the Black Panthers. And by December, nihilistic Weather Underground children of the upper-middle-class would endorse Manson's actions as "revolutionary." That part of the radical white Left was unraveling as a force of moral leadership, though it could hardly compete with the acceleration of the war in Vietnam for immorality and unthwarted violence, as U.S. planes dropped napalm and Agent Orange on civilians in villages, and on soldiers from both sides. The body bags of soldiers were returning to the U.S. with sacks of heroin stashed in them for resale in the increasing market of disaffected young people and former soldiers. In Vietnam, soldiers were so alienated, we were hearing, that some were murdering their own officers. I wondered if my friend Larry Jones was in the battle zones and if so, how was he faring? Like the rest of the youth movement, my grief escalated into outrage as the war spread and grew ever more violent.

In an attempt to get my writing voice moving again, I joined a lovely writing group of gay men who had gathered around the poet Robert Duncan. Robert never made it to the meetings but that did not deter the rest of us. This group included Paul Mariah and Richard Tagett, who put out a gay men's magazine together, *Man Root*. I was gratified that they included some of my work, though my attention was going elsewhere, toward women.

Our friend Beth had been married to a "star" in the white Left, Carl Oglesby, whose antiwar speech had so stirred me at the SDS peace march in Washington DC. Beth had put us up on her sun porch when we first arrived in San Francisco. Now, a year later, when this competent, smart mother of three called to invite us to a consciousness-raising group meeting, we said yes. She had left Carl and joined with several other leftist women who had turned away from the dominance of their men in the deteriorating and splintering antiwar movement in order to make a sharp turn. Women of the Left began to intensely discuss with each other the real circumstances of their lives, breaking the injunction of family secrecy—the age-old iron bit in the mouths of women like my mother, warning me, never tell anyone that your father drinks (or that your mother is nuts and dangerous, or that your brother and your uncle sexually used your body, or that you've known you were a lesbian since you were twelve), or *anything else* that might threaten the structure, the precariously out-of-balance family structure.

Now, in groups organized by Judy Knupp, Beth Oglesby, and Lynn O'Connor, among others, women at last spoke truths to each other. Wendy and I split up to join separate groups out of a pragmatic sense that we could then be more honest. But this left us isolated. I had no idea what a lethal bomb I was dropping by saying, "I am a lesbian." No one in the small group said anything to this, though I am sure the leaders welcomed the diversity, and adamantly wanted to intersect with working-class women like me. But afterwards a woman said she had waited through the meeting for me to "jump on her." Though she meant to convey that her fear had changed after hearing me, her fear passed over to me, and I felt terribly vulnerable, and dropped the group. Nevertheless Beth had recruited me into feminism, and like all the other women, my life took on a new commitment.

About a month later I formed my own fantasy CR group, writing it into a set of poems. Mulling over the lives of all the people in my memories, I thought of my life with Von and everyone we had known in DC, the black women from the rural south coping with urban problems, my bosses, my captains, Vicky Jacobs dancing through her life searching for "the feminine," all the closet lesbians. Now as I sat up all night writing, in particular I thought about all the women I had known so far, who inhabited the inner caves of my mind, transformed in the poetry by the flame of my desire for them to have power and be seen. The boss lady showed her bitterness, the waitress turned from victim to defender, the overburdened mother set fire to her neighborhood, the closet lesbian stood up to have her picture taken, the crazy intense hitchhiker set fire to herself, the fat woman with the delicate sensibilities got mad, and I made a pledge to my mother to put her all the way into the world if it took my entire life. I held the poem-portraits in a small group together with the word "common," which I used in the last two lines of each poem. And called them "The Common Woman Poems."

After the Common Woman poems arrived, the wind holding my life in position suddenly exhaled, and everything changed. Women wanted copies and I could hardly keep enough on hand.

GAY WOMEN'S LIBERATION: GETTING A MOVEMENT GOING

Late in November of 1969, a sizable gathering of gay people, almost all white men, met in a meeting hall on Bancroft Avenue, across the street from UC Berkeley campus near Sather Gate. One of the few other lesbians I met that day, Patricia Jackson, remembers this group as the "North American Homophile Organization," older and more conservative than the newly arising "Gay Liberation Front" that formed in several cities following the Stonewall riots.

Of course there had been several such organizations dedicated to furthering Gay rights for decades, including One (in LA), Mattachine, and others. Now, following Stonewall, gay people urgently collected together within the general atmosphere of opposition to the escalating war in Vietnam, as well as engagement in the escalating civil wars at home. Wendy and I attended the Homophile meeting with our neighbors, Linda Wilson, the handsome, restless, black activist dyke that we knew from Antioch, and her more at-ease-seeming white girlfriend.

At that meeting of mostly conservatively dressed gay men, I presented a paper I had just written. I had mimeographed fifty copies at the office of the Mime Troupe, that brave troupe of political street actors. My paper had a thin purple cover, and was titled, "On the Development of a Purple Fist," and consisted of a plea for gay people to unite across lines of difference, and to reach across to other movements. The piece reads a bit differently from more typical leftist tracts, as I had not yet dropped my homegrown countrywestern accent, so to speak, using images like corral, hogtie, horses "split off from each other in separate stalls." Of gay people in general I wrote, "Our sexual preference is so far underground that we cannot 'confess' it to our friends, our bosses, our teachers, our parents, or our preachers, and still hope to earn a living or be welcome in their lives. In short, we are a threat to *everybody*."

I went on to bring in other issues: the oppression of workers, the war, feminism, even ecology, with such descriptions as "the secretary who must rampantly waste paper making 18 copies of an unread office memo has no idea what the forest looked like when the loggers left, or whether it will ever be replanted." From here I went on to entreat that gay people needed to join with the greater Civil Rights movements of "Negroes" and of "black and brown peoples," or we would be "left with a bunch of splinters."

In my often skewed and overly sensitive memory, the speech was received with silence. I continued talking, looking for some emotional response, and receiving none, began talking about what our country was doing to the people of Vietnam, and broke into tears. As I left the platform I felt the old, deep, lesbian despair that I had no voice, nothing to say, even to these who were supposedly "my" people. The room was full of good men, sincere, some of them deeply radical, like Paul Mariah and maybe Winston Leyland, who would go on to found Gay Sunshine Press; certainly Malcolm Boyd was there, along with Will Inman, and Richard Tagett.

But something had turned. Since leaving the straight women's group and writing the Common Woman poems, I had a new hunger, a dissatisfaction, which I recognized, differences in pressing issues between gay men and lesbians. Lesbians needed to witness each other, to have simple face-to-face presence, as we did not yet even know what our own concerns might be. Now, drying my eyes and rejoining my friends, I learned that they too were feeling unseen. Truly, the men around us appeared to have a very different agenda from the women, as had been true in Mattachine during my old Washington, DC days with the Gay Movement. A sense of being tiny alien invaders futilely, inanely, gesturing to the air, having landed among a sea of creatures who had eyes only for each other. We had often found ourselves in these meetings looking blankly across the crowd of men at the other lesbians, then looking away. Who were women to each other, to anyone, to ourselves? We literally did not exist in any social sense.

Naomi Groeschel remembers that Wendy and I ran around that conference trying to gather the women together. In the hallway we coalesced with five or six bright-faced women, mostly from Berkeley, along with Linda and her girlfriend, who lived near us in the Mission District. Immediately our faces caught fire from the little sparks of attention we were finally focusing on ourselves as we expressed our sense of outsiderness. "Let's have meetings of our own," we concluded—just dykes. We exchanged contact information. One of the lesbians was very intense, with piercing, intelligent eyes peering out from frequently lowered eyelids and a friendly, if nebbishy, handshake. Alice Molloy was several years older than me, and had gone to school with Diane DiPrima and Audre Lorde at Hunter High School in New York City in the 1950s. The other lesbians were younger, and included nineteen-year-old Naomi Groeschel, in Civil-Rights-Movement-style blue overalls whose sturdiness was reinforced with rivets, her curly black hair cascading around her white, oval face, with her dark round eyes, heavy lids. Her grandfather had immigrated to California from an Eastern European Jewish family, so, unlike many of us, she had grown up in the state. Roaming around restlessly at the perimeter, then bursting into the center, was a tall, strong-jawed white woman with long blonde hair, blue eyes, quick flash of smile, and a dissatisfied face. Didn't we all have such faces? Yes, but she carried hers in front of her somehow, wanted action, had a stubborn chin to match; this was Patricia Jackson, up from San Jose, having moved there from Kentucky. Had no place to stay, she said.

"Come crash at our place," she recalls me inviting, so Patricia slept on the floor of our Capp Street studio apartment near the blue basinet of water, stones, and several little brown-speckled captive turtles, while Wendy and I curled together high up in our homemade pine loft. I doubt that we even had an extra blanket for the long-legged Kentucky woman on our floor. "That's okay, I have my jacket," she would have responded.

Within a few days we were visited by Alice Molloy, along with her lover Carol Wilson. They made themselves at home in the room, which we had reclaimed with bright white walls and sea-blue trim. They sat untroubled, side by side on the little log that served as a miniature surrogate couch next to our handsome, though deeply cracked, ship's hatch-cover table, whose round, sunken iron handle doubled as an ashtray, our only living room furniture, accented by the plastic blue tub of water and turtles.

Alice's small, short-nailed fingers twirled cigarette paper as she rolled tobacco into it. Carol, broad-shouldered and with her forthright steady western voice, was a drum half the speed of Alice's New York rattle. I loved them at once; they were smart, determined and intriguing. They had smoldering eyes. They had open hearts, though Alice hid hers under a layer of slightly bitter wit. The meeting was excellent, we were in agreement that we wanted revolutionary changes for everyone, but that separate lesbian political meetings—separate from straight people, separate from gay men, separate from everyone—needed to happen. We would make them happen. We planned our first meeting. We called ourselves "Gay Women's Liberation," and we'd organized just in time, as the peace movement was about to be rocked by one of the most socially explosive events of the era: The Rolling Stones Rock Festival at Altamont. And Wendy and I would be right in the middle of it, or should I say right in the middle of the edge of it.

Altamont Speedway Free Festival & All the Mayhem You Can Drink

As the final month opened in that momentous year, Wendy reported that her tall red-headed friend Peter Adair had invited us to be part of another film crew. On December 6, we were to help film a big rock concert featuring the Rolling Stones. We would be paid an astronomical amount—fifty dollars, or maybe it was four hundred dollars—for one day's work. I kept repeating the pay rate like a mechanical doll, "For one day? One *day*?" We were to work as grips, hauling equipment. In the middle of the night we drove to a gathering place in Marin, a big rough room with a table laden with bread and ham, where a crew of mostly men, some of them older, was assembling massive amounts of film gear.

After carrying black and silver cases of equipment, bags of cables, and backpacks of batteries and film out to the helicopter, we climbed in and spiraled up into the cold dark air, arriving at Altamont Speedway before dawn. Once landed, we gathered around a small white trailer and a tent that was used by the film crew, parked behind the stage. Shortly after sunrise, some kid came by with a glass jug half-filled with cheap-looking red wine, passing it to the crew. Wendy, always amiable, took a drink. I said, "No, thanks," I didn't want to be tipsy around all these men. A minute later the people who had drunk from the jug were slung out flat on their backs on the ground as though someone had come through and shot them. Wendy was pale, eyes shut, unable to rise. At least one guy had to be airlifted to the hospital. Later, we learned that the wine was laced with arsenic, or LSD that had been cut with arsenic. Friendly, huh?

Fortunately, like Wendy, most of the crew had taken just one slug, and were taken into the shade of the tent to sleep it off. Thus began a complete nightmare for all of us. And for me, a lonely one. With everyone either passed out or off in the crowd doing sound or camerawork, I had no job except to witness a deteriorating scene. The crowd was about 300,000, and by noon, several of the crew (I guessed that's who they were but maybe they were just passing by) had moved into the trailer, where they were busy tying their arms and shooting up, as I could see through the open door. I was probably the only non-stoned, non-drunk person among the acres of screaming humanity. Skinny and nervous, I stood biting my nails or pacing alone on the roof of the little white trailer, where I felt moderately safe, venturing once or twice to look at the front of the heaving, writhing, unpleasant crowd. The stage was a welter of ropes, cables and black box equipment. The music sounded thin, disjointed, and didn't interest me, even though some of my favorite bands were on the bill: Santana, Jefferson Airplane, Crosby, Stills, & Nash, and the great Neil Young. I also liked a lot of what the Stones had recorded. But that day everything seemed wrong and the music was grating. The musicians must have known early on that the organizers had let them down.

The notoriously violent motorcycle gang, the Hells Angels, had been hired to deliver "security," and they had stupidly been paid in cases of beer instead of cash, and so were raucously drunk by nine A.M. They were posted, like our film crew, behind the stage, resembling Viking extras in a B movie, with their big, white, naked arms, blue or black vests, shoulder-length hair, and small beards. By noon they were throwing full cans of beer, and punches, straight into people's faces. They were extremely frightening, but so was the crowd, which was out of its mind, trying to storm the stage.

Around noon or so I climbed down from the safety of the trailer to find a Port-o-Potty. Standing in the long line, I watched a man with an erection pissing onto the ground. He grinned at me. I grinned back as we acknowledged the freedom of the new sexual movement. Erection in hand, he crawled into a tent to join his friends. Returning to my own lonely post, I had to pass close by the back of the stage where the Angels were stomping around in states of rage.

A blonde kid in Levis and T-shirt, either drunk or stoned, staggered up to them; he was blathering loudly about Jesus, and he was small but really aggressive and obnoxious. The Angels started toward him and he avoided them, stalwartly wobbled onto the back of the stage shouting about peace and love; several Angels grabbed him and began to beat him unmercifully. I was just a few yards away, too terrified to move, as his blood poured down from their huge fists. A young femme woman came by in a halter and shorts, courageously tried to distract the Angels by shoving her pelvis and naked stomach at them, but they just continued to pound the guy's face. After a while the Angels were attacking the performers as well, and the Grateful Dead packed up and left without playing.

I retreated, completely sickened by the beating, by the whole writhing mess, as were others who witnessed this brutal side of rock-and-roll, and of the Sixties peace movement itself, with its heavy reliance on escape into oblivion. And here, people were drifting on tides of emotion laced with aggression-producing drugs. In retrospect, the war had come home right here, a war between those who drank liquor and those who smoked and shot up dope; a war between warriors without purpose and pacifists without direction or method.

The beating of the militant, or at least adamant, Christian man was a foreshadowing; late in the day the Stones finally got on stage. In the growing violence of the crowd, the film crew struggled to find a footing to hold their cameras; night lights came on. Some of our crew climbed poles or stood on a bus to gain a better purchase and view of the wall of black boxes on stage and the silvery, shimmery, powerful, and confused music men. I was on the ground again when one of the cameramen came back with a funny look on his face. As he came toward me, someone was shouting that a man had been killed on stage, the Angels had just stabbed someone.

The camera man said something like this, "I shot the whole thing, I just watched this guy being killed. He was stabbed right in front of me, and I just kept the camera going." He was shaking. The victim was a black man who had gotten on the stage waving a gun.

I couldn't believe this day would ever make any sense or ever end. Everyone seemed numb with shock—what of the dream of repeating Woodstock? What of those messages of peace and love? The film crew leaders loaded me, Wendy (awake and looking like herself at last), and five or six others into a car around nine o'clock and drove us out; it was hard to find any road in the dark as we wound through acres of stoned-out people rolled into sleeping bags and no lights anywhere; the driver kept cursing, "Jesus, there are no signs to indicate roadbeds." Later, we would learn that a number of people in the massive crowd had been run over by accident, two of whom died. Another had drowned in a shallow ditch. Four people dead for foolishness, for entertainment. The accounts later said that eight hundred and fifty were injured, many hit in the face with full cans of beer. Four babies were born at Altamont, on that terrible day that would be remembered as "the end of the peace movement."

Altamont had emphasized the need we women had begun to articulate. We would only do our own actions with other women, and we would define for ourselves what we considered effective activism. We never followed male leadership uncritically again. We were going to make a second place to stand, another place from which to act. We would kick out Freud and question Marx and Mao; we would turn our backs on Aristotle and Descartes; we would even forget Harry Hay and Frank Kameny for a while. And in some crucial ways we would help lead what became a genuine, if unfinished, nonviolent revolution.

But try as we might, we would be unable to completely escape the violence that had marked the earlier 1960s. That same December, the FBI continued its systematic destruction of black militant leadership, with the pre-dawn, cold-blooded murder of Black Panther Fred Hampton in Chicago, shot in his bed. Responding to a call from the Panthers that went out over KPFA's "people's radio," Wendy and I showed up outside a Panther office one wind-blown afternoon to serve as part of a small group, a "white buffer" between the black militants and the FBI. Later we would meet two other white lesbian organizers who did the same thing.

As though some international monster was panting for blood, the U.S. was delivering it, rampantly setting off waves of bloodshed at home and in other countries, as the killing in Vietnam, Laos, and Cambodia also accelerated.

We Saw Each Other

Early in 1970, Wendy and I moved out of Capp Street into a flat on Lexington Street, just around the corner from Valencia Street in the Mission district. The Lexington apartment was meant to have one bedroom, but it also had a large pantry, a front room, a dining room, and a narrow kitchen with a table—an unimaginable wealth of space. We used every bit of that space, including a wide part of the hall as a bedroom, and soon five people lived there. M., Anne, J., Wendy, and me. I had met Anne Leonard when we both worked at Presbyterian Hospital in the summer, and had taken her to a CR group; she and her husband J. soon took up residence with us. Wendy and I slept in the dining room, and our various art projects began to take up the remainder of our allotted space. Now that Wendy and I had more room, our projects, like goldfish in a larger tank, grew much larger. She built a real darkroom in the basement, so she could more easily develop her photographs, and we could use the bathtub for bathing. I had the valuable front living room, and its spaciousness allowed me to begin imagining a larger project than simply writing my own poems. Maybe Wendy and I could collaborate on a book of drawings and poems by women, for women. We had been talking about some kind of artistic collaboration for a while.

All kinds of intensely focused lesbians were now swirling around us as we held weekly meetings of Gay Women's Liberation, one week at Alice and Carol's place on Benvenue Street in Berkeley, the next week at our flat on Lexington Street.

The first all-women's dances of our movement were in Berkeley in 1970. Poetry readings were connected to them. As Cathy Cade, an organizer and photographer recently said, "The poets would read, and the poetry somehow united us as a community, and then we would all dance together." Women-only dances were happening at that time in New York and Boston as well, and perhaps other places, indicating that lesbians were on the move, outside the bar scenes. A communal erotic beat took hold of us, we began to dance with whoever was there, not as a flirtatious arrangement, but as a soaking up and spreading of a new exhilarating vibrational rate. The guarded quality of bar life fell away for a while; we saw each other anew. In that first rush of sexual solidarity, we saw each other as a group of warriors, Gay Women's Liberation's handsome warriors. We saw each other, and we liked what we saw.

Having been told so often, so many ways, how ugly we lesbians were how plain how old-maidish how "no man would want you" how criminal, unwomanly, undesirable, dishonorable, disorderly, filthy, manhating whorish inhuman insanely jealous and just yucky we were in our very existence, we were astonished to discover our collective beauty. I was not the only one to experience ecstatic exuberance and all-encompassing heart-opening desire at the women's dances; to feel again, as I had at earlier times, but never this strongly, swept up in a river of sheer beauty—sexy, powerful, gorgeous, clit-distending, nipple-raising, lip-swelling hair-shaking spit-flowing cunt-glowing eye-flashing, hip-rotating, knee twisting, thigh pumping, pheromone coursing, fingers expressing, sultry spicy sweat smelling complexly exhilarating female potentiality. We raised up storms of change with our dancing, not because we were dancing, but because our dancing celebrated our commitment to each other. Aesthetics begins with erotic love, and now because we had a viable movement we had an aesthetic, we had beauty and courage and loyalty, toward each other, and toward ourselves. We had hot hot desire, tongue-dangling nipple aching cunt surging desire, that seemed to start as a hunger in our blood, a pulse-pain in our hearts, and what was it for, what was it for, what were we going to do with it? That was our question.

Our solidarity was not an instant panacea, would not immediately restore us to full human status or make us less than second-class citizens. But our solidarity and respect for each other was the strongest weapon we or anyone can have, and while it lasted we would use it to its fullest advantage. We could see qualities we seemed to have in common and begin to associate them with what we meant by "dyke," like our willingness to be out in public with our clothes and postures and attitudes, and like the idealism that shone from our faces, and the honesty, plain-spokenness of our speech, and our willingness to fight for justice. Even now those of us who are activists trust each other's word, know we can call on each other in certain kinds of crises and we will show up.

This loyalty, I think, spread into the women's movement as a whole, where women had bumped into the stereotype about female friendship being impossible. There was a classic stereotype about women—that we could never be friends with each other, since all women were understood to be rivals of perpetually desirable men. Men would joke about women having "cat fights." This social disconnection is dangerous, as disconnected women will turn away when another woman is in trouble with a man or group of men—and by extension is in any kind of trouble—and will say, fearfully, cold-heartedly, mercilessly, "she must have brought it on herself," leaving the victim vulnerable and alone.

Our dyke households had couple relationships but very free sexual interactions outside of these commitments. Perhaps I just wasn't looking or didn't go to the bars enough, but I didn't see much sexual jealousy among us activist lesbians. The possessive jealousy so typical of isolated and frightened lesbian couples just vanished. We became suffusely eroticized, toward all of us; a sort of blanket of love permeated the air. Out of this we committed to take risks for each other, to show up and put lives on the line, just as we had done in other parts of the broader movement. But now, we were impacted very personally; we valued each other and thus ourselves as female beings. This created loyalty to each other such that many of us had never experienced. As Laura Brown put it, "I love that we were making it up, being as strong as you could be, and as kind and as loving as you could be. We had an ethic that love would make each other stronger…."

This love spread out to bisexual and straight women in a diffuse sort of way, that produced a new loyalty among women. Women who fell in love with each other even for a short time knew then what it was like to be intimate with another woman. This helped them love themselves more and it helped them understand each other empathically. As this love spread across different layers of society, women became capable of female friendships and loyalties many had not experienced in their lives.

For me this diffuse state of love never ended. Still today, even women from that tumultuous era with whom I had serious difficulties—I still love them. This wasn't about sex, I had sex with very few of them. Though maybe it mattered that the permission was there, that we *might* have had sex. Even now I still love all of them, including those with whom I have had major differences. Recently and somewhat mischievously, I asked Pat Jackson, not having seen her for thirty-five years, not having ever had sex with her or even cuddled all night with her, if she had ever loved me. She looked at the wall, looked at the table, looked at the wall again. "Love you!" she said. "Love you?" Another pause. She fixed blue eyes on me. "I would *die* for you."

Raising Consciousness with Men

In addition to our new women companions and sister revolutionaries, who were showing up sixty at a time to our meetings, Wendy and I belonged to a consciousness-raising group on Lexington Street that was half men. We joked about this, "How could you tell it was a *dyke* consciousness-raising group? Because it was half men." I had not spent more than two hours with a straight man since I left my father's house, and so was curious. What were straight men like? We lived with three men, Anne's husband J., M., who rented the tiny pantry bedroom, and S., who slept over at his girlfriend's house and just showed up for dinner and to work on the various cars he stored downstairs in the basement-garage.

We formed a group with the four of them, plus Gail and her man R. We talked a great deal about politics in general, but forced the discussions onto women's issues as often as possible. The men were very well-intentioned, loving guys, with plenty of problems of their own. They were actually quite tender-hearted, and genuinely wanted to learn about male supremacy. And they were starting from near zero.

"Oh, of course you can be a musician," S. and J. said scornfully to Wendy when she complained about women being excluded from the world of music. "Prove it," she replied, so they took her that night with her guitar, J.'s drumsticks, and S.'s saxophone, to a jam session. I waited up, so witnessed their drawn, pale faces when they marched in, single file, at 3 A.M. Wendy looked grimly vindicated, the others looked to be sadder and wiser men.

Thereafter S. said this: "Being a man is like being given a pile of money. And the catch is, you can only spend it on yourself. If you give it away to anyone else, you lose it."

This astute metaphor for male privilege could apply to white privilege as well. Racism and the Black Power movement were frequently discussed in our group, which was all white. S. was a huge fan of George Jackson's, and Angela Davis was our household heroine. We attended marches, rallies, speeches. Our group of four women and four men met weekly for the whole year of 1970. We grappled with such issues as why S. was refusing to use a condom, anti-lesbianism in R.'s family, men's resentment that, as S. put it, "a woman can just sell her ass."

Wendy finally said in exasperation, "Why don't you go out on the street and sell *your* ass?" On reflection, he dropped the subject.

GAY WOMEN'S LIBERATION: TERMS OF ENGAGEMENT

When our Gay Women's Liberation group began, Wendy and I had been together for two years, time that to me blended into one long, lovely, playful, meaningful day. We had (from my point of view) great sex, interesting stuff to do, lively interactions. She was more beautiful to me every day, and I was beginning to understand her when she spoke her radical New Yorkese. She was barrels of fun, creative, and loving of literature. Even our arts were coming into focus, though she was still mostly taking photographs rather than drawing, and I still did not dare to call myself a real poet because I thought of the "Common Woman Poems" as an exercise. What we did not have was reflection about ourselves as individual people and as a couple, as lovers, reflection we immediately received in Gay Women's Liberation (or GWL as we had taken to calling it). First question: Do you have a girlfriend? Second question: How long have you been together? Third question: Where did you meet, how did you get together? Fourth question: How old were you when you came out? We began to see ourselves, as a couple, as lovers, as real to the world, real to someone else.

Eventually some lesbians would go so far as to define themselves as a separate "race" because their families of origin had cut the bonds entirely. Within our group, members' experiences ranged from women fleeing from family-enforced incarceration and "treatment" such as electric shock or lobotomy, to milder yet nevertheless devastating splits like one woman's mother urging her—despite the daughter's years of committed gay rights activism—to drop lesbianism and get married to a man. There was not yet a social understanding of "sexual orientation" as something beyond choice.

To our families we were still anomalies. As far as I knew, my father was still not speaking to me, though he and my mother had stood at the foot of my bed as I awakened from my coma. But I had not visited them since then, and was estranged from everyone else in my family. Initially to Wendy's mother I was "the creep from Albuquerque" that she advised her daughter to "lose." As women out in the world we also had no personal identities. To the men in Newsreel we were "the girls." To the men at the *Express Times* I was "the typesetter." To my boss at work I was "the medical transcriptionist" (and somewhat suspect, as I had become surly).

To the Gay Women's Liberation women, Wendy and I were now respected as individuals, as persons, and also as a couple together, as lovers, the lovers, the stable model, the activists, the artists, the leaders—even in a movement that disclaimed leadership. "Lover" became a new title of distinction and connection. We were Lovers. This was a step into Outness from the old Washingtonian secrecy of the word "Friend," said with a slight emphasis. "This is my lover, Wendy." Across an ocean from "this is my Friend."

Wendy still did not claim the term "lesbian." "I am a woman who just happens to love Judy," she explained herself. Bisexuality was not a term of the day, not understood, not believed, and not tolerated. Our movement, like others, needed and demanded all or nothing, "the real thing." So in the Native movement some people dyed their skin to be dark enough to fit in, and in the black movement afros, formerly despised, now became the only way to wear one's hair. What had been only bad now became only good. In our movement dyke clothing and posturing were indications of the full commitment to dykeness that had become the acceptable, even glorified way to be, with little tolerance for variation.

So I would guess that at this time Wendy and others with her same openness, like Susan Griffin and alta, had to either surrender lesbian community or hide the part of themselves that loved, was lovers with, men. "I am a woman who happens to love women" was one definition of who we were. I did not think of myself as "a woman who happened to love women." I was a lesbian, a dyke, and a lifetime homosexual. It seems to me I was always gay, even in the womb, where my mother said "you kicked like a boy." For the first time I now had a license to be myself, and to be desirable as that self.

In 1970 I wrote a few stanzas in my poem "A History of Lesbianism" to encompass both positions, Wendy and me in the same poem, making up the term "women-loving-women" who "walked and wore their clothes / the way they liked / whenever they could." Some of us embraced the term "dyke" (dike, alternative spelling) while others thought it was a terrible, pejorative term. The poem continued, "in America we were called dykes / and some liked it / and some did not." Dyke is a good term because it refers to an individual and to her mannerisms and ways of being. A dyke is a dyke whether or not she is involved with lovers or a lover. Those of us from the old days, the bar culture days, tended to embrace this term; we had been called dyke by rough fellows, some of whom meant us harm, but we had also embraced the term as descriptive of our way of life. "I was a dyke by the time I was five" referred to, say, our fighting to wear pants and play sports. The poem ends with a feminist political statement: "the subject of lesbianism is very ordinary / it's the subject / of male domination / that makes / everybody / angry."

The line "in America we were called dykes" would be picked up and quoted, re-quoted, i.e., "In Amerikkka they call us dykes," for various purposes for decades afterwards. But in our 1970 GWL movement, those of us who had come out in earlier times or who felt we were "born that way" were called "bar dykes" or "old world dykes" by younger women who had another perspective, who thought that becoming a lesbian was a personal, and political, choice. The choice, they said, was to be free from male domination. Overnight, "dyke" had gone from the status of a Category 5 hurricane to the only possible site of rescue from harm. Our independent way of life was to be emulated, to be "chosen." The view from here was dizzying.

Standing Up for Ourselves as Dykes

More and more varied women were coming to meetings, like Red Jordan Arobateau, a mixed race, working-class writer and artist with street smarts who immediately began teaching self-defense for women. Middle-class white women came, like Marny Hall, who would become a writer and lesbian therapist, and activists from the old left labor movement, Brenda Crider and Louise Merrill.

The weekly meetings swelled, and we began to plan actions to draw the attention of straight, leftist, feminist women. For instance a group of us stood in a long line at the front of a NOW meeting holding hands and announcing ourselves into what seemed shocked silence. Some of us made T-shirts that read "East Bay Dykes" in big letters, and wore them, as Pat Jackson said, "to the ice cream stores"—meaning the places mainstream Americans gather.

Straight feminist organizers Beth Oglesby and Laura X began attending our meetings, listening to our heated discussions as we criticized every institution and every theory of social progress, trying to define who we were. Anne Leonard remembers going to the Benvenue meetings,

> [It was]a big room full of lesbian women, even though I didn't identify (yet) as a lesbian woman I was there; I remember the feeling the group had of wanting to be heard and recognized as a lesbian woman—by straight women and also by the Left. There was a lot of different opinions, and a lot of feelings, why were we doing this and how were we going to do this....militant, very enthusiastic, very devoted, very personal, each person....it was very personal that they were doing this. Everyone was there for personal reasons but something bigger was being created. I had no idea about left politics, I came from a small town outside Philadelphia, and even though I lived in LA for a time it was only when I got to San Francisco that I was learning, I was listening very closely while pretending that I knew what was going on. Though of course I knew what it was all about because I could feel it inside.

If theories of social change excluded, defamed, or criminalized us as lesbians, why should we accept their basic premises? We argued about our relationships to men, to straight women, to gay men, to the use of violent tactics, to feminism and socialism, to the radical left, to the psychiatric establishment. We discussed racism, including our own. We had no end of subjects. We continued our actions; a group of us attended a lecture by a well-known, thoroughly published psychiatrist, an "expert" in female homosexuality. From the audience, we questioned him, what was his authority based in? What real reasons did he have for pathologizing our lives? For emphasis, we stood up, scattered throughout the audience. There were at least a dozen of us, perhaps more. We didn't yell or threaten, just stood. At our standing up, declaring our sanity to him, he gathered his papers, and fled the room. We felt like Dorothy discovering the Wizard as a tiny man behind a curtain of false authority.

In that year of 1970 our group of determined activist lesbians took seriously the idea that we were a vanguard in behalf of all women, that we were a warrior brigade. We wanted women's bodies and sexualities liberated for each woman to inhabit for herself. We wanted battery and sexual assault against women to stop, we wanted the streets to be safe and pleasant for women to walk, we wanted mothers to be supported with childcare and in other ways, we wanted women's ideas and creative thoughts to be taken seriously. We wanted equality for all. We wanted women brought out of the Middle Ages. In short, we wanted a simple, but complete, revolution.

Woman to Woman—A Revolutionary Anthology

But this is a love story of course. It asks the question "What does it mean to love women?" And specifically, what would it mean if men loved women—really loved women? What would that be like? If women loved women, and themselves? How do I love women, and then one single woman? If you make a social movement that loves women, what does that accomplish? What does it mean? What if we had religions that loved women? A culture that cherished women and sought their leadership?

I handed out materials at the meetings, my own articles, including the satire "The Psychoanalysis of Edward the Dyke," my new article, "Lesbians as Bogeywomen," and reprints from *RAT Magazine*, a Left voice which had been seized by Radical Lesbian Feminists in New York. Martha Shelley and Rita Mae Brown had both published articles I thought were important, so I copied those and handed them out too.

Out on the West Coast, with so much activity and so many people avidly reading things we handed out at meetings, Wendy and I decided the time had come to start gathering material to do an anthology of women's poetry and graphics that would change the images and therefore the way women thought about themselves. We began gathering the materials from every source we could think of, including our neighbors, and of course women we were meeting through Gay Women's Liberation. We were perfectly coordinated in this endeavor, one of our best collaborations, and one in which we were inordinately creative as we had no idea what we were doing. What on earth was "women's poetry"? Who would decide? I collected some poems, some by well-known authors (Amy Lowell, Gertrude Stein), some by published feminist authors (Marge

Piercy, Marilyn Hacker, alta), and some by women we were meeting lately, our neighbors, people who heard we were doing such an outrageous project. I included my Common Woman poems. I gathered sixty pages of manuscript and handed it out to women, along with a form asking such questions as: Which poems affected you? Which do you consider poetry? What would you like included in a collection? The answers surprised, some of the biggest "names" didn't make the cut; some of the least "poetic" had the biggest effect. In the end, I chose for impact, positive *and* negative. Most liked my poems, though one responded "Common as a telephone directory....this is not poetry." I included them anyhow, as they were spreading around town; I would find pages posted on people's refrigerators in the new households consisting mostly of women.

Wendy's friend Vicky Jacobs showed up one day and pulled out some cash for us to buy paper so we could print our book. Then Naomi and Pat Jackson came over with money that Gay Women's Liberation had gathered for us to buy a mimeograph machine, an office copy machine that used ink; you typed the text on a limp, blue, waxy sort of template and then draped it over a fat rotating barrel. The ink squeezed through the letters and printed on the fresh blank pages. They had bought the machine from Diane DiPrima, who had been in the Bay Area poetry scenes for years. I was including one of Diane's poems in the anthology, though not necessarily with her permission. I was grabbing poetry from everywhere, taking the author's name off, going for pure content, and breaking down the elitism that I felt—despite the heroic efforts of the Beat poets—still dominated poetry.

The physical design of the book was inside out: we used heavy paper for the text, thin paper for the cover, and onionskin paper for the graphics. A dyslexic design sense on my part. I was certain that the ink on one side would leak through to the other, so insisted on backing each graphic with a blank sheet of the heavy, lavender-tinted paper. The cover, delicate as an aged leaf, was red, and carried a powerful graphic by Wendy and big letters for the title: *Woman to Woman*.

The boldness of the book described us as well. Our erotic connection was fueled by how competitive we were toward each other. When we struggled it became physical, not in any violent sense, just in the juggling we did for territory, our constant negotiations; who would run the mimeograph machine? We crowded shoulders and hips together to jockey for positions. Laughing, while knowing the seriousness of our personal quests for self-authorization, as well as for women's voices in the world. We wrestled heedlessly, testing and finding our strengths, exhilarated at the pitch and heave of our equality. Members of GWL came over to help us collate, so this became "our book," a collective enterprise. And the book, filled with women's art and poetic opinions, got printed, and was both strong and beautiful, if flawed in its design.

MEETING PARKER

One day shortly after we started this project, probably March or April of 1970, Linda Wilson stepped gracefully through the bright paisley cloth that draped the fine arch into my room. "I've brought someone to meet you," she said in her resonant voice, and in walked a tall black woman, neatly dressed in pressed slacks and blouse, high cheekbones, thick glasses, and handsome in her own striking way. Here was Pat Parker. Pat was gregarious, athletic like Linda and Wendy, while at the same time her thick glasses and high forehead gave her the intellectual look of an introvert, a book-reader or librarian. She emanated a wave of warmth, charming, like a lot of Southerners.

"I hear your drink is Southern Comfort," she said, handing me a brown bag with a pint bottle of amber liquid in it. Linda excused herself, Parker sat down (by now I had a couple of chairs) and, sipping the bitingly sweet liquor, we began talking about cowboy clothes, poetry, activism, Civil Rights, where we grew up, how we were with regard to feminism, the need for revolution, the bad deeds of the power structure, and by the time the bottle was empty we were connected.

I showed her the rows of pages Wendy had meticulously lined along the floorboards of my room, spilling into the room next to it. Pat promised to bring me some of her work.

I included four of Pat's feminist poems in *Woman to Woman*, which was ready for distribution in late summer of 1970. "Child of Myself" is a signature Pat Parker poem ending "I, Woman must be—the child of myself." Pat was writing black woman identity, black activist political, and feminist poems.

She was not yet writing anything pro-lesbian, though she had begun a love relationship with a woman.

Pat had been reading her antiracist and feminist poems through the second half of the sixties, in places like the Black Cat and other North Beach venues; she read with her second husband, a white poet named Bob Parker, as well as with alta and alta's poet-man, John Oliver Simon, and after divorcing Bob Parker, Pat kept his last name, dropping her father's name, "Cooks." Everyone in our movement called her "Parker," at her request. In 1968 she was reading a lot with another Berkeley white man poet, Charlie Potts. She and Charlie were lovers, according to Simon's memory, during the summer of 1968. By the time Linda Wilson brought her to meet me in spring of 1970, Pat had taken a woman lover; in January of that year she had turned twenty-six, and had already led a life full of black female landmines.

In 1970 there were of course no public venues for reading lesbian poetry (or doing anything else) to all women's audiences yet. In that year, Parker and I read together in an upstairs room of the Addison Street lesbian household in Berkeley, to a small though intensely attentive audience of militant dykes and friends. We both drank our way through this reading, yet in the energy of the moment stayed fairly focused. I read by candlelight, the golden glow giving a numinous cast to the faces surrounding and supporting us.

I took my shirt off at one point to display the nakedness one needs to tell new truths and then I set fire to my poems, in memory of Sappho and the historic burning of her work. That reading, in which I read virtually every poem I had written in my life, remains in my memory a liminal moment, sealing a partnership between Parker and me, a ritual that felt like setting lesbian poetry into a path of social change that would include us. Although Parker was not yet reading pro-lesbian poems, in her style she was definitely out as a dyke, her feminist poetry was an exhilarating confirmation of women's solidarity, and her anti-racist poems set our movement on an appropriate moral course.

Over the next two decades our friendship was close, very close at times, then further away, then close again. We never had a sexual connection, not even a flirtation. We both had rangey voices—a singing teacher once told me I covered five, somewhat quavery, octaves—and Pat's was at least as big a spread, with deep resonant tones and some good top notes. Of the two of us, she read much more expressively; I had adopted a flat form so as not to manipulate the audience, and I read slowly and deliberately—one reviewer described it as bell-like, another that it put her into alpha rhythm—but it sounds really dull to my ears now, and I've since changed how I read. Pat was more graceful and in the moment. Her nickname would come to be "the Preacher." Pat, offstage, had an easy, expansive manner and was persistently patient in reaching across to people. As one of her lovers, Ann Bernard, put it, to Parker breaking through prejudice was a personal matter, "she thought that if everyone got to know one another, things would change." No matter who you were she was willing to reach across to you.

The Trip to the East Coast

In the Fall of 1970, Anne Leonard and I responded to a notice from the New England Free Press, that they had internships for people wanting to learn printing. At the same time, Carol Wilson, Pat Jackson, and Naomi Groeschel had planned an epic cross-country trip distributing women's literature. They would drive us as far as Chicago and we would catch another ride to Boston. Big Anne Leonard and skinny me packed what little warm clothing we owned and came across the Bay Bridge from San Francisco to Oakland, sleeping on the floor along with several other women refugees of the movement, in the sprawling Terrace Street living room while Carol worked on repairing the van that would carry us.

The van in the driveway was a rare luxury for women to have. We had never seen a woman repair a car before. We were quite impatient about how long it took Carol, and how jealously she guarded her skills, allowing no one else to help. But Carol was a skilled mechanic. So, after three days of waiting, we bundled into the van and a number of us set out on the adventure.

The women of the radical New England Free Press were happy to see us but had no accommodations, and we had naively forgotten to ask about this. We had only our red copies of *Woman to Woman*, which we sold for a dollar, our only source of cash. Seeing that we were homeless in this already chilly city, I immediately bought wine. We walked around in a dazed condition, going to parties at night to keep warm, dragging a bottle of the anesthetizing red liquid everywhere, trying to figure out what to do. I'm sure we were allowed to sleep a couple of nights at the press, but the members made it clear this was a serious violation that could get everyone in trouble.

This semi-homeless situation went on for a few miserable days and then Beth Oglesby, who had moved to Boston recently with her three children, held a party for us. Specifically it was a poetry reading, and I read my heart out. When Beth announced that we had nowhere to live, two lesbians immediately volunteered to give us a bed in their place. They were both cabbies who lived in Roxbury; one of them was named Peaches. They were barely making a living. Their apartment had no heat, and they generously turned their bedroom, which had a barely functional space heater, over to us. I wish I could say that we valiantly refused and took the icy living room, but we didn't. We huddled in our California skins, sleeping in our clothes.

By now it was genuinely freezing at night, and as the weeks went on, we were perpetually shivering and hungry, living on doughnuts and wine; a tuna salad sandwich was a luxury. At the press, it's a wonder we learned anything. We must have been disheveled, stinking, wine-breathing, hippie-seeming, and off-putting to these buttoned-up, put together, mostly middle-class Marxist Boston radicals.

We did learn to print however, for which I am grateful; I also got my first glimpse of the FBI, tall tan raincoats who came to the press door and were admirably scolded by one of the women. "I won't say anything to you; it's within my rights to keep silent." I also noticed that many of the press pamphlets were dense intricate internal arguments of fine points about the proletariat. I could not understand them, even though I had passed courses in sociology, and had read some of Marx and Engels. Yet for all their obscurity, the pamphlets were priced low, at thirty-five cents, so the working class could afford them. But I wondered, who could read them? And renewed my vow to remain as accessible in my work as possible.

Some time in mid-November Beth invited me to her large, comfortable house on some pretext; I eagerly agreed to go, feeling horribly guilty at so readily abandoning my traveling buddy Anne and the two poor cabbies for a hot meal, a shower, and some personal attention. And, it turned out, a warm night in bed with Beth, who recently told me that I brought her out that night.

Bringing people out was not my specialty, though I heard some movement people excelled at this. I had a very difficult time with casual sex, not trusting strangers with my overly sensitive body. Beth was easy to be with, not demanding of an emotional commitment, and not distanced either, but invitational. I recall her surprise, "Oh! You have a *hard* body." Until the lesbian movement made them radical chic, muscles had been gendered, and also part of class structure. Now they could belong on any body, and happily on mine!

Just prior to Thanksgiving the white van showed up in Boston with Carol and Pat, radiant from their trip distributing women's literature, mostly alta's publications from her Shameless Hussy Press and our red-covered lavender-papered anthology *Woman to Woman*. We all went out to a bar, and on the way back to where we were staying we found a woman huddled on the street who said she had been beaten and raped by a taxi driver. I would describe this scene in my poem "A Woman Is Talking to Death" three years later: "My friends and I we left the bar / we found a woman lying in the snow / by the side of the road / her feet had turned the snow pink...." Pat remembers this incident, and that I covered the woman with my peacoat until the ambulance arrived.

On their historic trip Pat, Naomi, and Carol had covered a lot of territory. In Philadelphia they invited a black activist lesbian named Pat Norman to come home with them. Naomi told me they attended an important meeting in New York, which marked the founding of The Feminist Press, an independent publishing company run by Florence Howe. Pat Jackson remembers what their road tour was like: "In each city we connected with women...we met women in Lansing, Michigan, who had formed an Anti-Rape, Horseback Patrol. We met with Robin Morgan, who wrote *Sisterhood is Powerful*, met Rita Mae Brown who later wrote many lesbian novels. In New York we attended meetings of women trying to form a women's party. In New Haven, we attended the trials of Black Panthers Ericka Huggins and Bobby Seale. That November, we ended up in Washington, DC to witness the historic Black Panther Party conference, the Revolutionary People's Constitutional Convention (RPCC)."

BLACK PANTHER PARTY REVOLUTIONARY PEOPLE'S CONSTITUTIONAL CONVENTION, NOVEMBER 27-29, 1970

The Panther conference was indeed historic, an expansive attempt to unite in dialogue and common purpose the various movements that had poured out of the Sixties. Huey Newton had reached out to both the women's and the gay movements, declaring both to be oppressed groups. Anne and I rode down from Boston to Washington in the van, and met up with other lesbians from our West Coast Gay Women's Liberation. They had arrived with a fresh supply of *Woman to Woman*, which we easily hawked to the mob of radical women who showed up for the conference. Negotiations between the Washington chapter of the BPP and Howard University over use of buildings broke down, though another space was used to house about five hundred of us radical women. We spread sleeping bags, quilts and jackets on the floor. Anne Leonard and I stayed there, wrapped in our dark multi-purpose peacoats.

The Black Panther Constitutional Convention was an ambitious and idealistic meeting that intended to draw together common interests toward a single revolutionary goal, as the Panthers attempted to expand their base, calling themselves the "vanguard" of a broad movement. Newspapers reported that somewhere between three thousand and five thousand young people, mostly white, arrived in the capital city for the convention, having learned about the open invitation through the alternative left media including the widely distributed Black Panther paper. The newly formed Washington, DC, BPP had struggled all summer to find a hall large enough to hold everyone at once, with large workshop rooms so that issues could be addressed and the fledgling People's Constitution could be framed. Because of the violent rhetoric espoused by the party, including the phrase "Off the pigs!" and the Maoist war cry, "Power comes from the barrel of a gun," Washington's middle class did not trust them.

At the last moment, Howard University agreed to host the Convention, but only with a $10,000 advance payment. The Panthers were not organized to raise that amount of money. Lacking a place to gather, the Convention failed in its constitution discussions. Panther leaders delivered some speeches in smaller venues, but feminists objected to misogynist phrases, while Gay Liberation groups found homophobia in some of the rhetoric. Newton's invitations to both groups, each highly sensitive to language, was ahead of the reality of attitudes within the party.

Local churches opened their doors to shelter the attendees, and the fact that hundreds of feminists were housed in one huge hall provided a priceless opportunity for women from all over the country to make passionate speeches to each other. Women spoke up from a variety of positions—socialist, feminist, and the new voice of lesbian militancy, which our California group was especially vocal in articulating.

In retrospect the inability of the BPP to find space large enough to hold the disparate groups reflected the range of contradictory situations we were all in; this was much too soon for people to comprehend, let alone resolve each other's extremely diverse group needs. For example, just to take one issue, that of family structure: the people attending the conference had (at least) three very different needs from family that fell along the lines of African Americans, straight white feminists, and Lesbians and Gays.

Panthers of both sexes wanted to raise the status of manhood for black men, and worked hard for the solidification and security of black families that had been shredded since the deliberate divisions imposed on them during slavery and afterwards. Elaine Brown, who ultimately chaired the Black Panther Party, would write decades later in *A Taste of Power* of her efforts and motives for pushing black men to the forefront: "I had heard of black men—men who were loving fathers and caring husbands and strong protectors. I had not really known any."

Panther women in particular were addressing the needs of distressed children, running successful breakfast programs and educational programs for young people. Black people wanted police brutality and harassment, routine in their communities, to cease, and toward this end the party men had armed themselves and on certain occasions had fought back against the police in gun battles. The shoot-outs, killings, infiltrations, set-ups, arrests, and high-profile trials that resulted helped to publicize the behavior of police within and against black communities. And also helped to frighten mainstream white Americans, who looked the other way as the FBI, in conjunction with local police, harassed, hunted, and assassinated male BPP leaders. FBI head J. Edgar Hoover had been explicit in his orders that Panther leaders be taken down through false imprisonment and other methods, regardless of evidence.

In contrast, white feminists for the most part had encountered police clubs slamming heads only at demonstrations, not in their neighborhoods. Men and boys in white families were not gunned down on the street by officers in blue. White heterosexual women were critiquing their family system as a feudal institution in which the women had for many generations lost control of their bodies, and had as a primary or sole function supported a husband by taking a back seat, and providing him with heirs, preferably sons. While black men wanted the social support to head families, and to enable black women to stay home as wives and mothers, white feminists wanted to end the male-headed family structure. In order to produce the equal relationship they wanted, these women needed to separate, at least psychically, and more often physically, from the white men/husbands who had been raised to function as authoritarian heads of the family, and of every other institution. White women wanted control of their own bodies, and to gain economic and social independence, and they needed men who could change enough to become equal partners with them, as companions in life and in childrearing. These women were taking their families apart to reconstruct them.

Coming from yet a different perspective, many gay people of whatever gender were deeply estranged from, and sometimes in danger from their families of origin, needing to find a positive cultural group and individual safety first, a base from which to fight for basic human rights to live and love, rather than categorized as criminal, sinful, uselessly decadent, or mentally ill. Gay people were forming chosen community relationships that would protect them if necessary *from* their families of origin, and working for changes in social attitudes and practices that would allow their participation in society as themselves, and enable their families to understand them. Gay and lesbian people were looking for any kind of family structure that would work for them.

When I think of these examples of just one aspect of life—family—I understand why such a new constitutional convention could not go anywhere and why so often everyone seemed to speak at cross purposes. The Panther ideal of weaving together the intersecting strands of the same revolutionary, Marxian movement, had bumped into the contradictory histories and needs among us. There was no single movement. We were all fighting very different, sometimes overlapping, sometimes contradictory, revolutions. These movements were not yet, in my experience, about "identity." They were about trying to change power relations and varied forms of oppression that contradicted each other and impacted us selectively, and differently.

Coletta Reid was one of the East Coast radicals who was very impressed by the militancy and presence of the West Coast Lesbians. Reid told me a story that illustrates the general attitude of white leftist men at the time.

> There was a big Left organized demonstration against the invasion of Cambodia, which was announced in the spring of 1970 by Richard Nixon. Women from the Chicago 7 conspiracy trial came to DC, and brought a radical political consciousness. One leftist woman gave the women money for ten thousand free copies of *Off Our Backs*—but when they tried to distribute them at the demo the leftist men accused them of being bourgeois, suffragettes. At the demo, men tore the papers up, wouldn't let the women who were attached to them hand the papers out, said things like, "all you need is a good fuck, you women got it good," as though the women were simply being cranky.

Coletta understood from this experience that gender issues cut across all classes; she was never Left-identified after this. That summer, feminist and leftist women in the DC area began edging toward lesbianism. The Chicago 7 trial women were communal, so they held an *Off Our Backs* ten-day commune during which women opened themselves up to sexual feelings toward each other. Women thinking about their own condition and trying to change that was a million times more interesting than graduate school, where Coletta had been studying philosophy. She had a shift in consciousness, a realization "that men don't give women's issues any value." As indeed, how could they have been aware, given that women hadn't yet fully absorbed our issues ourselves?

Yet many men in my generation never did figure this out. Initially for white men, women's liberation meant "free sex." Max Dashu remembers attending a rally in New Haven for Ericka Huggins and Bobby Seale, where "Free Ericka!" and "Free Eldridge!" and similar slogans were being called out. Disgusted with the vacuity of school life at Harvard/Radcliffe, to which she had a scholarship, Max had been attending some feminist consciousness-raising meetings. She stood up and yelled, "Free women!"

The guy with the gramophone looked at her for a moment of potent silence, then announced the new chant, "Free Pussy!" At that moment Max left the Left just as Coletta had, having seen the enormous divide, the grand canyon of incomprehension. However much women wanted and needed social change, men were not going to be the vanguard for us or with us. We would need to vanguard ourselves.

BACK HOME TO A PRINTING PRESS

I arrived home in December to good news. Wendy and a few women who wanted to help us form a press had met with Ruth Gottstein, a representative from Glide Memorial Church. Ruth, who would five years later found Volcano Press, had handed them a $500 grant to reprint *Woman to Woman*. With this, they had immediately bought the biggest printing press they could find, an old Chief 22 that was going to give us a lot of excitement, much grief, some bad accidents, and several invaluable books.

Black painted, iron standing upright nearly as tall as we were, with a set of wide, impressive rollers, it could print a sheet that was 22 by 17, meaning eight pages, four on each side of the sheet, a great improvement for our speed. Probably that garrulous old machine had eaten the good hands of several printers, but we didn't know that. We didn't know anything. And no one was going to teach us. Only one guy in town knew how to run the Chief. We called him, he trucked his toolbox down the steps to our basement sanctuary, took a look at us seven eager-faced young women, pointed to one and said he would fix the press up if she would sleep with him. We ran him out, and began to take the machine apart to see how it worked.

At the opening of 1971, while this little collective struggled to learn how to use our newly acquired press, I was trying to figure out how to get out of the medical work that had been my primary way of earning a living for a decade. I craved economic independence that would feed my art, thought long and hard how this might come about. If I didn't need to buy work uniforms, have bus fare and lunch money, get my hair cut and look neat and clean, I wouldn't need much money. The ease with which we had sold *Woman to Woman* from hand to hand tickled my mind with another idea: why not put my own poetry into a book and sell it? Wendy was willing to supply her artwork as illustrations, including the portraits we had used in the *Common Woman* chapbook. Gay Women's Liberation was peopled with many graphics artists, so a young woman named Sunny sketched a portrait of me as "Edward" in the dyke hat I wore to an increasing number of highly political, all-women's poetry readings. I was learning to see books as artful products, as crafted objects. With the line drawing in mind, I chose a blue cover, tan page paper, and thin magenta paper for the illustrations.

I thought long and hard about the title of my first book. I had already made the decision to be public about being gay/lesbian—the decision to come out in a public and theatrical manner, to use the terms that were "underground," the words that dare not be said, the "bad" words. If people could not say "lesbian" then I would say "dyke" and that would make "lesbian" safer to say because the border of appropriate speech had been moved further out. So I chose the title *Edward the Dyke and Other Poems*. I thought it was ugly, which made me sad; yet I understood its necessary reach for power, the power to change habits and minds. I didn't like it, but I respected it. Sunny, not out to her family, painted the tail of the "y" out so it read "Edward the Duke" and proudly sent it home as an example of her artistic success.

I was nothing if not colorful in my design choices, and my poetry reading clothing was not far behind—I loved mixing various kinds of stripes and wearing a textured vest along with two or three shirts for a layered look. Goodbye horrible, badly-made, tacky women's clothing! Goodbye single-color work uniforms with no individual flair! Nor was I constrained to some version of "men's clothing." By prowling through the secondhand stores, often with Wendy or Anne Leonard, who both had great clothing design sense, I came up with outfits that suited my inner sense of self—paradoxical, going in more than one direction at once, layered and mysterious, unafraid of mixing colors, fearlessly placing a Levi's jacket with sheepskin lining over a velvet green vest over a vertical striped shirt or two over a turtleneck with broad horizontal sailor stripes.

No dull blue socialist workshirts for me! Up on that stage I wanted women to see possibility! And desirability. As the same. I wanted colorful striped turtlenecks and pearl-buttoned cowboy shirts; I wanted intricate plaid flannel shirts, pullover sweaters, and jackets that would keep me warm, warm, warm in our chilly apartment. Because of the hippie movement and the now-burgeoning gay movement, the city was stuffed with great clothing, and it was cheap, cheap, cheap. A quarter would get you a gorgeous shirt, a dollar some hip-fitting pants that showed off your ass yet let you stride freely. Now I had style. Soon I would dress like this a lot, wearing my soft-brimmed "dyke" hat that everyone loved and which I thought of as a poet's hat. I felt good about myself. And onstage my voice was coming in. "Bell-like."

Early in 1971 Wendy brought two more people home to live with us. She had met Helle on the street, and learned she was a recently arrived immigrant with no saleable skills except her body, so was hooking on the streets of the Tenderloin area of San Francisco to support herself and her four-year-old daughter. Short and stocky with straight blonde hair and blue eyes, from one of the northern European states, Lithuania or Estonia, Helle would do anything for the sake of her daughter. They sat together on the floor with Helle's hair falling onto Masika's curly brown locks, the delicate child's sea-grey eyes following the movements of Helle's pen on paper, teaching her to draw. We immediately turned my priceless front room over to them, where my handmade door now held court in the arched doorway. In a few days of concentration on carpentry, I had made a tall wooden door out of three slabs of hatch-cover wood Wendy and I had brought home from the docks on one of our scavenger missions. I covered it with eucalyptus nuts and Wendy arrived with a handful of brass fittings to hold it together.

Now, with mother and daughter installed in the room, I missed my space but could not begrudge its sweet new use. Wendy and I began sleeping on a couch in the hallway, and then when the lack of privacy drove us crazy we put down a mattress in a corner of the basement, avoiding the worst mess of S.'s ever-churning car collection, which now filled most of the space.

We were careful not to ask questions about his business, knowing only that he prowled out in the city for pink slips to match the cars and make them saleable. We were learning to live on a "need to know" basis, asking few questions, keeping our observations between us. So when he disappeared into the bathroom of an evening and came back to the kitchen table with his head drooping and eyes closed, we said nothing. For musicians especially, heroin lubricated the emotional channels, or so we believed, just as we believed that poets must drink lots of wine, artists must smoke opium, and that Van Gogh had cut his own ear off after being driven mad by the mistral wind of southern France. We were part of a very romantic era, full of excesses, artful with lively, nihilistic optimism and brilliance. We believed in beauty, theatrics, love, breaking rules, using art to whip up winds of rebellion.

While we lived in the uncomfortable basement, breathing air leaden with car exhaust and oil pans, I wrote a poem reclaiming Marilyn Monroe's body "for the sake of my own," a poem celebrating menstruation, and "A History of Lesbianism."

We had one dedicated straight woman in our early collective, and she gave our press its first home. Gail was tall and grounded, sure of what needed to be done, exactly what one would want to see in the mother of small children. Her role model of an adventurous female in her family had been her favorite aunt, who was a roller derby queen back in the day. Gail had rented a storefront on Valencia, which was right around the corner from our flat; she had made an apartment out of the back rooms, ignoring the papered-over front display windows. She had a huge, if damp, basement and offered it to us for our press. The mimeograph machine came out of our kitchen and found a place of its own in the front end of Gail's basement, on a long table where I could also stack the finished books. We were collecting other book-making tools as well—the long stapler Wendy and I had used to bind *Woman to Woman*, and a cutting board so we could trim the books and make them look more professional. I began to take great pleasure in solving the interesting problems of how to edit, design, typeset, lay out, and manufacture them.

Carol Wilson came down to our basement one day to make a jig, that woodworker's term for setting an action up to be repeatable; in this case she nailed a straight-edge to the table so I could slap one end of the cover against it and fold each cover perfectly with crisp blue edges. That month, February or March of 1971, as I completed production of two thousand copies of *Edward the Dyke and Other Poems* on the little mimeograph machine, while other press collective women worked across the room on the big stubborn Chief, we had a visitor from the East Coast—Coletta Reid. She was immediately excited by the blue stacks of copies of *Edward the Dyke* and asked to take some with her.

"They aren't finished," I said, "they need to be cut in half." (I had cleverly printed them two at a time, on what was called "legal-sized" pages—11 x 17.)

"I want them anyway," she insisted, picking one up to take with her. "The world needs to read these."

I had never met a woman so rudely determined. I grabbed the other side of the blue double book. "No, you aren't."

"Yes I am. I am taking quite a few of them."

I knew how to be stubborn. Didn't I? We tugged and argued for quite a while, and to my shock she held out the longest. She took a stack, a whole box of my unfinished books. This was not the last I would see of Coletta Reid, already one of the leaders of the East Coast women's movement, and a member of the Furies collective.

Through the first six months of 1971 Wendy and I worked every day possible at the press. Helle suggested we print one of my poems, "The Elephant Poem," as a coloring book, which she had designed with wonderful, fun illustrations, for Masika. So that was our first collectively manufactured book as a press "collective."

The year before, I had written an article, "Lesbians as Bogeywomen," which was published twice that summer, once unsigned in an issue of *It Ain't Me Babe* that Alice was helping to edit. That the article wasn't signed in the local rag is a measure of how influenced we still were by the Maoist cultural revolution in China, which held that individuality was a counter-revolutionary attitude. We hadn't yet absorbed the feminist idea that "anonymous was a woman," and that continuing the habit would simply continue the disappearance of women's impact on the world. "Lesbians as Bogeywomen" called for an end to categorizing people by sexual preferences, and can be summarized with its final line: *"Lesbianism isn't something you are...it's something you do...Specifically, it's the love you give somebody who happens, also, to be female."*

ACTIONS ON BEHALF OF WOMEN

Our dyke warrior engagements in behalf of other women accelerated during the first two years of our Gay Women's Liberation meetings, especially as lesbian households were forming and functioning as supportive underpinning to actions. Pat Jackson recalls that some of us (not including me) took action in behalf of a woman who had been hired as a dancer at a pre-wedding bachelor party, during which the groom had raped her with a Coke bottle to the cheers of his friends. Though rape was still considered by most of society as a joke, we took it very seriously, saw it as a crime that destroyed or threatened women's safe passage through this world. So the GWL group found out where the wedding was taking place, drove to the site and attended, handing out leaflets describing the groom's behavior. In this same period of time a change of consciousness was visible, as flyers appeared in neighborhoods, women posting descriptions and hand-drawings of their attackers, warning other women to stay away from men known to attack women.

Naomi, whose house on Addison Street had been from its inception a women's center, recalls that their household was part of a group that intervened. "We interceded with the battered women," Naomi said, "and sometimes it got physical. We fought with the men. We got into fist-fights with them. Some of the men complained to the police. Once we ended up in the DA's office. What we were doing was definitely extra-legal but what were we supposed to do? We wanted the battery to stop…" The District Attorney told them, "I'm going to throw you all in jail if *you* don't stop."

We changed tactics and persisted, undertaking "vigils" which meant that two or three women would stay with the battered woman (if she did not want to leave her home) to try to break up the emotional gridlock and prevent escalation. Once, when Wendy and I did such an intervention with Alice and Carol, Alice talked on the phone to the batterer. "We are the Women's Defense League of Oakland," she told him. "We know where you live, we know your wife's name and where she works, we know where you work." This particular fellow, desperate at the thought his wife would find out he had a girlfriend, stopped harassing her. Sometimes the intervention went much longer.

Early on in GWL, in 1970 probably, a straight woman in San Francisco, caught in a battering situation, asked for our assistance. We decided to do a massive intervention by never leaving her by herself, always two or three other women would be with her. Sixty women volunteered, each of us spending a few hours a week at the woman's apartment. Some of us took work with us, newspaper layouts or other work, jobs which we did on the premises. For six weeks, there were at least three people inside her apartment with her at all times.

The man with whom she had been lovers lived downstairs, and continued to threaten her. She had asked him to move entirely, and get out of her life. The two of them remained completely hooked into each other, tracking every move the other made. When we feminist activists moved in, the man, who worked as a security guard, which meant he wore a pistol, went to his boss for assistance. His captain said he would back him completely, and we were informed that he was supported by a group of men who were armed and would not tolerate any sort of action from us. We developed a rather typical anti-violence tactic—persistent and silent presence, strengthening the woman and getting her attention off the man and onto herself and her own development. Finally, some of the older women among us began directly reasoning with the man about the problem.

During the six weeks that we kept up our vigil, the woman's broken ribs and bruises healed. At this point in social history, there was not anything resembling a battered women's program that we could send her to, so Carol took her to the rifle range to give her the idea of taking care of herself. She and her ex-lover were on their own, and all at sea, as left to their own emotions they were well on their way to a downhill slide that could end with him killing her. They seemed locked in a deadly embrace, held in place by fear, rage, disappointment, pride, and their isolation together.

One night we arrived to find her with her ear to the floor listening to his every footstep downstairs. She could have moved to a different place, but the one stand she was willing to take was to keep her apartment; since he was the aggressor, he should be the one to move. We agreed. After six weeks we could not think of anything more to do that would not involve violence toward him; we had talked to him, to his boss; we had supported her independence. And so we left. Almost immediately so did he. Evidently he had wanted to leave after a short while of our vigil, but didn't want it to look as though we had driven him away.

As a community, we had put calm, steady pressure on the situation. Somehow, the presence of determined yet emotionally neutral women broke the negative connection. Women in other parts of the country, perhaps especially self-appointed "lesbian warriors," were also busy interrupting battery against women, and challenging men's authority, often in very physical ways. Using our newfound lesbian solidarity, groups of us began to take stands with our bodies to fight against the rampant sexism and assault of any woman, *including* us lesbians, assaults that had been completely part of our lives. We had never been safe in and around the bars or in public spaces. Now, lesbians began to resist in the context of the greater feminist and Gay Liberation movements.

Since being punched in Albuquerque, I had never thought of myself as all that tough because I was always so afraid of being hit again in the head and losing my brains, so I avoided the frontlines of demonstrations where police clubs fell heavily on people. But I was part of our lesbian actions. At a reading I did recently north of San Francisco, an old-time dyke named Betty P. told me that in the early 1970's we had helped her after she had been assaulted by a man at a lesbian bar. We stood in a line behind her while she confronted him, and, she said, "I felt so much stronger, knowing you were there." She added, "One of you had a gun." I don't recall any of us having a gun, but maybe we said we did, to appear more intimidating.

Resistance required a showing of strength, and being a dyke in warrior mode was never without its dangers. The activist Cynth Fitzpatrick told me about being one of a group of six dykes in LA that confronted two men who were hassling a woman. The men turned out to be street fighters, "who proceeded to take out the other dykes while I am running and ducking, saying 'No, no, no!' Later the men apologized, said they just went off. There were broken noses and cheekbones, I mean, it was a mess." Cynth added, "We were tough because our lives were dangerous and we needed armor."

In New York, activist and writer Martha Shelley was part of Gay Liberation Front in 1969, a mixed gender political group who among other actions did demonstrations protesting police harassment of gay people. Their group went up against a NYC mafia in their own behalf. As Martha tells it, "We demonstrated one time in a lesbian bar where women had not been treated very well; a lesbian had been punched out. And so we went in there and just danced around in circles. I was elected spokesperson—I felt like I was the shortest person on the block—because they said, you know, 'You go up there and tell them.' So I went up to them and said 'Do you know why we are here?' And the Mafiosi guy looks at me and says, 'Do you know who I am?' and I say, 'I don't know who you are and I don't care who you are, *we* are the *Gay Liberation Front!*' Meanwhile my knees were knocking...I was afraid they were going to come out with machine guns and of course they were afraid we were going to destroy everything in their bar."

What Is a House?

By spring of 1971 our Lexington street apartment had become an uncomfortable place to live. M. was drinking more heavily, screaming at times about witches chasing him around. He and his big friend Buzz had a sadistic game they played, sitting on the cellar steps drinking and shooting off bullets held between thumb and forefinger with a hammer. M. had shot himself in the leg. Despite our group meetings, the apartment dwellers had never come together as a coherent group. Though everyone considered themselves part of a greater American "movement," we had never congealed over any of the issues that we women brought up—the men were transfixed by the black revolution but didn't seem to bond with each other, while the women rapidly did; the men were sympathetic to our activities but had nothing to add. Lexington Street did not feel like home.

What is home anyhow? What is a household for? The usual image of home is of protective walls, warm hearth, welcome rug, soft light, fabrics of comfort, smell of dinner, little waggy-tailed dog. Home is refuge and family, first and foremost. Yet for many in our gay women's movement, childhood home had not been a refuge. Living together as lesbian lovers didn't always feel like "home" either—Wendy and I seemed to carve out only the most tenuous of spaces, a mattress on the floor or on a homemade loft, just slightly more secure than the deck of an unseaworthy boat. Maybe Von's strange choice to keep her house unfurnished was a powerful statement of the reality of our situation— we all had the hope of having a "place in the us," but for Von it had been a hollow promise....how would this be different if we moved into an all-lesbian household? Would we be disillusioned? Would it be true that women couldn't really get along? We took a breath, and took a chance.

Soon after Wendy and I moved into an all-women's household in Oakland, in May of 1971, I wrote to Von about it:

> [O]f course the people vary from day to day and many different things go on... sometimes the household publishes a newspaper. We make one third of the rent by selling hamburgers and enchiladas at our favorite gay bar so we cook a lot and Carol, Pat, Debbie and others fix people's cars for money and we always have almost enough of everything and too many cats.

Designed to be women-centered, activist, and lesbian, households like ours were appearing across the Bay Area and other parts of the country, like Iowa City. They each were unique and made valuable contributions to the women's movement. The ones I knew best were in San Francisco, Berkeley, and Oakland. For me, telling the story of my life would be incomplete without an account of these households because the revolutionary changes that came about for us could never have happened without the support they provided.

In late 1969, Carol Wilson and Alice Molloy had opened their Benvenue Street household to Gay Women's Liberation activists, taking on the biweekly mass meetings and taking in radical lesbian renters. It was probably the first Gay Women's Liberation household. Alice, Carol, and Natalie, had been living there with Carol's son Nick, now about sixteen. Carol and Natalie had been lovers for years, raising Carol's son. In the 50s they had been early members of Daughters of Bilitis, founded by Del Martin and Phyllis Lyon. Alice became Carol's lover in the late 1960s, moving into the Benvenue house and into an invaluable, if at times uneasy, coalition. As soon as we all met at the gay men's Homophile conference, Pat Jackson moved up from San Jose to take up residence in the big brown-shingled classic Berkeley house.

My first memory of the Benvenue house was driving over with Wendy for a GWL meeting, and being told by Alice that we were not to go into the living room, as it was currently inhabited by two monkeys who had been rescued by Carol from experimental labs at UC. This was typical, of Carol especially, who wanted to rescue every creature and human in pain. Peering into the dim recesses of that room, I saw crouched in the high drapery two frightened furry creatures looking back at me with round black eyes, their little hands wrapped in the beige fabric. Shades of People's Park! Carol and Alice wanted everyone liberated, including creatures and plants.

The landlord evicted the vibrant lesbian activist group within a few weeks, serving notice on Carol. As Pat explains, "There were a lot of women running in and out at all hours, and yes, some of us sat on the front porch without our shirts on; we were just so enthusiastic, feeling so free you know, and I think we played loud music, and the smell of marijuana smoke drifted into the neighbors' windows." And with her little smile, she adds, "Oh yes, and then there were those monkeys…"

Oakland: Terrace Street, 1970

What is a house? A cauldron of creativity and intellectual engagement. By summer, after the Benvenue eviction notice, the refugee monkeys were passed on to a suitable shelter, and the triumvirate of older organizers, Carol, Alice, and Natalie, bought a house in North Oakland. The house had four bedrooms and a vast living room big enough to serve as a meeting place and project center, as well as a spacious basement and an attic, which also became living spaces. Natalie lived in a rented apartment just two blocks away. Frugal and steady, she had worked for decades as an accountant, meticulously saving her money. She put up the $4,000 down payment. The three women agreed to put the house in Alice's name. Having lived as a beatnik in the Lower East Side, Alice was considered unlikely to ever be a grasping materialist, yet she was able to keep track of things, and so could be trusted to be the landlord in a collective living arrangement. Alice, Carol, and Natalie were an extremely stable trio, though Natalie preferred to live alone.

During the five years I lived in the Terrace Street household about forty other lesbians lived there as well, some for a few months, others for several years. Hundreds more women visited or attended the endless meetings there. The living room served as a meeting place for as many as sixty women at a time.

I consider living there one of the greatest privileges and learning experiences of my life, because I got to participate in helping to formulate a particular kind of revolution—a women's revolution. Only a few precious times in history have women been in a position to separate from the rest of society in order to describe the world as we see it, and to change it for our needs.

Probably our most important contributions were the projects we ran outside of the house. Carol, Pat, and Naomi's cross-country book distribution service had evolved into a large bookstore collective on the corner of Broadway and College Avenue in Oakland called the "Information Center Incorporate: or "ICI: A Woman's Place Bookstore." Alice was always quick to add "It's short for 'A woman's place is in the world.'" An actual press had evolved from our mimeograph machine, and would soon be moved across the Bay and named "The Oakland Women's Press Collective."

At the back of the living room Alice was often busy writing, editing, and doing layout for the radical feminist newspaper, *It Ain't Me Babe*, and the house also supported several book writing and art projects. Some of us were writers, including Alice, Willyce Kim, Martha Shelley, Connie McKinnon, and me. Others were literary in their interests, like Carol, and Paula Wallace, who also took photographs; Carol Seajay, with Paula's help, would establish Old Wives' Tales Bookstore in San Francisco. Later Paula would move to Albuquerque to establish Full Circle, another woman's bookstore. Wendy, of course, was resident artist at Terrace Street, but other artists like the painter Judith Lundgren lived in the house as well. Political activists like Pat Norman from Philadelphia lived there too, helping Del and Phyllis establish the Lesbian Mothers' Union, as she herself tried to regain custody of her children, taken away because of her lesbianism.

BERKELEY: ADDISON STREET, 1970

A house is a place where women are safe and their labor is valued. About a year after we began meeting, a group of Gay Women Liberationists moved into a house on Addison Street in Berkeley. Naomi Groeschel, who was about nineteen at the time, recalls that the woman who owned the house allowed them to live there in exchange for turning it into a women's center. Naomi, her bisexual friend Nancy Chestnut, the writer Jean Malley, and a lesbian couple, Louise Merrill and Brenda Crider and their two children, lived upstairs, while the downstairs served as a center for meetings and somewhat of a battered women's shelter.

Louise had spent her life fighting imperialism after being radicalized from a childhood spent in South America. She was one of the founders of the Workers World Party and would later help the movement to free Mae Mallory, a black woman framed for advocating self-defense against the Klan in North Carolina. An utterly dedicated radical, Louise had also been part of the "white buffer" that stood outside the BPP office, fending off the FBI. Perhaps, not yet knowing each other, we had stood in the same nervous little group.

Brenda and Louise had two daughters, one the birth child of Brenda, the other adopted. There was no possibility in the 1960s that an out lesbian could adopt a child, so Brenda had formally adopted little Judy Crider as a single parent. During the proceedings, the two-parent family pretended to the outside world that Louise was the housekeeper. At Addison Street, the family could begin to sort itself out as the other women of the collective tried to help with the children.

Addison Street household had a practical, craftswoman, hard-hat focus, in addition to writing and poetry. After a stint at the post office, Naomi became an electrician, volunteering to help with wiring problems on various women's projects, including the Women's Press Collective. Jean Malley co-edited a poetry anthology that was half women, half men for a mainstream publishing house. Then she went on to become part of a carpentry collective that remodeled and built houses, and did fine carpentry work. They called themselves "Seven Sisters" because they were graduates of various East Coast women's schools. After working a lot as a waitress, Louise now decided to attend trade school. A close friend of the household, Gail Atkins, opened a car-repair garage that specialized in helping women deal with their cars.

Brenda joined a group of six of us who co-edited an anthology of lesbian activist writings, *Lesbians Speak Out*. Louise, who left the Addison Street collective after a couple of years, founded a newspaper called *The Feminist*, and helped with an attempt to establish a "women's room" in the Berkeley Library.

SAN FRANCISCO: COLE STREET, 1971

What is a house? A crossroads for living with diverse people, and for confronting the injustice of the world. Pat Parker rented an apartment and rented a sequence of houses that served as lesbian households nurturing activism, sports, the arts, and a safer space for lesbians of color. The first of these was an apartment on Cole Street near Maud's Study, a rare woman-owned bar opened by Rikki Streicher in 1966. Maud's was of great social importance to the development of our political movement, and Pat was a solid member of its community, as well as a couple of others, like Scott's Pit. By late 1971 the people living on Cole Street were Pat, her best friend, a big blonde woman named Whitey, Whitey's lover, Pat Norman and her lover at the time, Dino, who worked at Maud's as a bartender. Keel, a black woman who was a bouncer at Maud's lived in a room of her own at the back of the railroad-style apartment. Downstairs, in a separate apartment, lived Pat's ex-lover Sandy with her son Michael. This was a completely mixed, black and white household.

As Patricia Cooks (her birth name) and then as Patricia Parker, Pat read poetry at small venues around the Bay Area, as she had begun doing after she and her first husband Ed Bullins moved up from LA. Esteemed black poet and teacher Adam David Miller included her in his 1970 anthology, *Dices or Black Bones: Black Voices of the Seventies.*

SAN FRANCISCO: BERNAL HEIGHTS, 1970

What is a house? Safety for children and growing things. Loveliness. Division of household chores. Hand-stitched designs on tea towels and a child's drawing taped up on the wall. Sharing of stories. Sandy Boucher's lesbian and straight feminist household in Bernal Heights had lots of sunlight, and a clean, sprightly appearance, with curtains and flowers, a tablecloth, nutritious food. Mothers and single women lived together, mutually caring for two children.

I had met Sandy because we both worked at Presbyterian Hospital, and our feminist antennae were up and looking for co-hearts. In 1970 Sandy had been attending women's liberation meetings at Glide Memorial Church, and was part of a consciousness-raising group there. After a while some of the women in the CR group created a household of four women and two children, as well as the boyfriend of one of the women. Despite his ideals of being a part of this household, every week when it was his day with the kids, he somehow "didn't feel well." So the women worked around this disability, week after week. As Sandy said, "We worked out a schedule with each of us having two full days with the kids and no one else, even the mother would not intercede, so if the kid needed to go to the doctor…you took him. I learned to like this a lot, it taught me about children."

They also published a women's newspaper out of the house, called *Motherlode*. Sandy told me:

> So then we went full out, way beyond our capacity to take care of ourselves; we worked twenty hours a day. Anyone who wanted to stay at the house did, all these dykes would come and stay. And then I had started a sexual relationship with one of the women. I was madly in love and it was very intense, so there was all this lovemaking going on.

This was all in addition to holding a full time job. Sandy says that despite the hard work, "Every moment of my life was for women, for all the women in the world, that's how I felt then. It was a great feeling, I was integrated. You know how people used to say 'Get it together,' well that's how it felt, that I had finally gotten everything together in my life."

Sandy's lover was Jeri Robertson, the artist whose work we had used in *Woman to Woman*. Later, Jeri teamed up with Karla Tonella, my lover from New Mexico, who had moved to San Francisco in 1968 to attend what was then called The California College of Arts and Crafts. Now, immersed in the burgeoning women's movement, Jeri and Karla, along with some others opened a women's art gallery on 3rd and Brannan Streets, in an upstairs loft, and it ran from 1974 through 1976. The "Women's Art Center" was a gallery with classes and workshops, and grew to over five hundred national members.

I asked Sandy what she thought was most successful with what her household was contributing to the world. For Sandy, creating a model for successfully raising children communally was one of the biggest contributions her household made. The children would wake up and ask, "Whose day is it?" They were happy. One of them told Sandy after she grew up that it was wonderful to have such strong female role models. They were also a model in their commitment to women. As Sandy puts it, "Anything that came up where some women needed something we would just go and do it. We didn't ask ourselves, 'do we have the energy?' We just did it. This is one reason people would burn out."

Sandy also wanted to describe the idealism that she considered not constructive: "People would be a hundred percent in it and then there was disillusion; people think institutions last forever, so if it fell apart then we have failed. I didn't think about it that way, to me the natural trajectory of the thing is that it builds and then falls apart, naturally disintegrates, so I thought we were a great success."

She isn't ideological, doesn't think ideology furthers, and when she described *Motherlode* newspaper, she said this:

> Our little newspaper that we put out, it wasn't political, it wasn't polemical, but it was a paper that described certain women's lives, so we thought of ourselves as giving voice to people who were voiceless. Of course we thought the whole world was going to change, and be different. Now not that much seems that different. Yet, everything we did then was important, it had its consequences in the world, I believe that, I know that.

OAKLAND: OAKLAND FEMINIST WOMEN'S HEALTH CENTER, 1972

Ideally in a house your health needs are looked after. You and others know the workings of your body and help track its concerns. Someone peers down your throat and touches your head to see if you are feverish. But women have an entire set of health needs, needs that had not been addressed at that time, as science had not really studied women's bodies. Women themselves had lost touch with their bodies, which had become sites of shame. As a "nurse" in an internist's practice in the early 1960s, I had seen many women in trouble, with menstrual ailments, with vaginal infections and cysts that could have been simply treated if caught earlier. The bitterness in the face of one devastated young woman remains with me: she had been date-raped and had miscarried on the plane returning (alone) from an abortion procedure in France.

In 1971, a group of working-class, fed-up feminist women in Los Angeles decided to adopt a slogan, "Putting women's health in women's hands." Carol Downer and Lorraine Rothman called their movement "self-help," and opened a walk-in clinic for women. They developed menstrual extraction as a procedure women could do for each other, which influenced the *Roe v. Wade* decision. They softened the experience of vaginal exams, abortion, and other procedures by changing from hard metal to more flexible plastic materials. Laura Kay Brown, Carol's oldest child, was seventeen years old when she began to participate in the self-help movement, which sent small groups of teachers around the country to show women how to see inside their own vaginas, how to discover what a cervix looks like, how to chart their periods, and how to take care of their priceless organs. On a mission to educate, teams of women went out into cities and countrysides doing self-help workshops, equipped with speculums, mirrors, and flashlights.

Barbara and Laura's household was set up in Oakland by Laura in summer of 1972. Barbara Hoke was living in Florida when a self-help team from LA came to town, and she immediately fell in love with the charismatically vivacious Laura Brown, who reciprocated her feelings.

Laura had come up to Oakland alone from LA with the idea of opening a health center. She sent a letter out to about thirty people, saying October 5, 1972 would be the opening of a clinic "I had rented a little place over on 48th Street." She smiles wryly: "Drive down Telegraph, turn left down a really grungy alley, go right past that collapsed building with the junked car in front of it…and right behind there was the Oakland Feminist Health Center. I lived there, and it was the Health Center too." She was soon joined by a lesbian couple from LA and Barbara.

During the day they transformed the living space into a clinic. Barbara described how they would cover the big boxes of menstrual pads with towels and use them as chairs at night, when they moved everything around, brought out dishes and bedding to turn the place into a house, a very busy activist house. They also harbored an underground fugitive from Iowa City they called Robin and just pretended she wasn't there. "She was our underground person, it was just wild, like having a non-roommate…. We had countless women coming through, the 'movement' part of our movement was very real, we had visitors from all around the world, expanding our view from our little world and we were sending people out into the world too." Laura was nineteen years old at the time she founded the Oakland Feminist Women's Health Center, and abortion was not yet legal.

The Oakland Feminist Women's Health center was part of what would become a group of centers that provided health screening, family planning, birth control, abortions, and simple treatments such as yogurt for yeast infections. They practiced "menstrual extraction," which Laura says the lesbians especially undertook because they wanted to know more about their blood, examining it under a microscope, painting with it, and so on.

Like the other lesbian households they were answering the feminist question, Whose body is it? Whose life? Whose choices? Do women, like men, get to make powerful life and death decisions?

Berkeley: Essex Street, 1971

A house is a place where a new generation has the support to envision social change and take it out into the world. In the early 1970s, Jane Lawhon, Karen Garrison, and Nancy Feinstein—three idealistic young white college graduates—bought a house on Essex Street in Berkeley. They describe attending a big women's liberation meeting at Glide Memorial Church in 1970. This just happened to be a meeting that GWL activists disrupted by entering as a group and insisting on standing in a line across the front of the room, telling stories about our lives as lesbians. Jane remembers, "We chattered away in the car going across the Bay Bridge to the meeting, but on the ride home we were all completely silent, absorbing what we had just witnessed." Karen adds, "We had never realized that a lesbian relationship could be an option until we heard you all speak. It changed our lives."

The position they took, that lesbianism is a political choice for liberation from male supremacy, was the source of some conflict with those of us who were older, and considered ourselves "born gay." In time of course, we all learned to have more sophisticated ideas about sexual orientation and transgender.

They all belonged to the initial group of women in the Women's Press Collective, when we had our first press in the basement on Valencia Street in

San Francisco. They brought youthful energy and enthusiasm, and raised money for the press. Karen contributed drawings to a number of Press Collective books, while she, Jane, and Nancy had contributed drawings to *Lesbians Speak Out*. Karen, Jane, Wendy, Willyce Kim, and I were instrumental to the Women's Press Collective's publication of Sharon Isabel's white working-class lesbian novel, *Yesterday's Lessons*, in 1974.

Along with Nancy and Jane, Karen was an avid socialist, staying active in the leftist group "Berkeley/Oakland Women's Union." Jane had written in 1973 that she then worked for both the Women's Press Collective and the socialist feminist organization, and that "It's still a struggle to integrate the personal and the political in each place."

For a while at least two of the women in the household had extremely low-paying jobs of delivering newspapers. This outraged Louise Merrill, who wanted to see women with real jobs paying real money, so they took jobs in the printing trade. Later, they would take up professions in order to make impact from the inside: Nancy as a therapist and advocate for lesbian and gay mental health, Jane as a labor lawyer, and Karen as an executive in water management, eventually becoming a leader in founding underwater sea parks. Karen says the extreme pollution in printing drove her into ecological activism.

The Essex Street women tried mightily to civilize the single-minded work-driven chaos of our Terrace Street household, by, for instance, suddenly showing up with a birthday cake. They used their own collective house as a place to encourage each other in major accomplishments, and as a place of integrity and caring from which to impact other institutions in the larger world.

OAKLAND: 61ST STREET, 1974-75

Parker moved from Cole Street to a narrow white house on Mississippi Street in San Francisco's Portrero Hill neighborhood, at that time a run-down area, with her lover Ann Bernard and her best friend Whitey. Pat was very proud to show me the garden she had put in among some concrete slabs, now green with collards, tomatoes, and corn. Ann would practice bass in a downstairs room with a little broken window, while upstairs Parker worked on her poetry.

But after a run-in with police that resulted in lots of stitches, Whitey wanted out of the city, and moved up to the northern California countryside. Parker and Ann rented a house in Oakland, managing to land a sizeable three-bedroom wooden house with a dining room and a much larger yard to grow vegetables. And of course Pat's big, easygoing black-and-brown dog Andy went with her. During this period of time, Parker and two other women founded Gente, a separatist support group consisting of lesbians of color—black, Hispanic, Asian, and one Sicilian. Many, if not most, of them had white lovers, which helped toward integrating the movement. During the years they met together the Gente group's numbers swelled to thirty-five or forty.

"Gente" is a Spanish word meaning "people." In addition to meetings where they all shared stories about their lives, Gente members also formed a softball team, no doubt at Parker's urging. She was always tickled to be an athlete as well as a poet. Later, they sponsored the singing group "Gente Gospeliers," to heighten their profile and give the movement a cultural boost. The importance of Gente as a support group in reflecting the experience of lesbians of color in the context of a largely white movement is captured in the ending lines of Pat's poem, "gente": "it feels good / to sit in a room / and say / '*Have you ever felt like*—?' / and somebody has."

Some of the Gente people became lifelines of closeness. Joanne Garrett was nursed through her cancer death by another Gente member long after the group disbanded in 1976. Already an established professional singer and musician, Linda Tillery and a number of other African-American lesbians lived on the same block in Emeryville, creating helpful neighborly bonds, according to Ann Bernard, who also lived there for a while. A picture taken about 1975 features Linda and Joanne belting out a song while in back of them Anita Oñang is clapping, singing harmony along with Parker, looking cool in dark glasses.

To me, our households centered on particular aspects of women's existence needing reclamation: self-defense, a safety zone from battery and rape; childcare assistance; health screening and advice, abortion and birth control information, reclamation of women's rights over their own bodies; a bookstore as both vital community space and brain food; printing press for independent publishing of crucial ideas and fomentations; arts, including imagery of how women saw themselves; poetry readings that led and focused movement attention, and fed hearts; newspapers to spread radical ideas and tell what women's lives were really like; art; music and performance to spark a sense of belonging. And always the continuing development of group activities, like the Gente support group for lesbians of color, like the Lesbian Mothers' Union, like the socialist women's groups, and like the group meetings around the anthology that Carol, Natalie, and I instigated. Households were centers for ongoing radical activity, as women poured into California from all over the country and parts of the world, looking for methods and new theories of social change. Households were also a base from which organizers engaged the rest of the country, sending us out on trips with literature and performance, sending people out to do self-help workshops in restoring women's connections to their own bodies, sending organizers out into the countryside to establish women's land and places where women could conduct community spiritual rituals and study wicca, herbal healing, organic gardening, goat-keeping, and so on. Some women engaged in hard-hat occupations, and learned trades: electrician, carpenter, plumber, auto mechanic, construction, line-work for PG&E. Nearly everyone became a teacher of some kind. Women taught their skills and gave each other a way to accomplish something or even gain a trade.

So What Is a House Anyhow?

Does it care for the children in every imaginable way? Does it care for everyone? Does it feed the women and protect them from being raped and battered? Does it give the mothers sanity and support? Does it feed women's minds, intellects, curiosities, and sense of themselves in the world? Does it care for women's health, including reproductive health? Does it set women on a path to be leaders in the world? Does it nurture women's artistic expressions and encourage them to be public and communal rather than individual "stars"? Does it enable women to reach across their differences and take care of themselves and each other in a racist, colonialist, imperialist society? Are people of all classes welcome? Does it engage women in sports and the outdoors? Does it care for women's emotional lives? Does it engage women with the natural world and enable them to help tend nature appropriately? Does it provide self-defense and other protections such as legal help when women engage with the world? Does it give them psychological support?

No one of our households covered all this territory, but the several I have described together covered a wide range of these needs—or "issues" as we called them—and more. Households like this, feminist and lesbian feminist, sprang up all over the country during the 1970s. And to the extent they did, we had a powerful economic, social, political, and familial network. We had changed the geographical landscape for women, and we had begun the revolution we needed.

A Simple Revolution

To get to sleep I nightly fantasized that I was part of a guerilla cadre; we had dug tunnels and lived underground; our tunnels were in a forest that was also a military camp, occupied by "enemy" soldiers—always white men in camouflage uniforms with stern faces. Martha Shelley and I (inevitably Martha was my comrade in these imaginary scenes) slipped along the tunnels "our side" had made, slithering up to ground level in order to fire our weapons, which were blowguns, tubes armed with tiny darts the size of sewing needles. The tips of the darts had a sleeping potion on them, so when we hit one of the soldiers, he would lie down and pass into unconsciousness. About the third soldier to collapse, and I was asleep.

In retrospect, and using a bit of psychology, these soldiers were me, my Joan of Arc self trying to be St. George the dragonkiller, my relentless misuse of myself, my sense of never accomplishing enough—accomplishing some, yes, but never enough to make a real difference, to say something all the way out, grab with all my teeth and successfully drag the culture into its own future by the scruff of its neck. In these fantasies perhaps the guerilla warrior maiden was trying to tell the knight to be still before he stupidly killed someone.

At the Ash Grove

In October of 1971 a young white musician with a shaved head named Cynthia Fitzgerald was working as manager at the Ash Grove in Los Angeles; this venerable folk music club had featured all kinds of great musicians, Muddy Waters, Joan Baez, Bob Dylan, June Carter, and The Weavers. Socially committed jazz and world musicians like Ravi Shankar and Jackson Browne also played there. Poets like Charles Bukowski read their antiwar poems at the Ash Grove.

As the seventies opened, in keeping with the club's reputation of being at the forefront of the times, the owner wanted a series of women and the blues. At that time Cynth was playing music with Renee "Peaches" Moore, who was a Panther—had even been in the LA Panther shootout, Cynth told me dramatically. Cynth was working as an ally for the Panthers in LA, and had also been part of the white "buffer." Cynth described Peaches as "brilliant, she could sing, she could play anything." Cynth played flute and saxophone, and the two women had opened for Albert King, the great blues guitarist.

Now with the women's movement gaining momentum, and hearing what kind of program the owner of the Ash Grove Club wanted, Peaches, according to Cynth, had said "Fuck the blues—it's a downer, let's stamp out the blues." Peaches wanted to hear songs about women's power. So the two of them invited feminist artists, including seventeen of us Bay Area lesbian cultural radicals, to the esteemed Ash Grove, putting together a spectacular women's festival of twelve nights of performers. Cynth remembers that Wanda Coleman did one of her first readings and Judy Chicago did a little play featuring a giant penis.

By now Wendy and I were part of a band, led by a singer named Pat Shelverton, a working-class white woman from Oakland, who named the five of us "Wailin' Pat and the Teardrops." Our band was part of the Bay Area contingency, as was Pat Parker.

Cynth saved our group of seventeen for the last weekend, "so you could really kick ass." And, at least according to Cynth, we did: "You blew everyone away. The Bay Area women brought a radical content that LA didn't have." I was onstage a few times, read my "Common Woman Poems" and sang my "Strikin' Dyke" song, a rewrite of a country western tune, with Wailin' Pat and the Teardrops. Wendy and I had sung it often together for lesbian events: "you made such a strikin' dyke / when we went riding on my bike / and with all yer young heart / you learned to care. / I brought you shame and disgrace, / the world has crumbled in your face / because they call our love / a back street affair."

There was a lot of conflict at the Ash Grove event. For example, Pat Jackson and two or three friends drove into town in a pickup truck from Arkansas where they had been looking for land that could be lesbian-owned and run. They showed up country-wild and loud and wrote "LESBIATE" all over the walls. This upset the moderate feminists, who Cynth—caught between the two factions—calls "Jane Fonda types." (Actress Jane Fonda was one of the supporters of the women's event and had performed there with material protesting the Vietnam War.)

Pat does not now recall this wall-writing episode, though Cynth and I both do, and Pat willingly acknowledges, "of course we *would* have done that." I remember the huge letters on the wall, "LESBIATE." My own thrill at this open advocacy. (The full phrase is "Lesbiate and Smash the State.") And I remember two nicely dressed, middle-class women sitting in the front row at the club who thought I was "cute" as I sat on the stool in my little vest and reached for the mike to read my poems. However, they found these so distressing they rose to walk out; sitting nearby, Janet said to them, "Still think she's cute?"

They did not.

MOVING INTO A NEW MOVEMENT

How did we effect this revolution? For one thing, our economy. We were intellectually and emotionally enriched from nearly every strata of society because our easy "who needs what?" economic exchanges enabled working-class and even very poor women to participate—along with (often disinherited) daughters of the upper middle classes and beyond. The solid foundations under these crucial collaborations were the households, as well as the collective commitments to form projects utilizing everyone's input. This maximized our pool of confidence, knowledge, creativity, sexual interest, and experience.

As an extension of the hippie, black activist, and white leftist values of sharing resources, we lived within what would much later come to be posited as a "gift economy." A gift economy is not reciprocal, there is no expectation of direct exchange of goods for goods or goods for value. Rather, gifts are given to those in need, who pass this on by giving in their own time what *they* can give to those in need. Some women were putting money into it, and all of us were putting labor into the movement.

Artists frequently live their entire lives within a gift exchange economy. We poets did dozens, eventually hundreds, of benefit readings to raise money for women's projects, and through this our work became known. The readings created a sense of unity in our audiences, which were not always women-only. As poets, we were willing to read anywhere for any number of righteous causes. For example, a poster among Parker's effects advertise a Benefit for the Council on Religion and the Homosexual, held at Glide Memorial Church, April 17, 1973—the readers consisted of four men, four women. Harold Norse, Rich Tagett, Paul Mariah, Jim Mitchell, Elsa Gidlow, Parker, alta, and me.

In the households, we received material gifts, some of them anonymous. Mysterious shoes and boots would show up at the foot of the steps at Terrace Street, or a stack of flannel shirts. In later years, under Naomi's influence, Louise Merrill would arrive with a box of organic vegetables and the news that food was political and we were endangering ourselves by not eating properly. She restrained herself on the subject of our smoking, which was obsessive enough to drive away all but the most devoted of our sister warriors. In turn, someone else was no doubt helping Louise with her newspaper, or telling her where she could find a job to get some cash.

After we moved our press into the back of A Woman's Place bookstore, individual women or organizations began arriving with money or supplies. Secretaries brought in boxes of paper they had lifted at work. A woman from Daughters of Bilitis arrived one day, announcing, "We voted to give this to you," placing a check for $500 into my ink-stained palm. Academic Sally Gearhart, who also lived in a lesbian-only household, generously began in 1972 to send us a check each month for $25 to help support our efforts. This would buy food for a week.

We each volunteered thousands of hours every year and didn't mind that people made fun of our cross-class "uniforms" of practical plain clothing, blue work shirts or checkered flannel shirts and Levi's, tennis shoes and vests. Potlucks became a way to spread dinner around without judging who wasn't in a position to bring anything. In the years of 1970-1976, I lived on as little as two thousand cash dollars per year, partially made possible by shopping for clothing at the Goodwill. In keeping with the one rule of Terrace Street house, that every woman was to have a room of her own, Wendy and I each had our own space. My rent was $60 a month for my handsome little room.

We also developed what might be called a "knowledge economy." We had a certain amount of public space in the form of health centers, bookstores, women's dances and meetings, and the press movement, which had quickly become capable of publishing anything, even full-length books. In addition to meetings we held "events" where knowledge was formally shared. By at least 1972, the movement took on the feeling of being "our own college," as Laura K. Brown put it. The founders of A Woman's Place had deliberately set this up by prefacing their name with the letters I.C.I., meaning "Information Center Incorporate." It was an embodied place for sharing knowledge, as Alice and other collective members never tired of explaining to the endless stream of women who came into the store, avidly hungry for what was there.

Into the space within each of us, created through the intense critique that we were continually doing—of power, of all knowledge, and of all social institutions—flowed the molten fluid of questions and ways of expressing our newly found and experienced knowledge. We learned, embodied, absorbed and exchanged this new knowledge as quickly as we could. In the Terrace Street household we discarded theory after theory that seemed to us ineffective, or misogynist, or antihomosexual, noninclusive, nonecological.

Alice, who was understood as the household intellectual and theorist, was inspired by Wittgenstein, but I was now turning only to women writers. I would hitch my little wagon to the tail end of their thin line and see where it took me. I was reading, among many others, Doris Lessing and Ursula Le Guin. Alice, ever the generous teacher, brought my attention to Mary Daly's *Beyond God the Father* and Marija Gimbutas' *Gods and Goddesses of Old Europe*; and also *The Secret Life of Plants*. Carol brought my attention to her favorite poet, Audre Lorde, whose second book of poems, *Cables to Rage*, had come out in 1970 from Dudley Randall's Broadside Press in Detroit. I was also reading other women of color published by Randall, like Sonia Sanchez and Nikki Giovanni.

Many of us were electrified by *The First Sex*, by Elizabeth Gould Davis, a librarian who saw compelling patterns in women's history and prehistory. We were seized with a nationalist type of fever over *S.C.U.M. Manifesto* by Valerie Solanas. Though the men of Olympia Press printed the small book as a joke, the joke was clearly on them. Never had we seen such a clear statement of the emperor, in the form of the superior sex, the First Sex, having no clothing, no scepter, no crown of approval. Men were lazy, she said, and unoriginal. We howled with laughter and a great relief. Men were human, not gods, we could level the playing field, play on it. Prior to this we had been taught in a thousand ways that only men were original; what now did this reversal mean for the originality of women?

Alice would get on the telephone to New York with feminist activist Ti-Grace Atkinson, sitting on the stairway rolling cigarettes, the coast-to-coast dialogue helping to guide our continual analysis and our scheming; this was no doubt a two-way street of influence. She would report these conversations with glee, as we continued to hotly debate: How could we change the world? How could we change anything at all?

Wendy was changing the view of "feminine" by making drawings of powerful-looking women, using heavy black lines with no shadowing, no subtlety, emphasizing character, strength of purpose, emotional state, and presence. We put some of her drawings with the Common Woman Poems into a chapbook, using beautiful, soft-looking tan paper and bold typeface; fifteen thousand copies would sell. A chapbook is a brilliant invention of free speech, dating from the decades following the invention of the printing press. In England, fellows called "chap-men" drove horse-drawn wagons from town to town selling various household goods and small self-published pamphlets called "chapbooks." People making use of them included religious thinkers with sparkling or dreadful new theological ideas, women selling their family recipes for cash, prostitutes advertising their trade, and poets. Poets trying their luck with the public.

CHILD OF MYSELF

Wendy and I now drove a handsome white and blue VW van, which we used to haul boxes of paper and printing supplies as our publication capacity expanded. We had bought, at a low price, this highly useful vehicle from who else but Diane DiPrima, that irascible New York and California poet who is the closest thing to a fairy godmother I have ever had. (She may be irritated that I have said this.)

Lucky for me Diane didn't hold grudges. She had given me a poetry manuscript for the press to publish, which I thought would be our privilege. Unfortunately, I took it to the collective group for a decision. They said "no," and, disappointed and embarrassed, I realized then that I did not want to spend my precious time processing emotions and arguing political positions interminably. I withdrew from group meetings of the press "collective," instead spending my days printing and talking to visitors, and my nights researching and writing in my room. When a few younger members of the group approached to say that we should not print Parker's second book, *Pit Stop*, on the grounds it was "politically incorrect," I said bluntly, "Too bad. I'm already printing it." And quite literally at that moment I was churning out crisply inked pages on the multilith. Worker's power trumped groupthink, I was thinking. Now, I wonder why I didn't ask them what they meant by that decision.

One of Parker's lines spoke to the problem of women's slowness to just act: "sometimes I think the tactic of this revolution is to *talk* the enemy to death." On the other hand she may have been thinking of all of us at Terrace Street, as we loved to engage in intellectual dialogue and in vain invited her to join us. She obviously thought we were wasting our time when we could be acting.

By 1972 Pat was reading at least one pro-lesbian poem at our community gatherings, and by then she was also willing to publish it. This allowed her to come out completely to each of her communities. Once a lesbian poem was published in a broadly available book, it was no longer possible to be straight to the black community and gay to the white community, a stance that had worked for her since 1970. Being out, yet continuing to write about black and female experience, also meant she was positioned as a flashpoint and change agent in three movements; she stood at the crossroads where they intersected. In 1973 we published, as part of the press collective's new edition of *Child of Myself*, her poem that overtly celebrated oral sex and careful love-making, "a woman's flesh learns slow by fire and pestle / like succulent meats, it must be sucked and eaten." She ended the book with a poem calling for the feminist ideal of equality in love relationships, "let me come to you naked / come without my masks / come dark / and lay beside you."

For the illustrations of *Child of Myself*, Wendy had looked at photographs and had drawn several illustrations, including the striking cover graphic, a long, serious African-American face with crown-like hair. We printed the cover in dark blue on light blue cover stock, Parker's favorite color. To help Pat choose the graphics Wendy had invited her to stay in the middle bedroom at Terrace Street, which was conveniently empty at the time. (No doubt Alice was in on this decision to keep the room for Parker for the sake of this experiment in embodied illustration.) Up for the artful adventure, Pat agreed, and moved into the room for a month while Wendy pinned various graphic options up on the walls. After living with the drawings, Pat made the decisions with Wendy of which graphics to use with which poems.

The new edition of *Child of Myself* was a handsome book, sturdy. Having Parker in the press collective line-up gave us an immeasurable boost, and gave me comradely company. But in my carelessness and greed in grabbing Pat for our press, I had really hurt my sister-poet alta, who had published the first edition of Pat's book for her courageous Shameless Hussy Press, the earliest feminist press on the West Coast. None of us at the press collective had even told her this second edition was happening. The ethics of publishing never occurred to me, I saw only the political implications of actions, not the personal or the ethical. That's the last time I would make that mistake. At least in publishing.

Besides publishing the new version of Parker's poems that established her as a public dyke leader, and ruining my relationship with alta, I also spent nine months of 1972 writing a new set of poems in a different style.

SHE WHO, 1972

Portrait poems had run their course for me. Artists, poets, and songwriters had brought several feminist ideas and formerly unspeakable subjects forward, not only male supremacy with all its violence, and not only lesbian lives as common lives, but also masturbation, cunnilingus, menstruation, and birth control. For instance, alta had written, "I am a woman / if you come in me / a child is likely to come back out."

Given all this specificity, what should happen next? I wanted to expand beyond individual portraits to speak a more collective idea, a counterpoint to idealized notions of "womankind," as earlier artists, poets, and theologians had been moved to change a definition of "mankind" to include peasants in the fields and poor men. I wanted to include all kinds of women, and also get to something "central" to women as a category. During this time I was closely reading Gertrude Stein, inspired that she had broken through so many linguistic barriers in a search for new meanings through altering syntax. To change *what* is said, I needed to change *how* it is said, how anything is said.

I thought that music might be a place to start, to change my poetic by expanding my inner "vocabulary" of rhythms. I invented some exercises for myself. Walking down the street, I would suddenly change my pace, start off on a different foot, skip, place my feet differently, anything to break my rhythmic habits. Anytime in 1972 if you saw me sitting in a café or even a meeting you would notice my fingers moving on my knees or the table as I tapped out rhythms constantly, especially the breathing patterns of people speaking, coughing, laughing.

Then, I tried older folk literary forms such as limericks and fables, as well as various uses of rhyme. My favorite was a reversed phrase: "red webs, webs red" which forced me to slow down and hold my mouth differently. Though I had sworn I would never use a list in poetry, as Vachel Lindsay had in his chants for the labor movement, I did this several times. In the She Who series, "the woman whose head is on fire" is the first line of a list of women whose qualities are not valued or acceptable as "beauty" or even power. For instance, "the woman with enormous knees, the woman who hates kittens, the woman who plants potatoes, the woman whose toes grew together, the woman who screams on the trumpet."

Later that year I would write in a poem, "Plainsong," "was I not ruling / guiding / naming / was I not brazen / crazy / chosen" with dramatic spaces between the words. This poem, not autobiographical, reflects collective women's imagined powerful past time conflated with the feminist and lesbian liberational experience of present time. The title poem of the series is ten lines, using just two words, "She Who." I put these thirty-two poems on 3 x 5 cards, along with a couple of Stein's paragraphs. After reading each one I slung it across the stage; sometimes I preceded this by tearing off my Levi jacket and throwing it too.

By the end of 1972, though I was reading "She Who" to enthusiastic crowds of women, an artistic unease coiled around my hips and shoulders, and the voices of political activists haunted my ears. Was I misleading women, setting up a romantic idealism, taking them off the path of, as the street chant goes, "justice for everyone," not "just us"? I determined to write a balancing poem, one that directly addressed political issues.

A WOMAN IS TALKING TO DEATH, 1973

At the opening of 1973 once again I searched for a change of voice that would hold the content that felt so pressing—war, racism, rape, poverty. I was reading Doris Lessing, admiring the relentlessly serious tone of her South African, leftist activist-feminist voice, her absolute refusal to let the reader off the moral or emotional hook. I wanted to stay in such a serious zone to do the writing, using memories of things unspoken from my own experience. So, the need to use an autobiographical voice, as Lessing did, and as Parker had in her 1968 poem "Goat Child." This meant learning to turn oneself into a character. Yet I also wanted to stay rooted in community, to tell stories that were not specifically mine.

I wrote "A Woman Is Talking to Death" in February of 1973, staying secluded in my little orange room, pacing back and forth on my disheveled, book-filled mattress, sitting deep in the chair within the closet, staring at the bare limbs of the magnolia tree outside the little window. Lurching up to pace and mumble out loud, reading sections to the air. Smoking hard, staring hard at the inner walls of my experience. To stay focused I brought a bottle of apricot brandy into the room, whose color tone clashed with the bright orange of the walls. Staying just on the edge of tipsy, I wrote on a yellow legal pad for three days.

In every way for me it was a culminating poem, the sum total, in a sense, of what I had come to understand about the complexities of western civilization, gleaned from our kitchen table and bookstore meetings. I decided to name the fifteen-page poem with a phrase in continual present tense, "A Woman Is Talking to Death," as a play on the trivializing notion that women talk a subject "to death." The title is making a serious claim of addressing "death" as "social death," the death that precedes actual ending of life, and destroys its quality of living.

The poem begins with a primal event, the collision of a car driven by a middle-aged black man with a stalled motorcycle on the Bay Bridge, the impact instantly killing the young white man who had been riding it—what Wendy and I had witnessed that February night in 1970. I added numerous other scenes that I had either witnessed or had been influenced by. A poet steeped in myth tells facts in the form of myth; if the facts are "new" then so is myth. But this poem was also a critique of the old myth of the sacrosanct "rights" of white men over those of anyone else, resulting in harm, or the "death" that is oppression.

My poet's and activist's desire was to reveal this old myth and suggest a crossing over into new ones, and a new place. The events are viewed through an overtly lesbian-feminist lens, giving the poem the mythic dimension that makes it a culturally and historically transitional poem, a poem of the transition from patriarchy and its violent, antilesbian, misogynist and racist/colonial history. I say "transition from" because it is not yet a transition *to* the next place, because the "next place" had not yet, in 1973, emerged in words or images. We were on the bridge leading to this next place; the poem told us what we were leaving, and that we were on our way to somewhere else. The poem also demands that we take responsibility for our own racism, and for our contribution to the suffering of others. The poem defines oppressed peoples as one's own charges, and the relationship as "lovers," the responsibility as one of love. "Was the general their lover?" the poem asks, of the absurd deaths of soldiers caught in the machinery of battle. The poem asks what our commitment is to other human beings if we think of ourselves as "lovers" to them. Once a group has coalesced around love, which is always an erotically charged atmosphere, how far in any direction does this radiate? The poem expands love beyond couple relationships to love that encompasses layers of commitment, even to strangers, and especially to those in need of compassion and resistance to whatever is oppressing them.

Immediately after I had completed "A Woman Is Talking to Death" I began the work that I hoped could help begin to define that new place, on the other side of the bridge.

PRESS, OH GLORIOUS PRESS

Up until we bought the Chief, Wendy and I both had long hair; so did the others now that I think of it. Some of us tied our curly locks casually into ponytails and blended in with the hippies. Others were like Janet, who let her hair hang in a long curtainy sheet so it could be flipped in various appealing gestures. The Chief changed all that, as one day I came down the stairs to find everyone gathered around Janet.

"She caught her hair in the rollers," Wendy explained. The heavy, foot-long, ink-drenched rubber tubes, inexorably revolving against each other to spread the ink evenly, had snagged the end of her straight black hair, slamming her head into the machine. I could only imagine the whole team of women, someone screaming to instigate the panicky leaping for the red "off" button to stop the monster and get Janet loose by removing the rollers carefully with their hands. That was our first accident. A second happened when Suzanne clipped a live electric wire that was drooping across the cutting board with the blade, shooting electricity through her body. Neither of them was seriously hurt, and they both tossed their accidents off with bravado, but printing was not without physical cost. From now on we would wear our hair short. We were well into learning firsthand about the hazards of the industrial revolution, and we would have more accidents.

By 1972 the press collective had hauled all our equipment across the bay to Oakland, to a generous section of space at the back of the bright and beautiful bookstore—how glorious to be warm and dry at the broad base of the isosceles triangle-shaped building. A thick wire wall separated us so customers buying books wouldn't accidently wander into the heavy machinery. We were, like the bookstore and the health center, far more than our description, far more than a press. We were like an art gallery because Wendy would hang up displays, of say, Cathy Cade's photographs of women working, so all the editors of *Lesbians Speak Out* could see them as they were selecting them for the book.

Membership of our collective expanded with East Bay lesbians, Willyce Kim, Karen Sjohölm, Anita Oñang Taylor, Paula Wallace, and more. Martha Shelley would soon move to the West Coast and join us. We bought a small second press, a Multilith, that was faster and safer than, though not nearly as eye-catching as, the big iron head-eating press, which loomed impressively near the tall window on the Broadway Avenue side of the building.

Like most of the women's movement, we rejected hierarchical leadership. When someone asked, "Who are the leaders?" we answered, "You are. What do you think we should be doing?" We were suspicious of the hierarchies of leftist organizations and of the Panthers, who had constructed a paramilitary organization with titles such as "Minister of Defense" and "Minister of Education" which, we felt, made it painfully easy for the FBI to pick off their leadership.

We felt intuitively that communalism, with its large numbers of circles and networks, would be a better method to organize women. Cultural work proliferated, and for a while we even adopted the Maoist tactic of making all cultural work anonymous, and though we soon realized this wouldn't work for us, many of us had lost control of some of our earlier work as a consequence of not always having our names on it. Nevertheless, our constant efforts to break the spell of "star power" and the tokenism of the media's singling out individual women for praise while ignoring everyone else, though somewhat hard on me, on all of us, at times, were more or less effective. Many more people participated in, and contributed leadership to, our movement than would have otherwise. Moreover, our non-hierarchical structure enabled those who did the hand labor, or "women's work" of cooking, shopping, and cleaning, or the emotional intelligence work involved in community building, to be recognized as contributing certain invaluable forms of leadership.

We were also a kind of training center on display for women who had never seen other women operating machines. People would line the floor-to-ceiling window on the street, watching us as we oiled and inked the presses, stapled or glued finished volumes, and hauled interminable boxes of paper. On any given day, six or eight of us might be in the space collating pages, dipping the spines of books into the hideous glue pot, and running in and out of the big darkroom, with its old camera that ran on tracks like a miniature train. Seen through the wire wall, we must have been as fascinating to look at as a construction project—but all women.

Laura Brown—who all her life has resembled a tall slender gracefully classic blonde Hollywood movie star until she opens her mouth and out come surprising Marxist references that frame her speech the way cowboy jargon framed mine and Willyce's—Laura describes meeting us at the press when she was fresh up from her mother's self-help group in LA. She needed to make leaflets to let people know to come to a meeting and support her opening of a health clinic for women:

> And how was I going to do this? Getting your message out to the people was the whole goal. Lenin really shook up the world with his group putting graffiti on the wall, getting your message out, and I really wanted to get my own message out. So getting hold of the technology for reproducing stuff was a really big deal in the pre-Xerox world. So—there were these women I heard about, the Women's Press Collective. It was a very hot day, I walked from 48th and Telegraph, just a handful of long blocks, to the bookstore and there were all these lesbians, walls lined with books and lots of loud outspoken talk, Alice directing me all around. And in the back was this wire wall, and behind it there were these machines and these women and these inks. And without any ado, no grilling about political lines or anything—I had simply appeared and said what I needed—and I'll be darned if Wendy and you didn't whip out a mimeograph machine, and set it up on a table, and your idea of solving my problem was to teach me how to use it.

WHAT WAS THIS MOVEMENT ANYHOW?

Younger people have asked me why lesbians, and not just lesbians but radical lesbian separatists, self-named as dykes, put so many of the public structures of the women's movement together and held them in place for two or three decades. Was it because we had no children? But many of us had children. Did we have a lot of leisure, privilege, extra money? No, we were almost all working, sometimes two jobs at a time, as well as doing political work; we had scraps of money or no money. At that time many of us were alienated from our families, and as separatists we were now independent of gay men who, for the most part, had many more resources. But we had ferocious commitment to each other, and we made some kinds of alliances with feminists of every description.

We had built an architecture of love—erotic, loyal, and sometimes contentious, but more often than not enabling us to set aside our differences for a while.

Sexism, that is to say male supremacy, does appear historically to be the root of the other oppressions, stemming from developments in the earliest empire at ancient Sumer. Nevertheless, experientially for women of color, as articulated in the lesbian movement initially by the poets Pat Parker and Audre Lorde, racism could never be separated out from sexism nor considered a lesser oppression. As they taught me to understand, the relentless daily experience of it places a huge burden that must be constantly countered, in any interface with the white world. Likewise, having class and heterosexual privilege can mitigate the impact of male supremacy. As for lesbianism being a political choice, that is also open for question. That too is a "yes, but" sort of thing. I had expected that raising the issues of lesbianism would lead straight people to become more accepting and understanding of us as a group. I never anticipated that lesbianism itself would become heralded as a doorway to women's freedom from certain kinds of oppression. Yet it did, for a time.

Those of us from the older movement, who were known as "bar dykes" because as lesbians we had had no public space except bar culture, thought the younger women talking about lesbianism as a "choice" were insanely naive. That's because bar culture was so limited, and so full of risks, of beatings and arrest and publicity that could cost women their jobs; and because bar culture pushed us to be alcoholics. Who in her right mind would *choose* to become a lesbian? Some of us could not go home again. The more out we were, the less likely that we could go home again. We were at risk of suicide, police brutality, despair, severe substance abuse. We needed to save our own lives. Our most powerful tool was separatism itself, because it gave us freedom of engagement and some measure of self-reflection (as warriors!) in a historic moment that needed us. Our chosen separatism was a reclamation, a transformation of the forms of exile that had made us hunger for engagement with each other and made us eager to prove that we were valuable to society, even as it was rejecting us. Yet younger women were claiming lesbianism as a method of defeating patriarchy's sexist imperatives, and they were driving the movement forward with this stance.

Lesbian, bisexual, and heterosexual radical feminists set about constructing the institutions that could support community with women and children at the heart. "Women and Children First," as one (lesbian-owned) Chicago bookstore would title itself. Health centers, karate classes, garages where women would fix your car without talking to you as though you were an idiot, or cheating you. Coffee shops with performance artists to confirm who you were. Skills classes to help women become independent from the deadly tie of enforced roles. Childcare centers. All-women bands that *wanted* women who played drums, electric guitars, and saxophones. Concerts with audiences who were thrilled to see women sound engineers and stagehands. Bookstores and presses were the intellectual heart of what we were about—to expand our minds, to engage, to learn. And more, as the full name of the Oakland bookstore put it: "A Woman's Place is in the World."

Where else in society could we do this? The more we were pulled into our own movement, the less we wanted to engage with the workaday world where our ideas were unwanted. So we leaped. We chose for life, and mind, we chose for what we saw was a revolution in and of itself—that women could matter, that we could own our own bodies, minds, and souls, that lesbian power could be harnessed and turned toward the social good.

Between 1970 and 1980, ferociously determined lesbian separatists in alliance with bisexual and progressive straight feminists built women's community on volunteerism, using some of the ideologies of socialism, of small business, of cooperatives, of entrepreneurial marketing, of the same charitable feelings that had built other utopias in an earlier America. Some aspects that we made up on the spot, based on our reality. We overlapped with all the other movements, yet ours had unique qualities.

Having a movement that held for a decade or two gave us the opportunity to develop ideas and express them in various ways, including the arts. Rarely have working-class women had such sustained support or had our ideas embraced, critiqued, and tried out. Never to my knowledge has such a large group of lesbians, including those from virtually every class and a wide variety of cultural backgrounds, had such focused purpose and such sustained support for each other.

A Simple Dream and a Simple Revolution

This book is called "A Simple Revolution" as an adaptation from Pat Parker's poem, "i have a dream." In her poem, published in 1973, about four years into Gay Women's Liberation, the narrator describes that she doesn't want a revolution that is of the vanguard, or of the masses, or that turns the world all over, that she as a black gay woman just wants to walk down the street holding hands with her lover, go to a bar, use a public bathroom—and not be arrested by the police, harassed by white bikers, beaten by her black brothers, screamed at by ladies (that is to say, "straight women") in bathrooms. She begins by describing her movement past: "I have placed this body / placed this mind / in lots of dreams / in malcolm's and martin's / in mao's and huey's / in george's and angela's."

Parker's poem "i have a dream" articulates a position taken in behalf of lesbians and gays within leftist movements: "I have placed this body & mind / in lots of dreams / dreams of other people," and then continues emphatically: "now I'm tired / now you listen!" This is a reference to the Left's insistence that homosexuality was a result of capitalist decadence, a side-effect of the indolence and corruption inherent in the capitalist system. But families of any class, from the richest .001 percent to the bottom-most homeless poor folks, have homosexual members. We are hardly explainable as "decadence." I had been grappling poetically and in articles with this wretchedly incorrect analysis for several years. Now Pat was directly addressing the Left and demanding that gay people have full authentic entry into leftist movement: "now you listen! / I have a dream too. / it's a simple dream."

It's not a simple dream of course, and therein lies the power of the poetry. And the power of our movement, which promoted what I want to describe as "a simple revolution" for very complex purposes. To solve, or at least seriously address, all at the same time, issues of racism, classism, queerness, and feminism. Parker's examples of how she had placed her body and mind in Maoist and Marxist movements make it clear that anti-imperialism also must be part of this revolution. In addition, gay women's liberationists were confronting ecological issues, and researching and devising new definitions of spirituality. We were on quite a roll, as were militant feminists all over the country.

The lesbians who turned out for Gay Women's Liberation meetings and actions had been involved personally or as allies in lots of movements, from Civil Rights to the Black Panthers, to the labor movement and the antiwar movement. Some women who had been in Gay Liberation Front saw themselves as advocating sexual liberation, while embracing broader feminism. "Women's Liberation," of course, was one of the terms flowing easily from our tongues. Many more of the people attracted to our meetings had probably never belonged to anything resembling a party or a political affiliation, yet had been drawn to antiwar demonstrations.

To escape labels, at Terrace Street house we often called ourselves "anarchists," as to us, "anarchism" didn't mean mindless violence; it meant militancy without ideology. Non-affiliated militancy. And "militancy" meant absolute insistence and persistence. We were activists, we weren't laid back, we weren't waiting for anyone else to liberate us. Opposed to the Vietnam War yet not necessarily into Peace and Love, more like "No Justice, No Peace." Not having an ideology also meant that the broad base of activist leaders, in roles that shifted personnel constantly, would stay in touch with what the people around us wanted to see happen and said they needed, rather than imposing *shoulds* from theories and tracts of the 19th century—though everything was up for discussion.

Now, bonded in loyalty to each other, we would help to open the floodgates to multiple forms of feminism, those tempestuous, lively mass movements that have continually redefined themselves as they spread worldwide, with as many fractious factions and additions as rivers have feeder-creeks. We helped develop some terms, phrases and images that would initially stand in for ideology: women-loving-women, woman-centered, rape culture, male domination, patriarchy, male-identified, sisterhood, sister love, gyn-ecology, lesbian nation, army of lovers, dyke, common woman, commonality.

Perhaps Pat's poem was suggesting that the closest thing we had to an ideology was that contained in a line from my "She Who" poems, written in 1972: "when She Who moves, the world will turn over." In her own poem Parker is responding, calling this (and at least momentarily rejecting it), "the dream of women."

A "simple revolution" has no ideology, no blueprint, and no preconceived outcome. It also has no idealized leaders, though everyone involved is encouraged to take leadership. A "simple revolution" asks, "What do people say they need? What do I need? What do the economy and the earth and the spirit in people need? What does the ending of prejudice need? What do our authentic selves need?"

Though our revolution has few figurehead leaders, it does have poets and artists who both reflect and add the artist's own experience and insight. Artists both reflect and galvanize. While the hippie movement expressed itself most frequently in visual art, design, and music, and these certainly impacted the women's movement, it is striking how very much the women's movement was immersed in the words of its poets, especially initially. Recent anthologists and critics have identified many poets who drove the movement forward; unfortunately they have seldom included Pat Parker.

Pat Parker and Working-Class Poetry

At ground level, hundreds of women wrote useful poems, published in the dozens of journals and newsletters that flourished across the country. Poetry became a grassroots tool for joining women in common expression. As I had learned from collecting poems for *Woman to Woman*, nearly every woman of the times wrote poetry, often expressive of hidden or forbidden thoughts.

Skillful poetry, however, is different from expressive poetry. Because Pat and I carefully advertised ourselves as working class, people often didn't understand how much care we put into our work, and how many skills we had meticulously honed to create poems that sang out when read aloud, and also read well on the page. Parker and I had both studied the craft of our poetic art from an early age. We had each used John Ciardi's *How Does a Poem Mean?* before Parker gave up using English poetry techniques and gave me her copy, as I had lost mine. She told me she made this change because she was following the poetic style of Don L. Lee. A radical black poet and professor who co-founded the very successful Third World Press, Lee constructed his poetry with speech rhythms, direct statement, repetition, and references to contemporary events impacting black people. Lee thought that black poets of the past had relied too heavily on metaphors and that metaphors just caused confusion, they didn't really make their point directly enough. Get rid of metaphor, just go for facts and observations, give people the dramatic emphasis that rhythm and repetition bring to poems. His poems were often formed around emphatic speech, using a black vernacular, and as he advised in his poem "Destiny," "not bitter songs in european melodies."

By 1973 Lee would rename himself Haki Madhubuti, from Swahili words meaning something similar to "accurate justice." Among the black poets who took up his stark yet effective method in the 1960s was the young Pat Parker, who at that time was still known as Patricia Cooks. She kept the storytelling of her earlier work but dropped the style, imagery, traditional English poetic cadence, and rhyme in favor of repetition, rhetorical questions, dramatic line, bold statements, irony and sarcasm, funny or emphatic punchlines, excellently timed release of information. Like Don L. Lee, she used black vernacular, for example "him" instead of "he," for particular familial emphasis.

With her early (1971) poem "Goat Child," Parker took an autobiographical and feminist voice that would continue, taking strong moral positions that suggested how people could think and feel, often conveyed through irony or suspense. Hence, a poetics. Some critics, including Audre Lorde and later Cheryl Clarke, suggested that she needed a strong editor, perhaps thinking of an outspoken person like Audre who would order her around, as I could not. But Parker, like me, like any politically motivated poet at the time, was not interested in outside advice about her poetic choices. Her poem with the line suggesting we "lay matches all the way to Nixon's ass" was Pat's response to the fact that Black Panther David Hilliard had been arrested for threatening to kill Nixon. But when I said to her, "the reference to Nixon is going to date your book," Pat didn't care about that. I think she probably wanted the solidarity with Hilliard. So the poem stayed in. She wanted her work to be oral, accessible, political, and effective. Both Parker and Lorde were "griots" in the sense of not only speaking directly to and to some extent on behalf of "community," but also pulling their subjects from and making critical commentary on, current events.

As Parker's editor, I sat beside her while we selected poems out of her black unlined handwritten notebooks, and I typed them (our version of typesetting).

We discussed everything about the structure of her poems, every line and punctuation. I was faithful to her desired punctuation, line breaks, capital letters, and so on. I made a few suggestions, changed one or two spellings, but only with her permission. I suggested the order of the poems, and she concurred.

Pat had led a traumatic life by the time I met her. She was the youngest of four sisters with a father who wanted sons and was a harsh disciplinarian, as she wrote, "I did want to please him." She was raped at ten, tricked into performing oral sex on a white man at about the same age. As a teenager she had a baby named Donna that she gave up for adoption, and during her first marriage she had a miscarriage requiring medical intervention.

Her mother was certain that Pat's uncle (her mother's brother) had been killed by the police while in jail, and that the family was falsely told he had committed suicide. One of her cousins died in the Vietnam War. Then, a gay friend, "the only boy I ever loved," who had escorted her to the high school prom, was murdered by local black youths. They called him a faggot, beat him, stole his money, and threw him in front of a car, an episode that haunted her poetry and underlay her fears for her dear friend Blackberri, the gay singer. Her first husband, Ed Bullins, titled "the Buddha" in her autobiographical poem "Goat Child," was abusive. She tried to leave him several times, but well-meaning (pre-feminist) friends kept telling him where she was staying, so he would find her and demand she return. He denigrated her writing, especially her fiction. She also did not like the forced marital sex. Eventually she managed to get away from him, and she married Bob Parker, a white poet, only three days after her divorce from Bullins became official, in January of 1966.

At the opening of 1970, when she had just turned twenty-six, Pat had taken the big brave step of forming a relationship with a woman lover. Lesbianism at first scared her—her first poem on the subject ends "you shudder and take one aspirin." She later changed her style, becoming publicly very butch, carrying a great deal of authority. Her new look was striking: black pearl-button shirt, black boots, black western pants, very slick. (She joked about her cowboy garb that when she went to her first gay bar in Houston, she found everyone in cowboy clothes, so thought that was a dyke look.) She just looked great in this get-up. She looked focused and leaderly, very different from the softer "Patricia

Cooks" look of earlier times, when she wore button front sweaters with girlish designs, and wore her hair longer and worked over, severely straightened.

Parker brought her feminist voice to the leftist audiences that embraced black and Latino power, but saved her lesbian voice for the mostly white lesbian activists. Only when this group expanded in size, was willing to support her voice, and was swelled by increasing numbers of lesbians of color did she dare to come all the way out to "everyone" (except her mother). Until then, Parker would arrive at the Black Cat in North Beach for readings to her straight audience in skirts, and show up to her lesbian readings as a dyke in cowboy boots and pants. She must have done this from 1969 at least through 1971, before allowing herself a completely dyke public identification to all her communities by 1972, when we published the revised edition of *Child of Myself.*

Now that she dressed like an out militant dyke in a vest and a short Afro, the librarian-in-thick-glasses look vanished, her fabulous forehead with receding hair line, her high cheekbones and brilliant smile came forward, and when she used her long fingers for emphasis in the readings, along with her deeply resonant, woody oboe voice, I don't see how any woman in the audience could have resisted her.

Besides sex appeal and serious political views, Parker was witty in her poetry, and she also had a slapstick sense of humor. Once, she took Willyce and me to the Berkeley Marina for an afternoon of fishing. Out of the trunk of her car she hauled two reeking crab traps, outfitted with very ripe fish heads. With these in the water we baited hooks and lines, stood around joking for what seemed eternity, pulled up empty traps and lines, and drove toward home. Suddenly Parker pulled the car to the curb, jumped out, ran into a fish store and emerged with a package. When we reached Terrace Street, she proudly displayed "our catch" to Carol, Alice, and Wendy, who had begun to ooh and ahh over the fine whole fishes. Finally, bending over laughing, Pat spilled the beans.

Grandchildren of slaves and, on her mother's side, a native woman, Pat's parents endorsed education, achievement, and the arts. Despite the racism and deprivation of black schools in Houston during the 1950s, her teachers encouraged her, and one wanted her to be "the next spade lawyer" to help her people. It was a given for her that she would improve the world for black people, and she went far beyond this. So some of Parker's poetry describes distinctly black experiences, from segregation policies of her youth to the Black Power Movement's stances of her young adulthood, and her sense of needing to capture her personal and family history. Other poems reach across, critique and advise: "For the white person who wants to know how to be my friend," one poem counsels, "The first thing you do is to forget that i'm Black. / Second, you must never forget that i'm Black."

Pat maintained a loving presence in her poetry and in her interactions, that was persistent and that wanted to shine on everyone who would reach back. She was a unifying force in our movement, challenging difference to engage in alliance. Her poetry and her example helped galvanize the participation of lesbians of any description who felt "othered."

We published Pat's second book, *Pit Stop*, in 1973. After this, she began to carry press collective books with her when she traveled to readings, and to speak up about the Press. Wendy made her an honorary member of the press collective at this time.

Pat repeatedly had been invited to join the collective, but she had said no. I was shocked. "Why not?" I finally asked. She was standing in the doorway of the wire fence that separated our messy shop from the neatly arranged shelves of the bookstore.

She looked at me standing with a red solvent-drenched, ink-splotched rag in one hand and a small oil can in the other. My pants, shirt, and face smeared, I was reeking of the industrial revolution.

"I can't stand to be that dirty."

"What?" I felt outrage crawl up my spine, especially as she was sneering her lip.

"I had enough of dirty work with a father who cut tires for a living. And besides that, my mother kept a pen of pigs right next to our house. My sisters and I hated those stinking pigs," she said. "We had to take care of them. Now talk about dirty…"

Pat wanted a white-collar job, had worked at the Post Office and then in a recycling plant. Of course what she wanted most was also what I wanted: to be paid to write from her heart. Pat also wanted something that seemed impossible at the time: she wanted to be an out lesbian with a middle-class job and a family, with children of her own.

PAT PARKER AND AUDRE LORDE

Carol Wilson was in love with Audre's poetry, so we all went to hear her read when she was in San Francisco, and invited her to stay over at Terrace Street. Wendy recalls that Audre came to one of our mass lesbian meetings, but stayed in the kitchen playing with Brenda and Louise's children. Before she left, Wendy took her to Cole Street to meet Parker.

On Audre's next trip, Parker had a discussion with Audre that she was sure had persuaded her to become a public lesbian poet, probably in 1973. Shortly before Audre had withdrawn an overtly lesbian poem, "Love Poem," from a forthcoming book, after her publisher Dudley Randall had questioned including it.

I remember the particular morning when I trundled downstairs from my room to find Pat and Audre sitting on the long couch in our sprawling living room. The early morning Oakland light illuminated their intense figures as they leaned toward each other in deep conversation, books open on the couch between them, avidly talking and gesticulating. Not wanting to interrupt, I dipped up a cup of Alice's super-strong campfire coffee steeping in a lidless pot on the stove, and sleepily headed back to the stairs. Pat ran after me, out of earshot of the downstairs bathroom at the back of the house, where Audre had gone.

"Isn't that Audre?" I said, by way of opening. I sat down on the stairs to sip my brew and clear my mind. "I didn't know she had spent the night."

Parker was standing, moving around as she told me excitedly that the two of them had sat together on the couch all night, reading to each other, discussing poetry, politics, their lives, and lesbianism. And, as she put it in shorthand, "all kinds of other shit." She was elated by this.

"And that's not all. Audre has decided to come out with her poetry!" Pat exclaimed. "I talked her into it! Audre's going to come out!"

She was ecstatic, looking up at the ceiling, letting out a big breath, then flashing a big smile, as happy as I ever saw her. I thought she was going to begin dancing (or Parker's version of dancing) right there on the landing, and no wonder—she would now have companionship in her lonely bravery as the only out black lesbian poet. In the world. As I knew well, once overtly lesbian poetry is published and available to the world, there is no place to hide. All of her communities, including the anti-lesbian members of her audiences, from leftists to conservatives, would know everything. It must have been deeply frightening for both Parker and Lorde to risk losing their black and Third World audiences, and possibly alienating some of the antiracist straight white feminists who were supporting their emphatic voices. Now Pat was not so alone in her position. Audre's willingness to be public supported all of our radical lesbian voices, so I was almost as happy as Pat was. A major poetic player had declared solidarity with us, that was how we thought about it.

Now, just to be clear, Audre *was* out, in that she had published an overtly lesbian poem, "Martha," in 1970. But this was now a louder-roaring seventies, and she was an emerging black feminist poetic voice, gaining attention in various political circles. Publication by Broadside Press was a major step in her career, keeping her in the circle of the black poetry movement, along with Haki Madhubuti, Gwendolyn Brooks, Nikki Giovanni, Sonia Sanchez, Amiri Baraka, and Alice Walker.

To publish an overtly lesbian poem sent a message about the strength of the growing lesbian movement. Later that year Audre mailed the excluded "Love Poem" with some other poems to Diane DiPrima, who published them under her own imprint. Audre then went a step more public and published the same poem in *Ms.* magazine, and insisted on its inclusion in her next (and last) book with Randall (*Coal*, 1976). And thereafter, Audre became completely public with lesbian poetry, no more juggling between one movement and the other.

A COMMUNITY INTERVENTION

In a recent conversation, Cynth Fitzpatrick described a scene from the Ash Grove adventure when she connected to Pat. "One of the festival days I was sitting on a couch between you and Wendy, and we were making out, we were drunk and stoned, and we were all kissing each other. Then Pat Parker walked into the room and lightning hit me. We just looked at each other and a huge current surged through us. I remember you and Wendy getting up, saying, 'Well, I guess it's time for us to leave…' and sneaking away. Pat and I stayed in bed for three days. I moved up to San Francisco to be with her, moved into her room on Cole Street."

Notice how Cynth had no trouble spotting a dragon's fire, a huge current surging through her and Pat. But the dragon had teeth: "I had never been a drinker until after Ash Grove, and getting involved with Pat, and the Maud's scene—it was, for me, just like lighting a match to kerosene. I didn't sober up until years later."

The bars—even the great, community-building Maud's—were a double-edged sword. They provided a place to gather, financed by our too-heavy drinking and out of control behavior. Some lesbians got into fistfights or engaged in battery. GWL organizers tried to change the bars; at first we tried this from inside. Pat Jackson and I persuaded Rikki to hire us to do fry cooking, and to provide a monthly free Sunday dinner. We persuaded her to put a book rack in so we could stock it with our liberation propaganda. Jean Malley made a gleaming dark wood stand and we proudly put newspapers, flyers, and chapbooks into the racks.

But while we hoped that people would sober up some and turn the bar into a place of political discussion and interaction, instead, everything heated up socially as more and more women came out and joined the lesbian subculture. They crowded into Maud's and several other San Francisco lesbian bars, eyes on each other and nowhere near our little newsstand in the corner. The music got louder. Janis Joplin roared about taking another little piece of her heart, now baby, and we did just that. The liquor flowed into pent-up, joyful, hopeful, angry bodies. And back in the kitchen in aprons flipping burgers, Pat Jackson and I sucked on bottles of beer to try to keep up with the ruckus, leaning over the half-door to joke and flirt with the customers. I began drinking way more than I wanted.

Before long, GWL began advertising our events as alternatives to the bars, competing to get women to our political poetry readings, meetings, actions, and dances. We had found one of the enemies—it was us. And we were also the solution.

At first we were dragging the alcohol out of our bars and into our movement. As the activism spiraled up through 1971 and into 1972 and the demand for poetry readings accelerated, Parker and I became drunks at the readings. There were clean and sober people in our movement, though in general people fell into one of two categories of self-medication: dopeheads or drunks. The hippie generation put drugs, especially marijuana, at the center of social life. And the beatnik poets had read their poetry in notoriously altered states, which carried over into the San Francisco poetry scene of the late 1960s. I had not been to a poetry reading that didn't feature lots of wine, and sometimes poets so stoned they literally could not read the poems, like one woman who was so high on acid all she could do was praise the fabric of the curtain at the back of the stage.

So now, in this new era of women's political poetry readings, Parker and I both thought you couldn't do a proper reading unless the libations to relaxation had been poured down your gullet to give you confidence. If we had a ten A.M. reading in a schoolroom we were tanking up on beer at nine A.M. Neither of us had an "off" button in those days; fortunately I didn't drive much, so confined my drunken outbursts to the house or street. I assaulted strangers, innocent men who in my drunken state appeared to be sinister, raged with great regularity or sobbed inappropriately, threw up consistently, and tossed a quite large and beloved potted plant through the second story window of my room. Onstage I acted on drunken impulse, once even interrupting one of Pat's poems during a reading we were doing together.

Pat did an even better job of creating mayhem, including wrecking her car while drunk. She was driving several people home from a lesbian bar about two A.M. when one of them began talking about suicide. Parker became drunkenly enraged. "Suicide?" she said, "I'll show you suicide," and she ran the vehicle into a lamppost on the Bay Bridge, injuring one of the passengers. This episode, coupled with my potted plant violence, led to a community intercession. This was long before such interventions became well known, as the Gay and Lesbian Movements somewhat successfully coped with alcoholism in the 1980s through AA meetings.

Louise, Brenda, Naomi, Wendy, probably Alice, and others put an intervention together for Pat and me. Everyone crowded into my room, and

Louise and Brenda led the testifying as to what we had done and how it was affecting others, including Wendy, who to my shame spoke of her increasing distress with my bad behavior.

"Think about the children," Brenda urged. "You're models, community leaders. What kind of models are you being for them?"

Parker and I sat in chastised states, soaking in the information that we needed to change our ways. For me stopping drinking was a matter of going cold turkey and spending a few months getting through the naked feeling of reading while sober—which I discovered after a few uneasy weeks meant I could actually relate to the audience and talk with people afterwards. For Pat everything was more complicated; she had an addiction, and began to write about it in poems addressed to her community.

After the shock of the intervention she tried to get help, going to an out white lesbian therapist (one of the first), who evidently didn't know how to relate to a working-class, militant black dyke, and instead put her on an antipsychotic drug; this was a disaster. When next I saw her she was thick tongued and flat-voiced from the drug, her usual vibrant skin tone dulled, her emotional life line flattened. After only a week or so, Parker told me she was going to have to give up on this solution, and I could clearly see why. Also, Pat continued, "the therapist is a white woman, and middle class,"…a cultural disconnect. "I can't talk to her."

The occasional intervention of other activists was the closest thing we had to professional help for our inner turmoils and the pressures we were under. The expressive arts we were doing helped us modulate our emotional states, as did the presence of certain kinds of women who served as a friendly ear for many of us. One of those people was Anne Leonard, who provided a coherence among the various households. She was a community builder who freely traveled from place to place, helping out as needed.

Anne's kind of maternal midwifery of group and individual feelings helped us stay located and in touch with each other despite the rigor of our work schedules and the differences in our needs. She was in the press collective helping to collate pages, she was in the She Who chorale group helping with the sound art of its staging, she was at Addison Street helping Brenda and her housemates deal with two troubled children, she was in the bar scene, and always she was patiently listening to everyone, gently offering advice. Anne was, in a way, a community therapist before there was women's or lesbian's therapy.

Not all lesbian activist groups were this therapeutically challenged. My academic friends from the East Coast, Blanche Cook and Clare Coss, were part of an extended family of about ten lesbians that included Audre Lorde and Frances Clayton, and Audre's two children. Also, Joan Larkin, Adrienne Rich, Michelle Cliff, and more. What an incredibly powerful group! Ultimately I would meet and, to varying degrees, get to know nearly all of them, as our movement wove its fabric across the country. The members of this community did not live in collective households, perhaps because they were middle to upper-middle class. They lived in separate couple relationships, often miles apart, yet stayed in very close connection. Their group began because they all became clients of the same therapist. Both Frances and Clare also became therapists, giving their extended group a solid relational basis for understanding themselves, an enviable resource in an era when self-medication with drugs and alcohol was virtually the only way of handling emotional eruptions.

On the West Coast, in our primarily working-class and extremely anti-authoritarian movement, therapy was an unpopular subject. First, we had to harshly critique all of psychology in order to get out from under the diagnosis of homosexuality as a form of mental illness, curable by going straight or, that ultimate stupidity, by "becoming attractive to men."

As part of her political analysis, Wendy wanted nothing to do with psychology of any kind, using a communist argument that it was a "band-aid solution" to deep social problems that had their source in economic hierarchy and class and race stratification. I had written my scathing satire "The Psychoanalysis of Edward the Dyke." Alice frequently said, "Ever notice that the word 'therapist' actually spells 'the rapist?'" Ugly words intended to protect us from any further degradation and mistreatment at the hands of the psychiatric establishment. But these stances were also going to leave me stranded in a pit of demons as soon as the movement gave me some breathing space.

Fortunately, Marny Hall and others took a different path. From GWL, Marny would go on to become licensed as a therapist and would eventually write up her unique perspective on appropriate advice for lesbians, especially lesbian couples. In her book, *The Lesbian Love Companion*, Marny challenges stock (heterosexually romantic) ideas about relationships, including that they need to be monogamous. She doesn't believe that the length of a relationship has anything to do with quality of life, or love. I like her viewpoint, won from listening to hundreds of real lesbian lovers in her office. Most lesbians don't stay with their first, second, or even third lover. And, she suggests, "break-ups create community." Ex-lovers can turn into family, can be the long-term friendships of a lifetime. Everyone you love is your love, not some mistake you are making. They are the love you need for that time, and they teach you how to love better the next time.

NEW YORK AND NEW MEXICO: PARENTS

Going to New York City meant either I was alone and doing a reading, usually in the West End, sleeping on couches of lesbian organizers, or that Wendy and I had gone together to visit her parents in their luxurious brownstone on the Upper East Side. Vivian Cadden had achieved success as a writer and senior editor of both *Redbook* and *McCall's* magazines. By 1978 she would be given *Working Woman*, her own magazine. Joe did contracting work, painting houses and apartments. Walking with Joe on the street, I was immediately aware that every third person knew him and called out a greeting. Smart, charming, and politically savvy, Joe Cadden should have been the mayor of New York, but he was prohibited from running for office because of his radical past, a nasty vestige of the blackballing McCarthy era.

The Caddens had open, warm patterns of hospitality, yet accepting Wendy's "choice of lifestyle," as she said, and even more challenging, her choice of partner, was difficult for them for at least the first decade that we were together. Vivian perhaps felt puzzled by me. Maybe she simply found me ugly, in my dyke outfit and combat boots, scrawny, intense, and with a mouthful of crooked teeth, in contrast to her gorgeous daughter. Vivian thought that our refusal to set prices and wages at our press was a form of "scabbing." Gradually Joe warmed to me, triggered initially by his liking of my poetry.

Wendy delighted in showing me the town, the garment district where her Russian immigrant grandmother had worked, the Lower East Side, Fifth

Avenue's elegant store windows, the Village where she had once sat on Bob Dylan's lap. More than once after midnight we hiked from the lower end of the island, winding our way through the cavernous emptiness of the Wall Street district and through Central Park. Holding hands, we would run for blocks, our fingers locked in a bond that overcame class judgments and political opinions. We knew we were involved in a revolution as real as any, but different from anything the older commies-turned-liberals could ever have imagined.

In my life I have been privileged to meet three people who knew Gertrude Stein well. The first was Jo Barrie, a close friend of the Caddens who was at the dinner table on one of the first occasions that Wendy took me to stay with her parents. Wendy and I were both wild about Gertrude Stein; we had bought *A Primer for the Gradual Understanding of Gertrude Stein*, edited by Robert Bartlett Haas, and spent many delightful hours reading it to each other, along with *The Making of Americans* and *Three Lives*. We would have loved her work even if she and Alice Toklas weren't also the only model for a long-term lesbian "marriage" that we had ever heard of.

Jo Barrie appears as a character in Stein's play, *The Mother of Us All*. He told us that while Stein was writing her play, he and his fiancée Lillian visited the Toklas-Stein household in Paris. Young, in love, and sexually progressive, Jo and Lillian sat on the couch discussing whether or not to marry. Stein, who was busy compressing historical figures into contemporary, everyday life in her tribute to Susan B. Anthony, later swept this lovers' dialogue into her play.

Jo Barrie talked about Stein and Toklas. "You wouldn't have liked their politics," he said. But we were lesbian-feminists, we didn't like anyone's politics. Boldly I asked if he thought Wendy and I would have been welcome to visit them. He looked thoughtful, selecting his words, "All kinds of artists and intellectuals visited them." He was diplomatic, not saying what I suspect he thought, which was "no."

"They weren't like you," he cautioned, addressing our militant enthusiasm. "Don't imagine she would have been sympathetic to you as radical leftists. They were extremely anti-communist, hated the communists. Gertrude Stein was very conservative, a Lincoln Republican, and Toklas was even more conservative— she loved Franco! Can you imagine this? But Alice loved everything Spanish, she was a romantic."

He took me aside after dinner to tell me that he really liked my poetry, that it was "real art." I was flattered by this attention. Later, I would meet Samuel M. Stewart and correspond with Robert Bartlett Haas, two other men who had known Stein, childishly thrilled that they each liked aspects of my work as well, giving me a strong sense of being with Stein, of being related. It also gave me confidence. Of course, at that time, I had no idea just *how* conservative and libertarian Stein was, how ambivalent she was about Franklin Delano Roosevelt and his social policies. How ironic to be discussing her politics in the house of two of the most prominent activists in the Communist Youth Congress of the 1930s, activists so supported by Eleanor Roosevelt that she attended their wedding, a fact of which Vivian was very proud, showing me pictures of the occasion.

VISITING MY PARENTS

Whenever Wendy and I went traveling to New Mexico in our VW van, we visited my parents, who adored Wendy. Everyone adored Wendy, and why wouldn't they? She was unfailingly warm, kind, thoughtful. Like me, my parents considered her beyond beautiful with her lustrous complexion, which we all referred to as "alabaster."

On our first trip, my father engaged with me again, giving me a big hug. "Some things don't matter," he repeated about three times. He hadn't seen me since he stood at the foot of my bed wondering if I would ever recover from the effects of encephalitis. Now he was saying he just loved me, was okay with my lesbianism, had come to terms with it after his shock of hearing about it from government officials banging on his screen door, twelve or thirteen years before.

Though my father had gotten over his years of miff, I still wasn't sure how to connect. Wendy took me shopping for them and gave me a clue how to relate to them as friends.

"Don't talk about yourself. Talk about them." What a lovely, grown-up idea. I wonder why I never thought of that?

So we brought them a picture book of radio-era stars that they would remember from their own youth in the twenties and thirties. They went wild for it, and dropped all their hold-backs, eagerly telling us stories about their favorite radio shows like "Fibber McGee and Mollie," and remembering the comics and famous singers from a time they were really in love with each other. Suddenly my parents were vivacious and fun again, as I remembered them from days of old.

My favorite part of all our van trips were the times we got caught in a New Mexico thunderstorm with lightning flashing down on each side of the bus while the squealing wipers scraped away a small flood on the windshield. I would scream "Look, look!" into the giant cracking noise and wave a wet arm out the window at the ferocious, magnificent tongues of light hitting the ground only yards away, scattering molecules of electricity everywhere like a huge flash camera. Air full of the sexy musk of drenched mesquite. Knowing, as she hunched over the steering wheel with a grin, swiveling her head to catch the view from all sides, that she loved all this drama too.

New Mexico enthralled Wendy as much as it did me; we never tired of the long day drives, watching light change the mountain colors and textures like a restless artist who could never settle on a finished canvas, who was driven instead to revise, revise, and got it right every time. In the timeless, seamless high desert, draped in each other's arms within the steel, fabric, and plastic safety of the van, we seemed caught in love's promise of forever, out of sight of the relentless movement pushing us ever forward.

Music Swelled and So Did Von's Hopes

By 1973, women's music was beginning to surface—not just women musicians, but women creating music with overtly women-centered and lesbian content. The Berkeley Women's Music Collective formed a band that included our friend Suzanne Shanbaum with her lively guitar; the band would stay together for five years, touring in both urban and rural venues and cutting albums. Alix Dobkin's first album, *Lavender Jane Loves Women*, was an exhilarating voice from the East Coast.

Some time that year I was in Washington DC for readings, invited to the apartment of two lesbian activists, Ginny Berson and Meg Christian. I had met Meg earlier, as she had sung at one of our all-women's events in Berkeley early in the movement. Wendy and I also sang "Strikin' Dyke" that night. Ginny had been part of the already well-known Furies Collective, along with Coletta Reid, Charlotte Bunch, Joan Biren, Rita Mae Brown, and others.

Now addressing me in the living room of their apartment, the two women had something on their minds as they spoke of Meg's experience trying to be a folk singer in the music scene. Meg described vividly how tired she was of playing bars and coffee shops where people jabbered and carried on through her sets. She wanted to play for women audiences, where she could deliver content people actually wanted to hear. So she and Ginny were going to put out a 45 of two of her songs, followed by a full-length album. "And," Ginny leaned forward emphatically, "we want your poetry to be our second album." They said they were going to call their recording company "Olivia Records," after a lesbian character in a novel. I said "Sure, why not?" I was flattered, but just barely hiding my skepticism; lots of people had big ideas. Making them come true was the tricky part.

But ten radical women from the DC area, including women from the Furies and Radicalesbians, did indeed form Olivia as a company; their first 45 had Meg on one side and Cris Williamson on the other. And, in 1974, after they had moved from Baltimore to LA and then to Oakland, they produced a record of my poetry. They didn't know Parker's work, but I decided to exert a little pressure, so I said I wouldn't do the album unless they included Pat. We called it "Where Would I Be Without You: The Poetry of Pat Parker and Judy Grahn." Wendy designed the cover, drawing all three of us as very muscled women holding a cable, and either pulling something along (our movement) or getting out from under chains (our oppressive lives). She also photographed Pat and me standing in front of the mural commemorating the People's Park demonstrations. So we were actually Olivia's second or third album (I can't recall if they had already produced Cris Williamson's album). As poetry, however, our sales could not come anywhere near what they needed to survive, so we disappeared from their lists pretty quickly.

In the summer of 1973, Yvonne came out to the West Coast to visit us. She had exciting news—she had a new job and it was in Oakland. Since I last saw her she had gone from her odd unfurnished house in New Mexico to Philadelphia, where she finished graduate school at Temple University. I had stayed in contact with her sporadically, and had written her about being on the East Coast in 1970: "I was too depressed in Boston to go see you although I did call you once on a rainy street corner in Philadelphia with a car load of impatient people coming up from the Panther Conference in Wash. But you don't answer your telephone any more often than I do…"

Yvonne had now become a respected educator with a graduate degree, with a practice and theory devoted to engaging even the most alienated groups of children, and she needed to be in a supportive community. She had just been accepted for an administrative job in the Oakland School District, assistant to the new superintendent Marcus Foster, whom she had known in Philadelphia. He was now the first black superintendent of the Oakland schools, considered a brilliant and progressive leader. She was going back to New Mexico to pack. By January we would all be in the same place again, as friends at least, and more than friends, as comrades, as co-lovers, as part of a support network.

To celebrate, Wendy and I joyfully sang Dobkin's activist line "any woman caaaan be a lesbian" to her. She was more confident, more optimistic, than I had seen her for a long time, and we were very happy for her, though I had an uneasy twinge. What would it be like to have her nearby, was she still in love with Wendy? Would the two of them fall into each other's arms and abandon me as they had in New Orleans? Or would I, with my new sense of sharing love, find that I liked a three-way arrangement, that it strengthened rather than weakened all of our bonds? Would we have a strong and steadily militant triumvirate, as Alice, Carol, and Natalie had?

We worked on optimistically into the fall. Visitors came from all over to see our press and to visit our Terrace Street household. Susan Griffin brought Adrienne Rich in to the bookstore one day, and introduced us. At that time neither of us had yet connected to each other's poetry, so we simply exchanged warm hellos. Joan Pinkvoss and Joan Larkin each came, on separate occasions, to talk to us about starting women's presses. Joan Pinkvoss co-founded the Iowa City Women's Press, while Joan Larkin returned to the East Coast to start Out & Out Books. Marilyn Waring met with a bunch of us in the living room in Terrace Street, prior to returning to New Zealand to become the youngest member of parliament at the age of twenty-three.

Our books were selling steadily, and we expanded our repertoire with Willyce Kim's poetry book, *Eating Artichokes*. We made plans to reprint *Lesbians Speak Out*. One night early in November we came home late from the press. "Come in here," Alice called from the living room, "there's something you need to see." We watched the news. Some kind of militant group had surfaced, calling themselves the "Symbionese Liberation Army." They had just shot two black educators in Oakland, killing one of them. "That's him, that's the guy," I said, hearing their names. "What guy?" Alice asked, rolling her cigarette. "That's the superintendent Von was going to work for...Marcus Foster. He's just been killed."

"Oh shit!" Wendy and I each exclaimed grimly. We were thinking, why would a left group murder a black leader?

This mysterious group of white militants of the middle class, led by a black ex-con, Donald DeFreeze, and later by Bill Harris, seemed to arise out of nowhere. To our further astonishment and horror, two ex-lovers from a lesbian activist household, a house I didn't know though it was in our neighborhood in North Oakland, were part of this gang.

As for Vonnie, our song of hope in the summer must now have seemed bitter herbs to her, as her chance to have a dream job with a progressive educator, to move to California and the relative safety of our movement, was over. She would need to find her own way to us.

Last Trip, August 1974

But Yvonne's love life continued to fall apart over the impossibility of her ever "coming out" and having an actual life, or keeping a lover given various oppressive contexts—religious, academic, educational, and the culture of rural New Mexico. The liberations we were pressing for and (though we didn't know it) beginning to achieve on the West Coast and the East Coast, were not yet happening in any of her situations.

When next we saw her, the following summer, she was living in Las Vegas, New Mexico. Wendy and I drove our van to her place and spent the evening with her. She was thin, agitated, and sad. She had almost made it to be with us. She insisted on giving us an I Ching reading, throwing the hollow centered coins and reading a verse for each recipient. Wendy's spoke of her continuing with her revolution. Mine assured that I would continue with my art. Von's lover, who was breaking up with her, received the information that she would travel. When Von read her own, the hair on the back of my neck rose up, because it said that she would die. As Wendy and I drove back to California we stopped outside of Shiprock, New Mexico, the ghostly mountain outcrop visible from the van window. Exhausted, we fell asleep. The wind rose in the night, howling off the tall rock like wolves, and shaking the van, as though the air itself convulsed in rhythm to our sad hearts.

In November of 1974, just three months after her prophetic I Ching readings, Yvonne did, indeed, die. A childhood episode of rheumatic fever had laid down a heart condition that triggered blood clots. She had just turned thirty-five. Alerted by her lover that her illness was terminal, I flew to Albuquerque and was urged to her side by her doctor, a kind woman named Barbara. Von was already unconscious, and I could sense that her spirit was leaving. Within a few minutes, she was taken off of life support. I returned to California in a lather of grief, and turned selfishly inward, not noticing that Wendy also was mourning a lost love.

The Symbionese Liberation Army hit headlines again, in 1975, and Alice, Wendy, and I watched the television in horror as the LAPD bulldozed and then set fire to a house with SLA people in it, gunning down two women who, according to the family of one of them, were trying to surrender. DeFreeze, the figurehead of this otherwise all-white group had worked as a police informant earlier in his life. The group was confusing; they seemed to want to feed hungry poor people, demanding, and receiving, sacks of food as ostensible ransom when they kidnapped newspaper heiress Patty Hearst. Suffering from Stockholm Syndrome (which hadn't been defined at the time so no one knew that a kidnap victim can, in terror, identify with the kidnappers) it looked as though Hearst was a convert to their atrocious politics when she was photographed with a rifle during a bank heist. She was tried in court later for participating, and only then did her own story come out that they were terrifying and raping her. Why had it never occurred to us that they would be raping her? Even more disturbing, they were a mostly white group who had killed a rising progressive black leader. As I had felt so strongly at Altamont Festival, the Left had lost its way, and its mind. There were, as the Marxists would say, contradictions everywhere.

Violence swirled around everyone in the movement, as all the movements overlapped. And none of us could see if we were having any impact. We put out tremendous effort, but was anyone out there listening or caring? Was anything changing? We had no feedback loop; our own ceaseless activities seemed to build a wall around us beyond which we could not see. The more frustrated we became, the closer the violence wave moved toward us. I was extremely anxious during this period. The overwork, the continual stress of movement paranoia, most of it probably accurate—yes our phones were tapped, yes we were followed, yes those were trenchcoat men at the door asking questions. And yes we knew women who were part of the underground, who were participating in armed revolution. More and more of them identified as lesbian or bisexual. But, if two of the Symbionese women had been part of a lesbian household and then had joined a group that murdered a rising black leader, what the hell movement was I in, anyhow? I didn't want anything to do with that one. Yet it was also confusing that this group had imitated the Panthers in calling for children to be fed. We thought we were in favor of nearly any tactic that could make that happen.

One night as Wendy and I worked alone together late at the press, we heard a tapping on the huge windowpane facing Broadway. Shadowy figures gestured for us to come outside, and once we were on the sidewalk they spoke quickly. They were Weather Underground women they said, and they were making new contacts with people they thought were doing real political work. They had read "A Woman Is Talking to Death," one added. Would we be willing to meet with some of them? We said yes, and for years we met with the same four women, two at a time. They always set the time and place, so it was an odd one-way friendship. They wanted to convert us to Marxism; we wanted to infuse them with the zeal of feminism. In fact we wanted them to leave the underground and join the more militant factions of the women's movement. We wanted them to break away from the violence of their male-led groups, even though the Weather Underground had decided to target sites rather than people.

From what I could see, the violence began as soon as anyone picked up a gun and declared a war. Then you were vulnerable, not only to the designated "enemy" (who in this case would relentlessly work to stop you, catch you) but almost as much to yourself, your own clumsiness (the gun just went off, shot my foot) and your own comrades (Are you an agent? Tell us. Or we'll kill you). And then the people you had hurt, how could you recover from that? The trick was to somehow be a revolutionary who did not engage in violence, though fearlessly living amidst it, with the flames of action licking at your door. To send relentless messages that would land somewhere and do their work of change, to get us away from inequality and its poverties.

We Used Poetry to Fight Back, 1974

At the press, our distribution reach was becoming increasingly broad. We combined issues, showing their connections: women, people of color, gay people, soldiers. Our venues were bars, cafes, bookstores, parks, living rooms, college auditoriums, theaters, churches, halls, prisons, galleries, art centers, classrooms. We even went onto a military base and did some leafleting and a reading. I sold copies of *Edward the Dyke and Other Poems* on street corners; one of my early customers was the marvelous leftist writer and organizer Tillie Olsen. One of the men in that 1968 gay men's writing group was Henry Noyes, who owned China Books, a communist bookstore. In solidarity with me and with gay rights, he put *Edward the Dyke* in the window of his shop on 24th Street, its little robin's egg blue cover a paradox in a sea of red-covered books from China.

Willyce Kim came in to the press one day to tell me she had designed a chapbook for "A Woman Is Talking to Death." "I found the perfect illustrations," she said. "Look at these." She showed me photographs of drawings and a painting by Karen Sjoholm, who lived in a lesbian household nearby and worked a hard-hat job at the Pacific Gas and Electric Company. I immediately loved Karen's work, with its heavy lines and dark mystery. But the painting was in color, and I didn't know how we could reproduce it.

"Wendy says we can do it and I believe her," Willyce answered. She was Wendy's biggest fan, next to me. "Plus, we'll put it on heavy stock, we'll make the cover heavy stock too." So we lined up the settings on the multilith, bought colored inks, and as carefully as we could, we ran the stock through the press four times, laying down the colors in order, while visitors crowded around, amazed at the resulting prints, which were richly beautiful and had a great deal of variety. Each copy was a unique art statement, which helped that sturdy little green chapbook stay in circulation for the next thirty-five years, until collectors had snatched every one of what I would guess were five thousand copies.

One day women from the Essex Street household approached me. Would I please please come read "A Woman Is Talking To Death" at an international socialist conference in Berkeley? It would be a guerilla action, as they would slip me into a sequence of "reports" by various groups. "We will just pretend this is our report," one of them began. "Because in a way, it is," another added. "We need them to hear this SO MUCH," the third one finished. I certainly agreed that strong new thoughts were needed to counteract the anti-homosexualism of so much of the Left, and our movement needed to make alliances.

Ordinarily I face friendly audiences, and don't use a podium so I can physically feel the energy of the crowd and play with it through my voice. Ordinarily that energy is shaped like a big, welcoming, fluffy bowl. But except for one slender band of women about five rows back who were smiling and waving encouragement, this audience of about five hundred very serious people had a totally different feeling, more like a convex shield that would protect them from—me. As I swung into the poem the audience got it that this was a lesbian story, and hostility swelled toward me like a steel storm front. I upped my effort, willing the words to penetrate their resistance. Halfway through, the stage wall behind me collapsed onto my head and back. Stunned, I stood at the mike with the wall slung across my shoulders, waiting for my skull to stop throbbing. This was entirely too much! When the wall was taken off me by silent people I was ready to surrender.

A voice shouted out of the crowd, somebody sitting down in front and to my left. A tall black man. "Sister! Sister!" he shouted.

I shook the ringing out of my ears. "I want to hear the rest of that poem!" He said it twice before I understood, grabbed the mike, and delivered the last ten minutes of my poem directly as a gift to him. After I finished, the hostility continued, a woman got up to complain about my reading at length, and people with cold faces brushed past me as I left the hall. Nevertheless, we had made a mark and we would continue to make marks. Some on the Left would listen, as lesbian and gay leftists took courage, especially after the Gay Movement swelled on and on as a power bloc.

I'm sure many women's movement poets must also have experienced people standing in line to tell them the poetry had literally saved their lives, had given them hope for the first time, had taken them through a hard time, had spurred them to change their lives for the better.

Sappho said that poetry is only air. But sometimes that air can be a wind causing a sea change, especially if that change is personal and interior at first. Anita Taylor, who had worked with us at the press for about a year, and who now used her family name Oñang, went on a sort of ancestral pilgrimage to trace her motherline. She began in the Philippines, then found a grandmother living on a subsistence farm in Southeast Asia. When she returned she told me this story: She was staying in a hotel room in Shanghai when a man broke in and tried to rape her. When she fought back, he continued to attack her, chasing her until she was exhausted. Finally, he had his hands around her neck, choking the life from her. She was still resisting, so he bent her neck back and to the side, until it was as close to snapping as it could get without her losing consciousness.

"I thought for certain I was going to die," Anita put one hand flat against her own cheek as though to comfort her body. "All he needed was one more second of that terrible pressure on my neck. And then I remembered 'A Woman Is Talking to Death,' the poem and its warrior feeling just came into my mind. And then I had a flash of all of you here at the press, and I let out a death cry that you wouldn't believe. I just howled it out. And he was so freaked out, he dropped me and ran out of the room."

Parker's voice was getting out in the world too. In 1974, Dr. Diana Russell, a lesbian raised in South Africa and a fierce fighter against racial injustice and the violence perpetrated against girls and women, organized the International Tribunal on Crimes Against Women, a four-day testimonial in Brussels. One of the invited participants was Pat Parker, who described through her new poem, "Womanslaughter," the murder of her sister by her brother-in-law, and the complicity of the justice system in making the woman's life matter less than the crime of shop lifting at a convenience store.

VISITING FRONTERA WOMEN'S PRISON AND THE MANSON WOMEN

One day while working at the press, probably in 1974, I was approached by a small group of women, including two thin, intense organizers, Jeanne Gallick and Karlene Faith. They were working with women in prison, and would I please make the trip with them to Southern California and do a writing workshop inside the Frontera women's prison? Since the ethics of women's liberation was to try to liberate the hearts and minds of all women, including those who were incarcerated, I of course said yes. The car trip from Oakland to Southern California, with five organizers, was memorable if only because of the amount of tension everyone felt at holding the balance between liberation and incarceration. We all spent the night in a single motel room with the overhead lights on; I was probably the only one who slept a little bit, and the only one who had something even remotely like a prison experience, from my confinement in the military.

The next morning, the organizers coached me on what to expect when entering the prison, how it was a tightrope walk between two opposing sides, how we would be searched, how to keep our faces still and say only the minimum, how we must be careful not to be the least bit friendly to the guards, how the prisoners called the guards *screws*, that ugly term that kept it clear who could and could not be trusted. We would have to drop our stance of openness toward all women in order to enter this split world.

I was struck by certain similarities with military life, the uniforms, the hierarchy, the rigidly proscribed behavior, the deliberately plain, low-end cafeteria food, the "privilege" of the greasy, mustardy, and more sensually satisfying fast food and sugary pop of the canteen, the degradations designed to induce humility, obedience, and shame.

The women in the general prison population who came to the writing workshop struck me as just like any other poor women, only more distressed, having to be more guarded in body language. Many of the prisoners' convictions were drug-use related, some were crimes committed with a boyfriend who took the lead. A majority of the women were mothers, now painfully separated from their children. I remember having a warm and engaging writing workshop with the women; they had so much to say, so much vitality as soon as no one in authority was looking. I read a little bit of my work, and Parker's as well, which was my habit. We all talked. Then we all wrote stories and read them to each other while I praised and made comments. The organizers were upset that I abruptly threw my story in the trash on my way out. "Why did you do that!" I couldn't explain my feeling, but it was something like, if the women in prison couldn't get their work published, why should I? That mountain climbing episode again, the refusal to go on unless the women could go with me. A self-destructive impulse? Loyalty going berserk? A way to keep myself on course?

Frontera was deceptively designed not like a concrete bunker, but more like a college campus, with low, pleasant-looking brick buildings, even green grass. The women of the general population were housed in rooms, not banks of cells as in the enormous men's prisons in this prison-wealthy state. But Frontera was prison nevertheless, with cold guard faces, heavy locking doors, searches and arbitrary denials, lines and imposed silence. Women who fell in love within the population, I was told, passed romantic notes through trusted channels, but seldom got even one minute alone together. And lived for that precious kiss or embrace.

At noon we were taken to eat in the canteen, where the guards and other prison personnel had the (dubious) privilege of hamburgers, Cokes, and potato chips. On the way we passed through the line of prisoners waiting to get a tray and go through the cafeteria-style food line. I had a glimpse of the kind of low-level sadism that must have permeated much of the place. A smarmy-looking, sneering little middle-aged white man, a guard, stood at a central position and grabbed at the women's breasts as they had to walk past him. They locked down their faces, crossed their arms across their chests, looked the other way from him. I felt the familiar queasy feeling in the presence of sex combined with humiliation. I wondered how many of the women were coerced into unwanted sex.

Sitting beside me at the grey table in the canteen was a middle-aged white man who introduced himself as the prison doctor. I half-listened as he rambled until something he said brought my head up out of my plate. "They're animals, you know," he confided to me with no prompting. What was he talking about?

"What animals?" I asked.

"The prisoners, they're animals."

"No they are not!"

"Yes they are, they are not like you and me."

I thought about the kind of "care" the inmates could expect from his ignorant hands, thought about the dreadfully backward, incompetent, if not outright sadistic, professionals drawn to institutions like prisons and the army. Then there were the humanitarians, you could see it in the flicker on the faces of some of the guards, of women doing a job for which they could not be liked, yet doing the best they could. All swirled together, all part of the mix.

We were only half through the day, yet I already felt exhausted from the experience, the stiff vigilance of the guards, the searches, the flashes of anger and control over the most elemental of needs, like bathroom breaks and food. Then Jean approached me after lunch, took my arm and spoke earnestly and firmly. "We have one more place planned for you to visit, it's the maximum security unit, Special Security Unit." I must have looked startled, as I had forgotten she had told me we might be doing this. "The Manson women—everyone calls them 'girls,' but we call them 'women'—are on that block. We really want you to meet with them if you feel up to it."

Oh right. I took a breath, I hadn't prepared for who I might be meeting in that unit. A ragtag white gang, Charles Manson and his young followers lived communally, scavenging for food, on a ranch in Southern California. At first not different from many hippie communes, they took a violent turn in 1969, and were arrested and tried for a number of killings. Most notorious were the murders of five white people, including the well-known actress Sharon Tate, who was pregnant. Two days later the gang killed two more people, a white couple. In each case they wrote messages in blood on the walls, intended to implicate black nationalists. Their delusional intention was to create a race war, which they believed would annihilate nearly everyone in the U.S. They would hide in an underground bunker, emerging triumphantly when the war was over.

As we walked toward the building that held five of the women from this gang, I was thinking, What could I possibly bring to women who had followed Charles Manson's directions to spread bloody mayhem, who had kept one man captive for two days, slowly killing him, who had sprayed blood all over the

Tate residence the night they killed five people? What could these women possibly be like, and what could they possibly like about me? Here I was a dyke, a flaming liberation dyke, and these women had given body, mind and soul to this authoritarian guy. What could we have in common?

While the general prison population was housed in cottages with rooms, the maximum security unit consisted of a room of barred cells, three in a row with a space in the middle so guards and prisoners could get in and out. Each woman occupied one cell. I had rarely felt such unrelieved tension as permeated those 6 x 9 cages. I had the impression of enormous strength forced into a bottle, and also of disconnection. Jean introduced us and then left.

Two guards in blue, a man and a woman, stood in place at the main door to the block. The inmates were Mary Brunner, Patricia Krenweil, Susan "Sadie" Atkins, Catherine "Gypsy" Share, and Leslie Van Houten. I sat down on the chair Jean had set up for me, with Patricia, Mary, and Leslie on my left side, Gypsy and Sadie on the other, each in her own cell. Sadie was in a cell a little away from the others, or at any rate I had the impression she was separating from them, pacing around, turning her back. Calling out once in a while but not really engaging in the conversation.

The other four were eager to speak.

Gypsy sat on her bed, her body wound tight as a spring, talking fast about how she had nearly escaped, planned constantly her next move to get out. She thought it was ironically funny, and kept laughing about something a judge had read to them, their charges. Something minor at the end of the long list, that struck her as hilarious—"like, after all that list of terrible stuff, we jay-walked!" Gypsy had not been present at any of the murders. She was charged with robbing a gun store in preparation for hijacking a plane to ransom Manson out of prison. She had burst onto the street spraying machine-gun fire when the police arrived to stop her getaway car. She didn't hit anyone, and she was lightly injured when the police retaliated.

Leslie, tall, almost gaunt, with huge eyes, seemed completely removed from reality. She said, among other things, "Until I was arrested, I had never seen a black person before. And there I was in line behind one of them." I was dumbfounded that some of these people who were planning to pin their heinous crimes on innocent black people had never met any.

What Patricia and Mary especially most wanted to convey was how close the women were in their lives together, how they helped each other give birth, scrounged through garbage for meals together. "We nursed each other's babies," Patricia said, her blue eyes full of nostalgia. And, at one point, their eyes sideways glancing at each other, "we know who we love," a reference to their absolute loyalty and devotion to Manson, who portrayed himself as Jesus come to rescue the world. Meantime the cult's group childcare had kept at least some of the mothers in line by making sure they could not take their own child with them should they wish to escape.

At the time I believed they had all committed murder, felt them as fragmented persons who would keep spinning in that terrible place of mayhem, who needed to act it out, and who needed to stay attached to the skillfully manipulative Manson. According to one account, Sadie had said, "I have no mercy for you, Woman," as she stabbed the body of Sharon Tate. *I have no mercy for you, Woman.*

Whether this actually happened or not, it is an appropriate metaphor that a deeply alienated crazed being would say about herself, about her own category of person, as meaningless, as worthy only of suffering and death. Some of the national shock over the Manson crimes, besides the celebrity of some of the victims, was that *young women* had participated. Though the extent of their participation was perhaps minimal, as later they would talk about how they protected Manson by taking blame onto themselves. And, evidently Tex Watson and Bobby Beausoleil did nearly all the actual murdering.

Sitting on a folding chair in the Special Security Unit between the two rows of cells housing these nearly lost women, in my jeans and little dyke vest and snap-button shirt, I was shaking. "Look at her shake," Gypsy commented. "She's afraid of us." But I think my body was reacting to the amount of pent-up energy, not from fear, as I didn't feel afraid of these young women—they were in cages, and two guards were watching us. I was shaking perhaps because of my own keenly felt inadequacy in the face of what they needed, in the face of their real human craziness, their cavernous hunger for life, their disconnection from the effects of the atrocities they had participated in, had done or claimed to have done. What could connect them to themselves? Surely I should be reading to them from Tolstoy, Shakespeare, Martin Buber. I had only two hours to make a bridge across a chasm of shattered soul. Having heard what they had to tell me, I sat forward in my chair and my trembling fingers opened to a page of my little blue handmade book. I began reading to them from "The Common Woman Poems."

That day in the Special Security Unit I had asked Mary about her family and she described something ordinary, Midwestern, middle class. They were all from middle-class families, all trained to be obedient. In Karlene Faith's book advocating Leslie Van Houten's release, arguing she had been rehabilitated, the author describes being initially invited into the SSU by the warden, an astute woman named Anne Carlson. The warden urged her to set up tutorials, and to "let them benefit from some of the insights of women's liberation movements." She wanted to introduce the Manson "girls" to books, ideas, and arts not only from university artists but also grassroots artists, who might raise their consciousness to allow them to begin thinking for themselves. She saw the women as victims of their middle-class cultivated femininity, sweetly submissive to and being used by Manson, the self-appointed avenging knight in hippie armor. Carlson was disgusted by his "prostituting the girls to the bikers, the pretty boys, and the so-called businessmen he attracted." His sexual and food-deprivation abuse of them would trap them further. The drugs, including the newer one, Orange Sunshine, would distort their sensibilities and moral judgment. They were searching for themselves without a map, without self-authority, and so they had fixed their urgent need on Manson as their savior.

I felt challenged by the task of changing anything within these women, who did not at all present themselves as victims dragged along by brutal men. They participated, they engaged with apocalyptic plans. What they wanted to talk about, however, was how they took care of each other, and their children. They seemed like dissociated women who had bonded, for a time at least, into a cult closeness, and were willing to do anything to stay in that companionship. The Faustian bargain, from a female perspective. The visit left me drained and uncertain whether the poetry had had an effect.

In 1975, Parker also visited Frontera prison, and read her poetry to the general population of women (not the Manson women, I think, or she would surely have mentioned this). She wrote about her experience to Audre, who was at that time gathering material for *Amazon Quarterly*. Pat wrote,

> Went down to the California Institute for Women. The in-mates liked my poetry. The prison officials weren't so happy about it, they denied me the right to do my second reading. I did it anyway, but had to have lookouts watching for guards. Spent most of the second reading listening to their poetry. Some of which was really good. Told them to send it off to you. They seemed excited about that suggestion. The guards searched me and my briefcase. They had a woman searching me while another guard searched my briefcase. And used that opportunity to steal one of my notebooks, And i wasn't sure I had brought that notebook, so I wasn't positive they had ripped it until i checked my studio when i got home. It was my working notebook which i usually don't take to readings.

However strange and fraught our prison visits were for me and Pat, our teaching had the impact intended by the organizers. According to Karlene Faith, my work in the lockdown ward "inspired and energized" the women there. Karlene also thought that women in the general prison population responded "most of all" to Pat's and my poetry because they related to our working-class and antiracist voices. She goes on to explain:

> The women in our (prison) classes believed in resistance against victimization and identified with women who organized for their rights. But they had not been infected by the idealistic notion that women's bonding with each other, just because they are women, transcends the injustices of racism, colonialism, and class discrimination. All women are not created with equal opportunity.

Over the years I have heard of other times that my work was taught to women in prison; this is very humbly gratifying to me, as it reminds me of the time I was under arrest, and someone took the trouble to say to me, "Some of us are with you…"

GETTING A GRIP

While it is extremely rare for women to kill other women, it is not unusual for them to kill themselves; so it isn't accurate to say that women don't kill women—just that when they do, it is usually themselves. We don't think of suicide as murder, yet what else is it? By this time, I had known five lesbians who had killed themselves, and I already knew at least four more who would eventually do this. Those who had already died by their own hands included two members of our Ash Grove band, lead singer Wailin' Pat, followed within months by her girlfriend.

And then Peaches, not the Peaches from LA who co-organized the Ash Grove women's festival, not the one from Boston who put Anne Leonard and me in "the warm room," nor the one back in the mid-Sixties in Washington, DC who was rescued by a gang of dykes from her spur-of-the-moment marriage. This Peaches was a compact, focused butch whose car broke down on the Bay Bridge as Wendy and I were driving by. Peaches and her girlfriend were bent over the smoking engine when we stopped to offer a ride. We took them home to Terrace Street where they lived in the living room until they could get themselves together. Peaches was a wonderfully enthusiastic working-class dyke organizer, involved in renters' rights. Her girlfriend, in her twenties, had arrived from Cambodia after being lured into the sex industry as a very young runaway teenager. She had come back to the States after hearing there was a women's revolution going on, but she grew disillusioned with the pace of change, and went back to Cambodia. Depressed and lonely without her girlfriend, Peaches took her own life with a pistol.

We were driven into even more frenetic work and overwork by these hideously tragic losses. Our movement often felt like a race against annihilation, as though we were dragging—not only strangers—but literally each other out of swirling deep water. Sometimes our grip just wasn't strong enough. And sometimes it was.

We had not stopped the flood of despair that some women felt and acted out. We had not made the world safe enough for Yvonne to come out as herself, or for Marcus Foster to live to be the leader he could have become. We had not brought the war to a halt, and my friend Larry Jones was not bounding joyfully toward me on the sidewalk. But there were a few things on our long list that we *were* able to do.

Inez Garcia

On March 17, 1974, electrifying news flashed through our women's communities. A woman named Inez Garcia had shot and killed a man who had just raped her, or rather, she had shot the man who held her down while a second man raped her.

Our Gay Women's Liberation movement had helped bring to the surface the subject of rape. In the late 60s Pat had written in her fiercely feminist autobiographical poem "Goat Child" of being assaulted at the age of ten by "a really hard-up rapist"—reflecting the old belief that rape was a product of men's sexual urges going out of control, as though men just somehow couldn't control themselves (although they could fly to the moon or stand at attention for five hours or work fourteen hour shifts, etc). Later, feminists managed to change this to a view of rape as simple domination and punishment of women. In my antiwar poem "Vietnamese woman speaking to an American soldier" (1967), I had tried to politicize rape as the assault on a civilian population, a frequent connection made in antiwar sentiments. In "A Woman Is Talking To Death" I brought up rape again, the woman in the snow in Boston after a taxi driver "beat her up and raped her / throwing her out of his / care." In reading the poem I let the line prior to "care" hang in the air for emphasis, as I had left it hanging on the page of print.

The whole subject of rape enraged me and all the lesbians I knew. While Parker was explicit, and public, in remembering the rape that happened to her as a child, my own childhood sexual abuse was still buried in my subconscious, not to surface for another decade. So perhaps this shadow memory underlay my rage. Or, perhaps our anger was also fueled by the cavalier acceptance of rape, the "just lie back and enjoy it" kind of dismissal that dominated men's attitudes at the time, coupled with how maligned our own lesbian sexuality was. The combination was explosive for militant feminists, lesbian and straight.

Then, one day at the press we received an autobiographical piece called "The Rape Poem" from a white writer named Dell Fitzgerald-Richards. Holding our collective breath, knowing how important the subject was and how fraught with political landmines, such as racism, we read it. Dell wrote it as a first person narrative, so it had a very personal tone. A white man had come in her window and raped her. The poem included her courageous analysis, that she herself had recovered but her parents had not, had locked themselves fearfully into a gated community, had become prisoners of fear, and thus had succumbed to the attack on her in the worst possible way. It was a brilliant political and psychological poem. We immediately published it as a chapbook. With Dell's permission I read it all over the place. A few distressed women, reminded of their own unspeakable experiences, sometimes needed to get up and rush from the room. I felt terrible for them, but pushed on with my readings, to help open the pustulating social wound, to let it begin to drain and hopefully heal.

In addition to revealing injuries, we were also affirming the strength and beauty in all women, including the beauty of women's bodies. To counter male violence aimed at controlling us, we advocated women's sexual autonomy. At that time the press was distributing Tee Corinne's marvelous, ingenious *Cunt Coloring Book*. The flower-like drawings added to the sheer whimsy of expressing with crayons or colored pencils that women's genitalia are diverse and beautiful. Earlier feminist artists had taken on the same task, with poet Amy Lowell writing about lilies sticking out their tongues and, more recently, poet Elsa Gidlow describing her women lovers as various flowers. So *Cunt Coloring Book* was really in that venerable lineage and Corinne, a photographer and writer as well as a visual artist, was a leader at incorporating both the sexuality and the diversity of women's bodies into her art. She used an all-encompassing female gaze. Though I appreciated the meaning of the book, at first I cringed at the title as demeaning, shaming. I, who had reclaimed *dyke!* Strange. Later I learned that the root of the word "cunt" seems to be *cune,* related to "queen" and to a past time, many of us believed, when women were revered. And what other word is more appropriate? Vagina is only one part of the whole jewelbox. The coloring book, which continues in print, is subversively unassuming and cheerful, like Tee herself.

By 1975 we were distributing a book of poems by women in the underground. And a handbook advising women on how to buy and use a pistol. Martha was especially pushing for this publication; she was going to target practice. Soon she bought a .45 pistol. New Yorker meets the West. I had grown up with guns and the idea that they "protect" you, though I left this idea far behind after a neighbor accidentally fired Yvonne's "unloaded" pistol through the wall back in Washington, DC, something my father would not have predicted. Then too, Parker's experience of buying guns to arm her household on Mississippi Street, only to have someone break in for the sole purpose of stealing the guns reinforced my belief that guns attract violence and stupidity. And as a generation we were already attracting plenty of violence, the era was electric with it.

The line we were walking around the subject of rape was how to bring an issue into national attention without committing irrelevant violence. It's not as though we could lie down across the railroad tracks of the patriarchy, or demand that all rapists leave our country. The issue of rape was embedded within the culture of men.

We movement women had done everything we knew to make it clear to our society that rape was a crime against a person. Women were standing up for each other. For years, anti-rape squads had been organized to escort women in risky locations, wife rape was being challenged, and women were increasingly speaking up about this particular aspect of their oppression. *It Ain't Me Babe* included a cartoon showing a woman wearing a napkin around her neck, holding a fork with a skull and carcass on her plate with the caption, "My husband told me to eat him so I did." In a culture in which women were sexual servants, it was a breakthrough for wives to imagine saying "no" to acts that did not give them any pleasure. This cartoon was not about hating oral sex; it was about hating non-reciprocated sex on demand.

The drastic effects of rape on women was an issue on which we could agree, our band of dyke warriors was completely united on this—but unable to affect the national conscience. The Inez Garcia case would change everything.

Into our growing hope, which was accompanied by increasing impatience, resentment and dissatisfaction, a new voice roared. Inez Garcia, a Catholic farmworker and mother living in Soledad, a city in one of California's agricultural counties, had shot one of her two rapists, the 300-pound henchman who held her down in an alley outside her apartment. After the two attackers left, they called her on the phone to mock her and threaten her life. She grabbed her son's shotgun and went to find them.

Louise Merrill helped lead the Inez Garcia Defense Committee, to raise both money and awareness. Then came Inez's trial in Salinas, a farming town about ninety miles south of the Bay Area. Feminist and radical lesbian mobilization around the subject ratcheted up a few notches, and newspapers carried the story. A group of us got up at 4 A.M. to pile into the open bed of Louise's pickup truck and shiver our way through the predawn ride down to the Salinas courtroom.

We sat watching the proceedings, as Inez's lawyer, Charles Garry, who had made a name for himself defending Huey Newton and Bobby Seale, as well as antiwar activists in Oakland, was pleading her case. To our outrage, he paraded across the courtroom, a picture of aggression and arrogance. "Do you know who I am?" He postured urbanely and contemptuously to the rural jury. They didn't know who he was, why should they? Who would want to know? Inez herself was at odds with his representation of her as a female who had gone out of control. Garry had no idea how to plead a feminist case.

We were most outraged that the plea was wrong. Garry was arguing for something called "diminished capacity"—the antithesis of what we, her grassroots feminist supporters, thought of her, and most importantly of what she thought of herself. We thought of her as having enhanced capacity, and as displaying the real feelings women had about being raped. Inez confirmed this view when, during one of Garry's presentations of her as emotionally unstable, she stormed to the front of the court and addressed the judge directly, bursting out with a description of her consciousness at the time she pulled the trigger, "I did it and I would do it again!" A woman has honor, Inez said.

Wow! Imagine that, a woman has honor of her own, protective honor toward her own body, and the right to free herself from being property to her family or the patriarchy.

The prosecution painted a tawdry picture of drug dealers entangled in vengeance, and the jury convicted Inez. We were howlingly disappointed and enraged that the biggest leftist lawyer in the country could not adequately defend this modest and pious woman. Vindictively the judge had given her an indeterminate sentence, which for a proud person usually means a much longer sentence, as the prison guards will try to break your will.

Mouths set in grim determination, Alice, Carol, and Natalie along with other members of the bookstore collective vowed to publicize Inez's case in every way they could. They made sure all who came into the store knew about the case and so were swept into the general atmosphere of support for Inez. Posters and decorated cans asking for donations for her appeal were everywhere. We poets continued showing up for benefits to raise funds for a new trial and new lawyer. The press collective gave a precious $500 of our operating funds; the Health Center gave much more. To us, Garcia was a political prisoner. Louise organized a protest at San Francisco's State Building near Civic Center. They occupied the building, in defense of Inez Garcia and other political prisoners, and thirty-two women, both lesbian and straight, were arrested, along with six gay men. Louise then took on the task of raising funds to fight those charges. She felt this was a great deal of effort for unknown quantity of return. Was anyone paying attention to what women were saying, we wondered?

A few months after the first trial, Martha approached some of us, her trusted dyke comrades. She had a good friend who had been raped, she said, and the friend wanted action. The victim was P., a friend of Martha's; she had been out camping. The rapist had crept up on her in the night, had hit her in the face and threatened her with a knife. She wanted to call him out. We had no reason to believe that the police or any other authorities would do anything except laugh at us, ignore or further mistreat her, make a joke. Inez with her rifle and her sense of "women's honor" represented an end to this, a sea change of the seriousness with which women were beginning to take our treatment at the hands of men and at the hands of the society that hypocritically pretended to protect us. Inez was about women taking the matter on for ourselves. We thought that by taking an action, we could be supportive of Inez. We didn't want to kill this man; but we did want to capture him, take him to the judge's house, and tie him to the base of a huge tree along with a note about his crime. As Martha said recently there is something so archetypal about women and the tree, as though the tree would help us bear witness: to call him out as publicly as possible. (Eerily, June Arnold's 1975 novel *Sister Gin* contains a similar scene, except the women are old.)

Our group met several times to plan and to rehearse. We gathered what we would need, tape, chains, handcuffs, rope, wads of cotton for the chloroform, to render him unconscious. We rehearsed which of us would grasp which part of him while we did this. Five of us got into a car. Louise drove. Martha had brought her big blue-black pistol. I was very nervous about this. She had been agitated lately (we were all agitated lately) and I didn't trust that she wouldn't use the pistol, perhaps by accident. I asked to hold it and to my surprise she gave it to me. The weapon smelled sharply of gun oil, and hung heavily in my hand, much heavier than my father's little pistols, which I had played with so many times as a child. I should have been thinking, in dread, about the terrible size of the hole this big pistol could punch in a person. We drove, P. in the back seat giving directions. She had gone back several times to the town near the campsite, had located him, his car, his house. She knew where he worked. She had followed him everywhere. She knew his habits, his favorite bar.

We drove in the night, tension throbbing through the inside of the car like a heart attack in process. We drove through several neighborhoods in a woodsy town of northern California. We looked and looked; we could not find him, not his car, not a trace. The search seemed interminable. Finally P. said in disappointment, "He's gone. He must have moved." We turned back, and then I felt a sweep of great relief. In retrospect, I feel just the way Martha does as she holds her face in her hands when I bring it up now, thirty-five years after the fact.

"We could have gone to prison for such a long time," she says, shuddering. Indeed, we might still be in prison. We could have injured the man trying to subdue him. And had we been arrested, had we done some harm, I would have been the one holding the gun. And, most frightening in retrospect, we could have done damage to Inez's case and to the whole issue we had worked so hard to establish: rape is an act that damages the victim.

As it was, in early 1977, Garcia's appeal lawyer, a young feminist named Susan Jordan, dropped the diminished capacity defense, arguing simple self-defense, and Inez was found innocent and released, having been imprisoned for two years. The legal precedent was now in favor of women defending themselves from sexual assault.

We exulted, and ICI: A Woman's Place bookstore, for that single day in its eleven years of existence, closed its doors in celebration of Inez Garcia's victory.

By then there were battered women's shelters with paid staff, and hotlines for women in trouble. By then and in the years thereafter rape became a national and then an international subject, a real crime. We had all—dozens, hundreds, and then thousands—helped to disempower one of the most powerful weapons of male supremacy, and one of the major causes of human despair.

Dancing Into the Wind

...this is how we tried to love,
and these are the forces they had ranged against us,
and these are the forces we had ranged within us,
within us and against us, against us and within us.
—Adrienne Rich

Wendy was instantly certain she knew who had done it. *"The FBI,"* she said firmly. *I had been slow, years slow, to understand that our own government could plot against us. For one thing, I didn't think we were that high on the radar screen. For another, I had simply been naive. Though conspiracy theories had spread rapidly in the 1960s after JFK and Robert Kennedy's assassinations, I had remained skeptical. The Russians assassinated their leaders, as we had all learned in high school; but here, in a democracy? Nah. It didn't occur to me that just as adventurous women flooded into our rebel movement, they also poured into police and fire departments, and into the FBI, which recruited them to keep an eye on...us.*

One evening back in 1967 when I was in Placitas, gathered with fellow poets and artists over a bowl of Karla's thick lentil soup, a guy was there, just passing through, a fellow with a crew cut who said he had been in the military; he'd been an interrogator, he said. He was fresh from New Orleans. "People there are certain the CIA had something to do with Kennedy's assassination," he told us, "and I think so too."

Members of the CIA, he said, had combined with the Mafia, who were furious that Kennedy botched the Bay of Pigs invasion of Cuba. The Mafia wanted access to Cuba in order to resume its gambling and prostitution operations. "All the witnesses have mysteriously died," he said. "Not just Jack Ruby and Lee Harvey Oswald. All of them." He was persuasive, but still I was skeptical.

Now on this long night we talked in terse sentences about the vandalism, "Who do you think did it?" I asked as if she hadn't spoken. I shivered. An all-night wind was up, tossing the leaves on the trees over the skylight so the shadows danced in a frenzy against the dirty panes.

"The FBI," she repeated.

"I don't know..." I answered. I was thinking about the small footprint found near my desk and the argument Coletta had with a hotheaded lesbian group in the Pacific Northwest.

I put the small rifle next to me on the pallet. It had an ugly gunstock, not elegantly oiled brown wood like the rifles of my father, but rather painted a dull rusty color. I didn't like it. I didn't feel like clutching it for protection, or aiming it at the restless shadows on the skylight. I felt like throwing the rifle across the cement floor, just to hear its hollow clatter echoed by the tall still walls.

WOMEN'S SPIRITUALITY—ANOTHER STREAM OF RESISTANCE

The question of choices, whether to use the tactic of force or persuasion, continued to haunt our movement. Inez Garcia had fought back in self-defense. She was a religious person, and this helped give her credibility with the wider public. Susan Griffin put the feeling into repeating lines of poetry, "she is in a white dress kneeling," driving home the point of Inez's innocence and piety as a Catholic woman. For militants like Parker, however, "piety" suggested passivity, and she objected to Susan's poem.

I was drawn not to religion but to spirituality, non-religious practices drawing from earth-based traditions, combining love and respect for other beings with militant activism for social justice. Spirituality within our movement developed its own rituals to sustain those of us who sought its wisdom and its emphasis on healing.

After Von died I wrote the last poem of the She Who series, "a funeral plainsong" for her: "I will be your fight now to do your winning / as the bond between women is beginning..." As December dragged on I remained mired in grief, a kind of emotional paralysis that felt like my heart had the flu. Fortunately for me, cultural feminism was producing a powerful new set of practices and I turned to one of them at this time. While the political aspects of feminism continued to professionalize, especially as funding came in, cultural feminism continued creating a new rebellion, one that critiqued and opposed the entrenched patriarchal institutions of religion. More to the point, this rebellion would encourage women to find, create, or reinvent more independent practices of spirituality.

Z Budapest, a witch who inherited knowledge of old practices through her Eastern European matrilineal line, was holding solstice rituals on the open bluffs over Santa Monica. I was lucky to be able to attend her winter solstice ritual in December of 1974, just weeks after Von's death. Karla took me to the house where about twenty of us gathered, patiently helped me make the round wreath out of green leafy vines, fitted it to my head, and, even though she didn't want to participate in the ritual, waited for me back at the house.

That cold clear memorable night I was delighted that Z was so loose and interactive, dressed in thick gray wooly material, laughing and even rolling on the ground. The participants had made a circle of stones on the dark earth, the moon was far away and stark white. A police helicopter flashing dramatic red lights monitored us overhead like an obsessive roaring beast going round and round. Circle upon circle we danced, the cops danced, the moon danced.

Z announced only one rule in her Wicca practice: "Don't step outside the circle!" She led us in chants and a ritual to Diana, with each of us waving a gleaming knife at the full moon overhead. I was exceedingly noisy in my chanting, overly excited in my dancing, really pumped up with emotion. Some of the other women were casting looks of disapproval my way, and soon someone came over to tell me in a shocked whisper that I should watch my feet. "Look what you've done, you're outside the circle!"

Sure enough, my feet had carried me where they wanted to go. I hustled back inside the bright ring of stones. But a few minutes later, I drifted outside the parameters again. As usual, my first thought was that something was wrong with me. My second thought was how lines, rules, boxes, had never been anything I could follow.

Martha Shelley was in the circle that night too, I remember because each of us came through a double line of women to greet priestess Z with her open arms and broadly smiling, welcoming face. After my turn I looked back to watch the others. We were to "hug and kiss the priestess," which I had done in a sort of depressive perfunctory way.

When Martha came through the line, naked to the waist like the rest of us, she gave Z an embrace and a long kiss, a real erotic kiss, and Z shouted "At last! Someone who gets it!"

Her exuberant response signified that a circle celebrating Diana is an exchange of erotic energy, not some kind of serious anti-body suppression procession. Even alcohol was not prohibited, but I was still on the wagon so had to think twice about drinking from the Mason jar of vodka and hot peppers that Z passed around to keep us warm in the cold December air. The potion worked as an instant hit of warmth and of course didn't send me back to the bottle. Intention, intention, intention.

I learned two things that night, besides that Martha "got it." One was that I can't stay inside lines no matter how simple. The other was that rituals have real effect. I returned all the way back into myself through the ritual, and though still sad I was again functional, as if I could once again inhabit my body, and this world, even without one of my loves. I was convinced that Von had died of a broken heart, without the social support she needed to have love and an authentic life. The circle of women on the cliffs, persisting in dancing together even under the police helicopter's flashing red lights, reassured my own broken heart that we would all go on, do our activist work, and keep love alive within us and among us.

The lock of grief for Von was opened, and though I would continue to miss her all the rest of my life, I was able to go back to my work of making a world she might have been able to inhabit, rather than acquiescing to a world that I was certain had killed her.

SPIRITUALITY AND CULTURAL WORKERS

I had very consciously written the She Who poems, chasing after an ephemeral "female principle," a kind of collectivity of women's capacity for social change and change of worldview. Then came "A Woman Is Talking to Death," which defined "lover" as anyone caught in oppressive circumstances.

Following these roadbeds, as I imagine whole poetic thoughts to be, I gave myself permission to explore any female subjects I wished—whatever I could write that would help give women power. Thinking of my mother's admiration for science, I decided to explore menstruation, with its obvious connection to lunar cycles, intending to credit women with the invention of calendars, at least.

I found a haven in my large room at Terrace Street with windows overlooking Broadway's lights and the handsome, silent-at-night buildings and evergreens of Oakland Technical High School. Peace entered in, a relief from the relentless activity that was the press, the bookstore, my constant readings in support of the movement, the continual pressure to "be political." In the privacy of my room I talked out loud to the air, paced and waved my arms.

While studying Marija Gimbutas' *Gods and Goddesses of Old Europe* and Robert Graves' *The White Goddess*, I was feeling a ravening dissatisfaction. Besides the She Who poems, what contribution could I make to this exciting, mysterious, developing field?

Grassroots interest in women and spirituality was happening in both rural and urban centers. In 1974, two women, Ruth and Jean Mountaingrove, fell in love, militantly took the same last name, and founded *WomanSpirit Magazine* in Wolf Creek, Oregon. Their publication included a multitude of voices on subjects like herbology and goddess lore. Scholars like Merlin Stone (who had tried to place her manuscript *When God Was a Woman* at the Women's Press Collective, but we were too exhausted by then to imagine taking it on), Barbara Walker, and Monika Sjö were already well along in gathering material that would explode women's spirituality into the world as a largely unrecognized, but nevertheless popular, contribution to world religions. I already knew some of the key figures who would help shape it from early in our Gay Women's Liberation movement.

I recently asked Sandy Boucher about her connection to spirituality, and she immediately brought up women bonding in consciousness-raising groups: "I could feel in our small group, when one of us talked about something oppressive in her life, I could feel the different quality of the air as if we had touched into a place that was very deep… I am going to cry now… it saved my life. The kind of mental state I was in… I could function at work but on weekends I couldn't get out of bed. I started to have this thought, 'I could get up and have breakfast or I could kill myself.' And they were equal."

So Sandy first saw the movement itself, and the sharing of stories between women, as a spiritual experience. She undertook a lifelong practice of Vipassana meditation practice, and would later become a spokeswoman for American women engaging with Buddhism. Beginning in the 1980s, she wrote *Turning the Wheel: American Women Creating the New Buddhism; Opening the Lotus: A Woman's Guide to Buddhism;* and *Discovering Kwan Yin, Buddhist Goddess of Compassion,* among others.

Our understanding of our own roles in the creation of culture was greatly enhanced by the work of artist and archivist Max Dashu. She is one of the reasons we sometimes thought of our movement as a "college." As a kid in a working-class town in West Chicago, Max would play in the radioactive debris dumped by nearby factories. She escaped the stifling anti-intellectualism of her hometown on a scholarship to Radcliffe in the late sixties, but was disappointed by the competitive and vacuous atmosphere there. She fled to the Left and antiwar movements instead.

Disillusioned with both college and the male-led movement, Max began to search for another kind of knowledge. A professor had casually mentioned the existence of matriarchies, and Max began a forty-year journey of collecting images and stories about the presence of women in culture. She gave her early presentations at A Woman's Place bookstore, which our whole household attended. Her archive was originally named Matriarchives; she later renamed it the Suppressed Histories Archive to address the themes of anticolonialism and antiracism present in her work.

Max accomplished her archive, which is now 15,000 slides and over 100 fact-filled presentations, by living very frugally. I remember going once to ask a scholarly question, generously answered; she was sitting in a small cold room in a dyke household with the lights off, though it was late afternoon on a dim day. "To save money," she explained. Max's disciplined asceticism sustained both her prolifically artful and scholarly life, and our movement.

Reclaiming and Inventing: Gente and High Risk

Linda Tillery came of age just as Gay Women's Liberation got started. She was only nineteen when she joined a rock band as its lead singer, and played with such artists as Cream and Janis Joplin. Linda grew up in the Fillmore district of San Francisco, an eclectic, vibrant neighborhood intersected with black Muslims, black Christians, and white hippies from nearby Haight-Ashbury district. She describes her mother's house as full of wonderfully interesting people, and all kinds of art, especially music, every day.

It made sense that the young musical artist would seek her lesbian identity in community, across the Bay in Oakland, where Pat Parker, acting as mentor, took her on as a "younger sister" while she lived in Pat's women's households. Linda soon became an open lesbian activist, working in A Woman's Place bookstore behind the counter. She helped at the press as well, especially when we moved our huge and heavy paper cutting machine into a freight elevator as we shifted the press equipment out of the bookstore space in 1975.

She was an early activist in Gente, the gay women of color supportive group Pat Parker helped to form in 1974. Young and ambitious, Gente women spent precious hours in Parker's dining room sharing stories, discussing their lives, and doing consciousness-raising around their (often white) lovers. Many if not most went on to successful careers as political activists, educators, writers, musicians, songwriters and more. Among others, the group included political organizer Pat Norman, writer and educator Barbara "B.G." Glass, political activist Linda Wilson, musicians Sandi Ajida and Matu Feliciano, novelist and professor Dodici Azpadu, and world-renowned musician and professor of Africana Studies Judith Casselberry. Gente raised money for women in prison, and helped publicize political activists such as Joanne Little, who like Inez Garcia had killed her rapist in self-defense. Of course, as with other lesbian groups, Gente had its conflicts, but more importantly they gave each other encouragement to assert themselves in the world.

Linda and Ann Bernard both describe living on a block on Vallejo Street in Emeryville, a town near Berkeley. "Every house on the block had at least one lesbian." The women, many of them musicians, took care of each other. They made sure tools were loaned, cars got fixed, and food was shared.

Music, like imagery and poetry, easily conveys spiritual content, to which its history of association with religious expression testifies. The arts are by definition holistic and attached to the heart. Always collaborative and community-minded, Linda formed the Gente Gospeliers, whose stage presence as out lesbians of color helped heighten Gente's profile. Linda produced her first solo album with Olivia Records in 1978. Later she would form her own extraordinary group, the Cultural Heritage Choir, gathering spirituals, which are traditional folksongs, from older black people, teaching them to younger people, and touring around the world.

One of the most compelling of the contributors to the women's musical explosion was Gwen Avery. African American and openly lesbian, she was raised by her grandmother in a roadhouse in a black precinct of Pennsylvania, where she inherited deep southern blues and spiritual music, and delivered them in highly dramatic performance. She would take charge of the performance space with her entire body. One of my favorite memories from the seventies era is seeing Gwen on stage delivering a passionate song while lying on her back.

Another of the early members of Gente was Sandi Ajida, who had worked for civil rights in the South in the early sixties. Although she played in lots of bands, I knew her mostly because in 1974 she was part of a group of four musicians, two white and two black, living variously in the Bay Area and in LA, who recorded six of my "Common Woman Poems." They called themselves, appropriately for the times, "High Risk." High Risk also put out a 45 for which Max Dashu designed the cover, featuring three dark-skinned Amazons on horseback, charging forward with their black hair whipping in the wind. This was one of the first records distributed by Olivia Records. Recently Cynth Fitzpatrick, who played on the album, told me the record has become an underground jazz collector's item, a tribute to the vivacious and original musicality of the quartet.

The little 45 featured "Nadine, resting on her neighbor's stoop," a portrait poem from my days with women newly arrived from the rural south in NW Washington, DC. Ajida read the poem as well as doing the percussion. The bass player, Bobi Jackson, sang her own feminist song, "Degradation," on the flip side. The cover photographs said clearly that these women were consciously dyke-identified. Cynth Fitzpatrick has her head shaved and is so thin she nearly disappears behind her shiny alto sax, Bobi sports a tight-fitting brown WWI leather flying helmet, dramatically accented with her dark glasses, while Ajida stands under a tree with a serious expression, dressed ceremonially in the denim overalls of grassroots civil rights workers, topped off with an artful French beret.

As with movement lyrics and poetry in general, the deeply felt morality of both feminist and antiwar themes wove together in the music of this group. Virginia Rubino wailed out her own antiwar song in the voice of conscripted young men, using the street chant, "1,2,3,4, I ain't gonna go no more" while Cynth and Bobi rolled out a sustaining structure in tenor sax, flute, and bass, and Ajida held a steady bell and bullet rattle with her sticks on the cymbal. A poster, probably from 1975, advertises a High Risk concert with me reading at the First Unitarian Church in San Francisco, "women only" and "childcare provided." Cynth tells me this was their last performance together, and their best.

INVENTING A NEW REVOLUTION

Historians have said that the feminist movement developed along two major lines, cultural and political. While for most of us these seemed braided, for others they were two contradictory streams. Just as feminists were beginning to confront institutions that had oppressed them, women who were working in cultural mediums were trying to identify what was missing in the basic theoretical frameworks of history and in prevailing forms of activism. Our lives, our feelings simply didn't make sense when restricted to imagery of labor, suffering, outrage, history. Mary Daly created a language to embody her theology with which she intended to replace patriarchy. The term "patriarchy" itself gave us a new place to stand, as it became more clear that the revolution we had set out to make was not the one we were making.

We cultural workers were devising new origin stories to replace those of the patriarchy on every front. Parker stepped into this new stream with her lines, "I have a dream too. / it's a simple dream." The revolutionary theories that had gone before would not help sustain Pat's life; neither would the white women's movement. She was calling for a queer and multiracial revolutionary movement, a "simple" revolution based on what was needed, yet also a very complex one that no theory has yet been able to encompass.

Pat had an idea at this time that might have led us towards a different theoretical base:

> I'd like to see a history book in which every chapter is written by a different group. It's arranged by decade, so we could see, like, what was the decade of 1890 to 1900 for a black person, what was that same decade for a member of the white government, what was it for an Indian, what was it for a poor white person, and so on...

I thought this was a spectacular idea. We didn't have the resources to start such a project, of course. We could just wish.

But aside from one poem critical of the patriarchal god, "For Willyce," Parker did not venture into spirituality in her poetry as I did, and as Audre did in her metaphors and after her trip to Africa, in *The Black Unicorn* and again in her "biomythography" *Zami: A New Spelling of My Name,* where she introduces Afro-Caribbean-New York lesbian goddess Afrekete. Olga Broumas, meanwhile, would publish the 1976 chapbook "Charis," describing the view of a woman's cervix and vaginal walls as cathedral-like, and therefore sacred. Diane di Prima had been writing her poetic series *Loba* around an Italian wolf-goddess theme. As Ntozake Shange would write in her choreopoem, *for colored girls who have considered suicide / when the rainbow is enuf:* "i found god in myself / & i loved her / i loved her fiercely."

The cultural workers continued to explore and absorb the past from a woman-centered point of view, expanding what would become the field of "women's spirituality." Politically identified women howled and raged at us, certain that spirituality would make us passive, impotent, perhaps also co-opted by the male religions. Countering these fears, Daly refused to teach men in her advanced courses at Boston University. Z Budapest continued to hold her high-spirited pagan rituals, teach Dianic arts to groups of women, and began to initiate priestesses, who formed groups of their own.

Many feminist scholars and poets helped develop the field of women's spirituality: Marija Gimbutas, Merlin Stone, Luisah Teish, Charlene Spretnak, Starhawk, Carol Christ, Ntozake Shange. Theologians such as Rosemary Ruether, working inside mainstream patriarchal religious institutions, also effected changes, and for the next three decades women would fight to become rabbis, ministers, bishops, and even ordained Catholic priests. U.S. women, including huge numbers of lesbian feminists, would also pour into Buddhism and Hinduism in the 1980s.

To me though, the big news came from outrageously pro-women feminist authors like Stone, Daly, and Gimbutas, along with the grassroots researcher/ artists, as we surfaced with new imagery and information, and therefore new rituals and origin stories. This was a revolution we had not anticipated. The spiritual fire that breathed through our movement by 1976 buoyed me even as I exhausted myself, lost myself, in the seemingly endless struggle for any kind of foothold, any way to hold onto our hard won solidarity toward common purpose, to know when we were actually gaining ground and to successfully hold, as Lorde would so astutely describe the paradox, *common differences*.

My own spirituality remained an inner dialogue on the subject of love as a matrix greater than individuals, and more mystical than bonding or solidarity suggested. Love seemed to connect across impossible distances, and I wanted to know more about this. Besides having my father's gift of talking to a spirit in the air, I was now becoming aware of some psychic capacities. Once late at night I heard someone urgently calling my name in a deep resonant voice, and within a couple of minutes received a phone call from Parker—the only person I knew with such a voice—needing a place to spend the night. I had no doubt I had heard her psychically. Then, in the weeks prior to Yvonne's death, I repeatedly heard children's voices on a playground so clearly I would open my window and lean out into Oakland's still night air seeking the source. Only after she died did these voices cease, making me wonder if I had locked into her consciousness, a thousand miles away.

In 1973 I had made an artistic decision to write from a sensibility of connection within nature. The shaping of my novel *Mundane's World* led me to develop a voice of a shifting sense of time and point of view, and attempt to incorporate the lives of creatures along with the human characters. The book also has a glimpse of a fictional earth goddess who lives in a cave, and is visited by the women in the imaginary village. I felt great joy in writing *Mundane's World*, which took fifteen years to complete. As Wendy and I became more physically and emotionally depleted, it gave me a place to express the wonder of living beings in paragraphs that replicated space-time relativity, while retaining a whimsical love of life. In a way, the writing of *Mundane's World* was a form of spiritual practice that sustained me through years that became more and more challenging. This kept me somewhat aware of the "greater love" outside of myself, to which I longed to be connected.

SLIPPING

In 1975 I wrote a series of short poems, "Confrontations with the Devil in the Form of Love." Pressing the subject of love as a personification having agency, and thus attempting something mythic about love, I was trying for a broader storyline, but had not yet gathered enough information or inner resilience to create anything substantial. The poems begin with a romantic image of Love as a person, something like Eve with her apples, her vivacity, nourishment and seduction, her hopes and dreams. "What do I have / if not my two hands / and my apples" and, "look at my hands / they are apples / my breasts / are apples / my life / is an apple tree"—the innocence of understanding oneself as resourceful.

Then the set abruptly swings into a sarcastic tone that verges on bitterness: "Love came along / and saved me / saved me…. / and then one day / Love left to go save / someone else…" Expressing disappointment was not my intention, however, but rather to point out the incapacity of love and empathy alone to affect major change.

The poems continue with a (some might think, scathing) critique of women settling for too little: "Venus dear / where are your arms? / if only you were a tree / they have so many / and no one thinks less of them for it."

Finally, the culminating poem, while maintaining the sarcasm, speaks in a more sincere, urgent tone: don't be taken in by romance alone; solidarity just for the sake of being together will not get us anywhere. The poem entitled "My name is Judith, meaning" is about gaining resources, allies, and self-defense, said with strong words: provision, protection, power. That without these, "why would you call my name love?" Without these, we may as well settle for romance, "which is so much easier / and so much less / than any of us / deserve."

The poems in this series call for a militant stance in support of the woman-centeredness we had all created. Culturally, this woman-centeredness was finding expression in women's spirituality and political movements, both grassroots and academic. In reviving the mythic figure of Venus as Love, I was trying to stand on the axial edge between political/economic effectiveness and the emerging ethos of women's spirituality. In a nod toward the need for women to acquire resources, the final poem in the series states, "not until we have ground to call our own…weapons of our own in hand…and some kind of friends around us." How should this happen? We were adamant that money with strings attached was not acceptable. We argued incessantly about for-profit versus nonprofit, about business and capitalism, market and constituency, collective and hierarchy. I had long given up on consensus as a viable decision-making model at the press collective, and had settled for "worker's power" instead: whoever had the energy and charisma to get something done got to do it. This resulted in quite a varied publishing list. A moon calendar and a coloring book of women's vaginas sat on shelves next to *The Gun Pamphlet*, instructions on how women could arm themselves, and *Sing a Battle Song*, poetry of the Weather Underground women. "Confrontations with the Devil in the Form of Love" did not draw much attention for about fifteen years. In retrospect, the acid little poems mark a turning point for me, a restless time of searching for a new movement wind that could blow up some different action, could stir us in a new direction.

If you had seen any photos of Wendy and me in 1975 you would notice immediately that we were sliding toward ill health—her porcelain complexion was now mottled, I was too thin, almost emaciated from stress, and both of us look exhausted. The first injury since we had moved the press from San Francisco had happened. Earlier that year Alice and I were talking in the Terrace Street kitchen at about one o'clock in the morning when Willyce and Wendy stumbled in. Wendy was leaning on Willyce, who had one arm around Wendy's waist while with the other she raised Wendy's injured hand high, a hand covered in thick black ink and red blood.

"She got her finger caught in the rollers of the Chief," Willyce said. By the time Willyce had been able to jump for the "off" switch, Wendy's finger had split open. Foolishly, we let her go to bed instead of taking her to the emergency room to get the deep gash cleaned and stitched. By the next day she was running a fever, and when we got her to the hospital, they kept her for a few terrifying days as septicemia raged through her body. What I remember is my intense guilt that she nearly lost her finger and I had not rushed her to the emergency room. What she remembers is that the hospital staff would not grant me visiting privileges, unlike the kind doctor who had overseen Yvonne's illness, and had urged me to the bedside. "Also," Wendy remembers wryly, "they kept calling me 'sir'."

The pressures on us were only increasing as the years went by. Our poor pricing and devil-may-care marketing habits meant that the more we succeeded the more unpaid labor we had to do. The work was no longer a free-running beast energizing us. Rather, it was like an old locomotive whose motor had died, so we were hauling it by hand up the tracks of a mountain. We weren't singing anymore. Wendy, with a huge scar the length of her middle finger, didn't play guitar. A sadness and unease had settled in, and a sinister quality in the air seemed to be gaining strength.

At home, we were increasingly aware of surveillance. Men in suits came to the door asking questions we refused to answer, the phone made strange noises. The energy around us that had been so buoyant, so erotically bonding, was becoming erratic, even threatening. Alice made space in the house for a mentally ill woman escaping her family. One night I heard pounding, went to investigate, and saw her beating a butcher knife against the kitchen counter. Alice found another place for her to live.

Wendy moved into the attic after Martha moved out, and we cut a hole in the wall to make a window but never finished, sealing the gap with a piece of crude plastic. Two women stayed in the basement for a week, one helping the other kick heroin. Someone at the health center had overdosed and died, rumor said. We heard that a woman had killed another woman with a karate blow in Sacramento, found it had been in an argument over a cherished job. Ever vigilant, Martha drove to Sacramento to ask questions. "No one is talking about it," she reported. Women, with our still fragile bonds, could not yet bear to imagine our power turned against other women. We soldiered on.

Trips East

By the middle of 1974 Pat was again in love, with a thoroughly supportive white dyke from Mississippi named Ann Bernard. She played bass, so the two of them had an artistic friendship in addition to their love. She and Pat went on a cross-country trip by car, doing readings and distributing books.

Ann Bernard has a favorite story about Pat's reading at the Firehouse, that grand Manhattan lesbian venue that I remember as naked white brick and exhilarating high walls.

> There was a little window high on the wall behind Pat. She read that outrageous poem, "For Willyce," about making love to a woman who kept moaning, "oh god," and when she came to the line about "here it is, some dude's / getting credit / for what a woman has done / again" suddenly there was a big crack of thunder and lightning at the window.

They had been incredibly brave, the two of them, a black and white lesbian couple alone on the road, having to stop at the bathrooms, the cafes, to walk into a room full of white strangers, trusting that they wouldn't be confronted, hassled, punched, or worse. Sometimes they were taken as a black man and a white woman, equally sexually transgressive in that era and location. Ann describes the tactic they used while going into bathrooms: "We would both start talking loudly to each other about the best place to buy tampax and other intimately womanly matters."

In Denver, the white lesbians who had put them up unthinkingly advised them to go to a cafe that turned out to be dangerous for them. A drunken white man watched as their food was served, then got up and began to rage, calling them the usual scary names. Even more threateningly, he went from table to table urging action from the other white customers, pointing to the two women, shouting, "Shouldn't we do something about this?" No one moved one way or the other. Pat stood up to confront him and they argued face to face for what seemed like a very long time to Ann's nervously watching eyes.

At one point the drunk said something about people like Pat "trying to take our Cadillacs." Pat responded coolly, "I thought we black people were the ones who already had the Cadillacs." Finally stirred by Pat's refusal to show fear or irrationality, the waitress found her own bravery and interceded, pushing the drunk out the door.

On the East Coast, Pat and Ann stayed on Staten Island with Audre Lorde and Frances Clayton, which sealed a familial bond among them; thereafter Audre's letters warmly included Ann. Pat wrote to Audre about the trip, confiding her relief to have black faces in some of her crowds.

On some of my trips to the East Coast, I too was invited to stay with Audre and Frances in their Staten Island home, where Frances had a home office for her psychotherapy practice, and where Audre took me to the backyard to show me their little garden and the dramatic top of a freighter sliding past in the seawater just yards away. Extremely generous if overly excited, Audre drove me, cursing all the way, through driving rain on some ghastly New York interstate to a reading at Rutgers or Hunter College.

I was extremely nervous to do a reading on the West side of Manhattan with such notable authors as Kate Millet, Mary Daly, and Adrienne Rich in the audience. But Adrienne reported being changed by "A Woman Is Talking to Death," and afterwards she was increasingly bold in publishing work that could be read as lesbian.

MOVING ON

Alice rolled her cigarette casually, flicking her gaze up to Wendy and me. "It's time for you to move," she said. What? Why? Somehow I thought we would live there forever, hundreds of years. Mummified and buried with honors in a box in the dirt part of the basement. "Carol and I want a change, we want to fix the place up and rent it. We're tired of living in a collective."

Once past our initial shock, we were surprisingly ready to move on. Her timing could not have been better, as Wendy had just inherited some IBM shares from the grandmother on the wealthy side of her family. She had dumped the papers in the bottom of my bureau drawer where they had lain for months. "Let's buy a house!" I suggested. Houses in Oakland were beyond cheap, especially if you didn't mind a few bullet holes. We found a three bedroom stand-alone "rowhouse" on Ninth Avenue above Lake Merritt, with a cottage in the back, 150 foot lot, $1,800 down, total price $18,000.

We moved in and began to argue about what color to paint it, an argument that would go on for five years. In the meantime I took up gardening, as the last tenants had left a lovely patch of organic ground ready to receive nearly any seeds you put in it. The fresh little seedlings gave me much needed joy and hope.

The last book I typed and printed myself was Alice Molloy's oversize book *In Other Words*, a critique of scientific thinking and corporations. I was injured one night while doing the printing. A small bar attached to the woman-devouring Chief rose up suddenly under me as I poured oil into one of the oil holes. The bar slammed into my eyebrow, crushing a small section of my occipital orb. A half inch lower and I would have lost my left eye. I fell to the floor with my brain rocking while Alice leaped to press an oily rag to my head to stem the blood. At first it looked like a simple cut, which Carol taped shut with a butterfly adhesive bandage. But the next day I was dizzy and had blood in my ear. I physically and emotionally collapsed, and I think this precipitated my alienation from the press.

New language and styles continued to arise. Across the Bay from Oakland, gay men in the San Francisco movement adopted a new masculinity; they poured into gyms and grew moustaches. I missed the drag queens of my youth, who were now being excluded. The lesbian movement now began to include a few transwomen, asking for a place and encountering resistance. I experienced this resistance quite personally during the recording of my album with Parker. The Olivia Records women had just hired a recording engineer, and I found her very attractive. On being told that Sandy Stone was a transgender person I was dismayed, which hurt her feelings. I examined my response carefully and then wrote her a letter of apology. "My attraction to you threatened my lesbian identity," I said. I was shocked to think I might just be locked into something as simple as an "identity," which could become a place of rigid pride if I took myself too seriously. As a cultural worker, didn't I always need to remember that life is a story we are telling ourselves? And that terminologies for its characters and plots are constantly changing?

The women's movement had adopted the term "lesbian-feminist" and had dropped the term "gay," virtually giving it away to the men in order to distinguish the two distinctly different, though overlapping, movements. The term "liberation" was now attached to women, as activist lesbians continued to track feminism and the needs of women and children. We had challenged institutional definitions of "homosexuality" and "female" in education, jobs, the media, increasingly in history and in religions. "Gay Women's Liberation" now seemed far in the past.

But Wendy and I were about to embark on one last separatist adventure that would turn us completely upside down.

Feminist Economic Network: FEN

In 1975 members of two radical dyke households on opposite coasts put their heads together with a lesbian couple in Detroit and decided to lead an economic revolution that would benefit women, who continued to have trouble acquiring credit, by giving them access to small business loans. Laura Brown and Barbara Hoke from the Oakland Feminist Women's Health Center, Coletta Reid and Katherine Czarnik (Casey) of Diana Press in Baltimore, and Joanne Parent and Valerie Angers of the Detroit Women's Credit Union formed the Feminist Economic Network.

Using credit union funds loaned to them as individuals, they bought the old Women's City Club in downtown Detroit. The six-story building, built in 1924, had been an exclusively white, elite women's club in its early history, and later abandoned. FEN women restored it with a ballroom, pool and restaurant, and hundreds of suites that could be rented for conferences. The street level spaces housed services and other enterprises, such as karate lessons, a rape crisis center, a health center that did abortions, a dress shop, and a women's bank. The $100 yearly dues to the club meant that FEN owners were dependent on more prosperous women living in the suburbs to come into downtown Detroit, which had a mostly black and poor population. People from the neighborhood were delighted by the openness of the building to them, and Laura recalled that they had a lot of local volunteers and support, in addition to the black women they hired to help restore the building, and who served on its board.

But the FEN group underestimated the depth of the class/race split in Detroit. White women from the suburbs were reluctant to come into the downtown. FEN hired women guards to ensure women's safety going to and from the club, and they also lit the parking lot at night. So the irony: the club was appealing, but yearly dues kept working-class women away from membership, while perceived need in the downtown location for armed security guards did not reassure, but rather kept more prosperous women away.

As activists FEN put their economic plan into practice before anyone had time to absorb the theoretical basis of it, and the feminist media criticized them relentlessly as hierarchical, corporate capitalists trying to take over the movement, and as having betrayed "collectivity," which was sacrosanct to both the Left and to feminism. Perhaps also the pervasive sacrificial volunteerism and asceticism so necessary to begin the women's movement had acquired a moral status of ultimate goodness that was challenged by FEN's existence.

I don't think anything could have prepared the FEN women for the reaction they received. "People went nuts," Barbara told me. "I think we were infiltrated. There were fistfights the very first weekend the building opened." Angry feminist activists from Ann Arbor had arrived the day after the grand opening, which had featured a speech by Gloria Steinem. The Ann Arbor women stormed the building, and several women were reportedly injured in the melee. Laura says the FEN group was aware of the presence of agents throughout their time in Detroit, probably the FBI in collaboration with the local police "Red Squad" that for decades had been used to prevent more unionization.

Few could believe that FEN women were economic activists, not budding capitalists. In a welter of controversy, which included internal combustion, their enterprise was brought to a screaming halt. "We made some mistakes," Laura acknowledges. For one thing, they did not articulate their goals clearly enough to attract allies within the movement—what we did not yet know to call "public relations." And, the Detroit couple had a bitter and divisive break-up that forced people to take sides. Across the country the women's media lined up in opposition to what FEN was doing; at the same time the group fell apart from within.

Julie R. Enszer wrote in their defense that they were not capitalist elitists, as their critics saw them, but rather were pursuing genuinely revolutionary ends: "The goal of FEN institutions was economic self-sufficiency for the Feminist Movement, which would allow women an economic as well as cultural context in which to become free of patriarchy." In my opinion, the FEN women were grassroots activists who were seriously misinterpreted. While they were primarily working class, actively antiracist, and lesbian, the label "capitalist" marked them very differently. And they refused to soft-pedal their structural ideas. For example, they circumvented democratic processes in order to move quickly. They believed in and practiced worker's power. Whoever did the most work should make the most, and the most final, decisions. They had not taken the liberal stance that they were "helping poor women." Instead, they boldly stated that they wanted women to have money and power in order to be independent of the patriarchy.

From their point of view, seizing economic power by sharing sizeable sums of money to create sustainable small businesses for women was an extension of our earlier projects of seizing control of women's health care and reproductive rights by opening health clinics, establishing women's educational centers in our bookstores, and creating public voice through ownership of printing presses and distribution networks. They intended to spread FEN businesses across the country. Instead, they sold the building and dissolved FEN.

I visited Diana Press in 1976, as I happened to be on a poetry reading trip on the East Coast, stopping in Baltimore in order to stay with Casey and Coletta overnight and find out what was happening, as rumors were flying everywhere. Their ten-month enterprise with FEN had just recently collapsed, sending them back to Baltimore to regroup and comfort each other, try to sort it all out. I found a clutch of depressed radicals huddled in a dark house. They were all wounded-looking, haunted, exhausted, decimated by their losses in Detroit and disappointed that they had not pressed the movement forward.

What was clear to me was they didn't know what to do next. They had run their small businesses (minus the Detroit building) with great success; they organized the work well, supervised workers well, priced their goods and services well. I considered Coletta a superb businesswoman. Laura and Barbara had spent years learning to train skilled workers and supervise doctors. They paid attention to things like insurance and fire alarms. I knew I had failed at all of this with the press collective, and had created an enterprise with a sterling if stoic reputation at the expense of destroying and endangering the workforce, impoverishing the resources, injuring and burning out the leadership. I was certain these women could do a much better job. I suggested they come to the

West Coast and work with us, as they clearly still believed in Diana Press and its publications.

Wendy was in agreement that we invite them to move to California and merge with the Women's Press Collective, which had been mired in useless meetings for a year. The anarchistic organization of the press had always meant that leadership shifted according to whoever had an idea and was able to muster support for it. This, again, was workers' power.

Now, the remaining few members had loyalty to Wendy and to me as people who had put in the most work with the press; we had dedicated our lives to it since 1970. They trusted that we would do the right thing, and willingly conceded to the idea of the merger. Martha was on a cross-country trip when this decision was made, and no doubt she would have objected. She had heroically gone back to the press to make sure Alice's book was finished, as I had abandoned the project following my head injury, which may have been more serious than I realized at the time.

Unbeknownst to me (or maybe I just ignored it), Martha took a load of all of our books on a tour of the country, soliciting donations everywhere she went. She returned triumphantly with $9,000. But by that time I had already made the deal with Diana Press, and the Women's Press Collective was history.

A Merger

In early 1977 the Baltimore women with renewed zeal packed up the entire Diana Press operation and moved it to Oakland in a hired moving van, which Barbara Hoke drove across country. "The group trusted me to drive this enormous semi," Barbara exclaimed, "the most physically challenging thing I had ever done, and the amazing part is, I did it!"

Wendy and I now stepped back into the Women's Press Collective and asserted our earned authority to claim its equipment, mailing lists, and so on. We received no resistance, as Joanne and Karen made clear that the operation had completely stalled. None of the remaining members came with us to Diana Press, with the exception of Parker and Ann Bernard.

The new building on Market Street in Oakland was enormous, a former vitamin factory that was permeated with a nauseating chemical reek that would soon be overthrown by the petroleum smells our presses excelled at emitting—acrid glue fumes from the bindery would join with the (to me, delicious) smell of ink on fresh paper. Soon, the warehouse would shelter what was now an autonomous publishing operation with a front desk, six presses, a full bindery, and editorial offices. Once again Wendy took up her saw and hammer to help build a huge darkroom to house a Brown walk-in copy camera. Olivia Records rented the remaining space, about a third of the warehouse, for their expanding business.

In merging the two presses, we decided to keep the single name "Diana Press." Coletta's plan was to offer printing services that would help support the publishing and turn it into a thriving business. Casey's plan was for us to gather enough credit to buy a huge web press and publish mass paperbacks that would reach millions of women. We were already printing and selling larger print runs of books—five thousand was not unusual—than many long-standing, mid-level publishing houses on the East Coast.

The first actions we took were to get books of mine and Pat's moving into publication again, and to keep us both writing. Diana Press people encouraged Wendy to complete her design of the She Who poems, and the book finally came out that same year, in 1977. Oversized, *She Who* featured fifty-four really diverse and glorious drawings and photographs by movement women. Wendy's artist statement in the book reflects our desire to stay clear of ideologies:

> To move together means creating co motion—a commitment to women's publishing, printing, creating, contaminating (means together touching) the world with strong alive images of women—a desire to see women create structures and commotion for the overturning of traditions, the shifting of power relationships of the world to end the domination of men over women, white over black, right over left—a knowledge that images are power—a strong sense that "the love you save today may very well be your own" (a Joe Tex song).

Diana Press also immediately published Pat's third book, *Womanslaughter*, designed by Wendy. The poem described, in detail, the tragedy in Parker's immediate family, when in a fit of jealous rage, her brother-in-law killed his estranged wife, Parker's beloved sister Shirley. Domestic violence that ends in femicide is a common enough story, but what gave this one an extra knife twist was the attitude of the judge in the case, who implied that because the killer was a good man, a good worker, and that because the woman was also black, no real crime had occurred, no real sentence was to be given, this was "a crime of passion." Parker's rage comes through in her lines, "men do not kill their wives, / they *passion* them to death." She ends with an oath of allegiance to women, to sisters, in trouble, "I will come strong."

Within this same year, the team of Laura, Coletta, and Casey, with their strongly developed working-class consciousness, told me they had become alarmed that our work would disappear into the shadow of the middle-class East Coast poets, Audre Lorde and Adrienne Rich. Lorde and Rich had now come all the way out as lesbian leaders—Audre in her newest books and in *Ms.* magazine, Adrienne in her public activities and leadership (though not yet so overtly in her writing). Our team believed that the two of them were now being credited with leading the whole movement with their poetry, while Parker's and my work was languishing, the parts we had played in leading the movement were being forgotten, and if allowed to continue would ensure that much of the contribution of working-class women to that movement could disappear from history.

In response, Coletta, Casey, and Laura had decided to produce a double volume of hardbacks, collections of our poetry. These were conceived, appropriately enough, as sister volumes. Identical in design features, they were to come out simultaneously.

Pat and I edited her collection, and Coletta helped me as I edited mine. Wendy was recruited to design both covers, as well as the inside pages, and she did a beautiful job, putting a bold drawing of her own on my cover, and getting permission to use a sculptural piece by the late Elizabeth Catlett on the front and back of Pat's cover. I called mine *The Work of a Common Woman*, relieved I could finally have a title that moved beyond the "Edward the Dyke" label. Pat called her collection *Movement in Black* after the chorale poem she had written for multiple voices. The inside of her book had fine illustrations by the black artist Irmagean, as well as by Karen and Wendy. Kate Winter of Olivia Records took photos of Pat and me. Pat looks happy, and with a new look, a white vest, head high. I look better too, had lost the starved orphan look of 1975; I had managed to stop smoking and was eating better, growing—and learning to cook—garden vegetables.

In line with their strategy to give us the highest possible profile, Coletta and Laura recruited Audre Lorde to write the introduction to Pat's book, and Adrienne Rich to write the introduction to mine. Both poets generously responded, and luckily for me Adrienne wrote an introduction with real ideas that would be much reprinted, using the words "power" and "danger" and acknowledging that she had been transformed by "A Woman Is Talking to Death." Audre's introduction was not so successful, short and at times veering close to dismissive of the quality of Pat's work. Pat hated it, particularly that Audre painted her as having a can of beer in one hand when they first met at Pat's Cole Street apartment. Despite having written about her own alcoholism in *Pit Stop*, Pat was sensitive about her addiction, which she attributed to oppression.

Pat said to me, "Is this how Audre thinks of me? With a can of beer in my hand? No, no, no, this will never do. Plus, she doesn't even think I write good poetry!"

Evidently Audre, esteemed professor of literature at Hunter College, was being loyal to her academic and metaphor-rich poetic standards (and her class) when she wrote that Pat's work was uneven and, as she stated, that Pat's voice maintained, "even when a line falters." Of course she also said Pat's voice was strong and tender, vulnerable, merciless and far-ranging. But the critical tone stung.

Pat was devastated, feeling betrayed and undermined by Audre. This incident caused a breach in their friendship that did not heal until the 1980s. After first Audre, and then Pat, was diagnosed with cancer, the two of them wrote intense, passionate letters and poems of sisterlove and mutual compassion toward each other.

In 1986 they would read together at the Women's Building in San Francisco, and Pat would revise her story about their first meeting, telling a story of how Audre was so brazen that immediately after meeting her, she told Pat to change lovers, to find someone who could help her. "Who *is* this bitch?" Pat said she was thinking. It was a funny story, appreciated by their audience, and it both allowed Pat to take a sisterly revenge and to tell everyone how thoroughly Audre had taken Pat under her bold and protective wing. Audre tirelessly advocated for younger black women writers, though she did not always consider them her peers. Yet underneath her sometimes heavy-handed, always protective "older sister" posture with Pat was another and more secret thought. Audre wrote in her journal in 1976, perhaps after reading Pat's poem "Womanslaughter," that "Pat Parker illustrates to me again how much of a sucker harpie blowhard creampuff I really am."

I was approached by Coletta to write a different introduction. They would call Audre's a foreword. Though I did the best I could in the short time frame, I didn't think I did justice to Parker in this, my first assignment writing about another poet's work.

The paired hardbacks were generally quite well received when they came out in 1978; most people were happy that we had been given such a gift as working-class lesbian poets. However, true to the contentious times, other voices threatened to picket the press on the grounds that selling a hardback— for $8.75—could only be for the purpose of "making money off the backs of poor lesbians."

"Dykes want soft-cover books so we can fold them in half and stick them into our back pockets," we were told, along with other comments that were actually insulting to our judgment of what, as publishers and writers, we needed to thrive. You could see in this the rising conflict as women moved into jobs paying real money and as government funding began to slide in the direction of women's social services, creating a divide between the old-guard grassroots ethical position of economic liberty versus "selling out" and dependence. I was not immune to these pressures—Wendy and I both had "good" reputations as ascetics—and I can recall, to my shame, screaming for five minutes at some poor government-funded rape crisis center employee about how unjust it was that she was being paid for what the rest of us had been doing for nothing.

So as we slid uneasily through early fall of 1977, there was a rising swirl of dissention around us. At Diana Press we faced a familiar opposition as we set up the business. Some of the workmen who installed the phones planted propaganda in our desks that urged lesbians to change their sinful ways before

God punished them. Someone tied up our phone for days with garbled messages so no one could call in or out. And one late afternoon when Wendy and I came out of the press, we found that all four tires on our van had been slashed, which had once happened to Parker as well.

Though I was taking better care of myself, the strain of needing to be so on guard was making me paranoid and hallucinatory, sometimes thinking that strangers were talking to or about me, or that people at the press were saying negative things about Wendy. Intense fear accompanied these states, and the states themselves terrified me, since it wasn't just that I thought people were speaking, but that I could hear the words, as an intense whisper across impossible distances. Certain I was losing my mind, I became very secretive, telling my feelings to no one. I felt caught between huge forces that lived inside my chest, about which I could do nothing, and those forces building up outside. At the same time, hallucinating voices helped me understand my mother's schizophrenic experiences better, and to commiserate with her continual fright. What's real? What's not?

One night a dream came: Wendy and I were in a huge semi-truck, speeding down a highway. She was driving, and as she turned onto an exit she lost control; the truck plunged over the edge, falling down, down, and landing in a fenced-in yard. We got out and were confronted by large raging Dobermans with yellow eyes and open, snarling mouths.

Slick with sweat, I lay reviewing the dream while waiting for my heart to stop pounding. Casey and Coletta kept a Doberman but I don't think the dream was about them. Rather, I think I was pre-cogging an undercurrent of threat that was pressing itself all around us. Fierce yellow eyes were following us everywhere. And radicalism (Wendy driving the truck) wasn't working for us. I always imagined that Wendy was the more radical of the two of us, a trick to keep from being so afraid.

SYSTEMATICALLY AND METHODICALLY

As we plummeted toward late fall, my sense of heaviness and dread increased; I felt that I was dying. When Wendy came home one day to tell me grimly that the press had been vandalized, I went numb, suspended in space somewhere, a bubble of complete isolation. Pale and glum-faced, Coletta, Laura, and Casey showed us the damage, from one end of the press operations to the other.

The women's paper out of Denver, *Big Mama Rag*, which had suffered an earlier attack, printed our account of the October 25th break-in:

> *Diana Press, the women's press located in Oakland, Ca., was vandalized during the early morning of Oct. 25, 1977. The plant was broken into and the presses damaged and much of the equipment and stock of books were destroyed. Included in the destruction were 5,000 copies of* A Plain Brown Rapper *by Rita Mae Brown.*
>
> *Vandals evidently entered by a side loading dock that was improperly wired by the alarm company. They systematically and methodically worked their way through the shop, starting with Judy Grahn's office, which they rifled. In the bindery they poured gallons of solvent and every other chemical available on the 5,000 books plus ink and solvent on the 4,500 copies of the first 96 pages of* Lesbian Lives. *From there they moved into the press room where they poured paint, ink, solvent, and Comet cleanser into the presses.*

As our press release made clear, the damage had been very calculated. Chemicals and abrasive powders were poured into the delicate rubber rollers and other moveable parts of our presses; sticky ink, just short of the consistency of tar, had been poured over the desks and over big pallets of finished books waiting to be shipped. Ink was carefully slopped through the rolodex files of phone numbers on Coletta's and Laura's desks. A framed memorabilia sign with the initials "FEN" had been torn from a door, thrown to the floor, and trampled. Particular attention had been paid in the photographic section, where large sheets of film layout pages, representing several books in process, were piled into a calf-high clutter of debris. The pages, expensive to create and crucial to the process of making plates for printing, had been torn, crushed, and drenched in ink. Because of the way the damage was done, with nothing actually being broken, the insurance company paid only about ten percent of the actual loss. The press release ended with a plea for economic and moral support so the press could continue.

For two or three nerve-wracking nights, we took turns staying up, guarding our press with a rifle and a pistol. During the day we surveyed the damage and examined the evidence for clues as to where the attack might have come from. Opinion immediately divided, Wendy and Laura thinking the FBI had done it, others having different speculations. Ann Bernard said she had been visited by two strange-acting white women in recent days, dressed in overalls. They had asked many questions about lesbianism and the press, and insisted, indeed, demanded, that she give them a tour. When Ann, suspicious, continued to refuse, one of them slipped away into the back and Ann had to call for Becky, who was working in the bindery, to chase her out. Ann believed that these women, who she thought were probably members of a Christian right group, must have done the vandalism. We knew that at least one woman had been involved, as one of the inky footprints near my desk was a tennis shoe at least one size smaller than my foot, and I have small feet.

But surely a vandalism this serious and this knowledgeable about internal movement conflicts required us to look elsewhere, for more self-interested motives. The FBI might certainly be involved, as there seemed to be a pattern. *Big Mama Rag* had been vandalized and in Washington, DC, Women in Distribution had been broken into and its property damaged about six months prior to the attack on our press, and the New York offices of *Majority Report*, a national women's newspaper experienced a similar attack. The DC police also claimed the break-in was an inside job because the security system had been breached. Who else would know how to do this other than the FBI?

The FBI's infamous Cointelpro program supposedly ended in 1971, though it is believed that in the years following, the FBI continued to target radicals and dissenters—they simply moved the operations deeper undercover. The FBI was later revealed to have been recruiting women. It must have seemed quite an adventure to join the FBI and be asked to infiltrate women's groups. Who might have been susceptible to this?

Coletta and Casey suspected a renegade lesbian feminist group from the Pacific Northwest with a very radical rhetoric. They had been in the process of publishing a book with Diana Press, but only a short time earlier had suddenly reversed, saying they wanted publication to cease. They had changed their minds they said, as they had abandoned their former philosophy. Coletta had argued with one of them on the phone, the conversation turning vehement as she insisted the group would have to pay several hundred dollars to account for the amount of work that had already gone into their book. They had refused. The vandals had destroyed the film mock-ups for that book, among several others. This was certainly not enough information to go on, but we also couldn't rule it out.

Quite possibly the attack was political, and from within the movement—the vandals had focused on a FEN sign and the desks of FEN members, as well as the books associated with Diana Press from its Baltimore days, while the pallets of books by Parker and me were left pristine. This could have been a coincidence. Or, it could have meant that whoever broke in was fully aware of the huge split in the movement between FEN and its critics.

Martha Shelley had gone to Detroit to question people, some of them bitter and accusatory, in the aftermath of the FEN collapse. She had then written a heated position paper in which she was particularly critical of Laura Brown and implied that Wendy and I were puppets who had fallen under the spell of capitalist sell-outs. This paper was sold on the counter at ICI: A Woman's Place bookstore; Alice and possibly others in the bookstore collective evidently shared the analysis that FEN was evil, and that any approaches using capital, banking, and non-collective organizing principles were anti-movement.

Throughout the following year I was obsessed by this position paper and by the idea that it had fomented an atmosphere conducive to the vandalism. But in reality, though I did feel hurt and betrayed, I knew the position paper was just a matter of free speech and that it wouldn't give any random person, however ideologically driven, motive enough to figure out how to circumvent or dismantle our alarm system and inflict a hundred thousand dollars in damage.

But a Marxian group who didn't want to be associated with the bad rep of FEN, or who had stopped their radical politics altogether but owed hundreds of dollars to the press? Now that was closer to being a motive. And infiltration of women's militant groups by the FBI was also a possibility. Infiltrators were notorious for going way beyond gathering information and leading actions that were illegal and violent.

Another piece of this puzzle was revealed when, a few months following the vandalism, I had a reading in the Northwest and was invited to a women's party afterwards. While I was standing in the kitchen drinking a glass of water (still on the wagon), I was approached by someone who had once worked in the Women's Press Collective. She stood close and whispered that "there are some people in this town who know the women who did the vandalism—they are scary people, very scary. In fact, I am moving to another state to get away from them." When I told this story to Coletta years later she said, "Oh, so it *was* that group!"

But was it? Ann Bernard raised another possibility. Recently she told me she had later seen the two women who came to Diana Press ostensibly to ask questions just before the vandalism. "I was in a women's conference in LA, and I spotted them. They saw me and began to run away, so I followed them. I even followed them in my car; when they drove away, they were in such a hurry! But then as I was driving, I thought, 'And what will I do when I catch up with them?' and so I turned back."

Laura Brown had yet another intriguing explanation. Sometime soon after the vandalism she and other Diana Press people were approached through movement sources by a guy who said he was a reporter. He said he had been present at a meeting of undercover cops in San Jose, forty miles south of San Francisco. An officer distributed a list of radical Bay Area groups, offering bonus pay to anyone who brought them down. The list, the reporter said, consisted entirely of black organizations, with one exception—Diana Press.

So there are the theories. I don't know who did this vandalism; I am really curious about why it happened. I wait for someone to step forward to look me in the eye and say, "That was me. I was part of that gang. Here's who we were, why we did it." The way soldiers from different sides sometimes share stories after the war. But this wasn't a war, it was a struggle for social change and it has not ended.

In any event, the damage to the press was so debilitating that we were immediately out of business. Coletta especially didn't want to give up, couldn't bear to close the doors; she still had some hope of reviving the business. "Besides that," she said angrily, "I don't want to give them the satisfaction of knowing they destroyed the press." For years she remained emotionally devastated by what was for her a very personal loss.

Throughout 1978 Coletta stalwartly stayed at the press, keeping the doors open by taking small jobs, trying to make something work. Thanks to a generous outpouring of support from across the women's movement, she had enough money to publish a thousand copies each of the twin hardbacks for Parker and me, and our work again sailed out into the world.

But in the aftermath, Casey left her lesbian family, and the movement altogether, and began a different life married to a man. I went down sick for a year, and Laura was sick as well. Wendy became withdrawn and seemed perpetually angry. Parker also withdrew so that I hardly saw her, and the brown briefcase that she had given me, inscribed with my initials and "Diana Press," sat forlornly in a corner.

Other presses would step into the gap left by our collapse; demand for women-centered work had created a healthy women's press movement and what was now called a "market," but none of the rising presses were as avidly ambitious as Diana Press or as rooted in the grassroots, working-class radical politics of the 1960s. None knit together the cultural workers with the socialist-politicos, the women's history with the emergent spirituality, as we had done and would have continued to do. We had integrated so much of the movement, something quite spectacular could have emerged from our collective cooking pot.

But what we had succeeded in publishing was at the forefront of women-centered content that was—we hoped—spelling out the terms of our simple revolution. And that work nobody could take away from us—it was like little spiderlings blown out over the ocean, caught up in the air currents that would take it around the globe.

While I attempted to recover from the last twelve years, sitting in a state of unaccountable grief among the brilliant green life in my garden, Pat and Laura joined their formidable forces and embarked on a stunning new adventure.

Lesbian Mothers

I introduced Parker to Laura Brown just as Parker was about to go off to

Italy with someone she barely knew who had promised her a cottage where she could write. Very skeptical about this venture, I figured she would last a week and then get into a fight with a bunch of Italian village men that she would lose. So, rightly or wrongly I played matchmaker, and within a short time she and Laura became lovers.

Behind the one-story row house that Wendy and I had bought with her grandmother's money stood a little two-story cottage that Wendy had been using as a studio. It was coffee-with-lots-of-cream colored, had tiny rooms with an illegal bathroom connected to the kitchen. Steep stairs led up to a sweetly petite bedroom, tucked under the slanted roof with a window that swung out to overlook the garden. Not long after Laura and Pat became lovers they moved into the cottage.

Becky from Detroit, who had moved to California with Diana Press, was still part of Laura's life even though they had broken up after a brief relationship. Now she described in agony the plight of her two-year-old niece, stranded with caretakers in Detroit who were so badly addicted to alcohol they were neglecting the child, who wasn't learning to talk. "They even let the milk sour in her bottle," Becky said.

"She plays with trash in the street all day, sitting in dirty diapers," Laura explained to me. "So Pat and I've decided to adopt her."

I was astonished at this amount of daring, which I was not feeling. I had reason to believe that the world wasn't ready for their action. Wendy, Ann Bernard, and I had recently attended the government-sponsored women's conference in Houston, with five thousand other women. Patricia Jackson and her lover were outside the convention center, standing shoulder to shoulder with Ericka Huggins, director for eight years of the Oakland Community School (one of the most successful of the Black Panther Party projects). Along with other women, they physically fought against what Patricia calls "the KKK"— aggressive white men who attacked them, breaking teeth and jaws of some of the women. This aggression was perhaps due to the most contentious issue on the floor of the convention, lesbian rights. Though the measure of support passed, because Betty Friedan reversed her previous opposition, the general public would be a lot less accepting.

Yet this beautiful, head-turning interracial couple who delighted in going to the local Denny's, kissing and hugging noisily in the booth, were going to challenge one of the biggest taboos in the U.S.: lesbians and children. Lesbian mothers all over the country were fighting in the courts to retain their right of motherhood. Pat Norman was the first lesbian I knew who had done this, forming the Lesbian Mother's Union in the process. Lesbian parenting was going public—this was about the time that Nancy Feinstein, the founder of the San Francisco Center for Feminist Therapy and Education, decided with her partner to conceive a child using artificial insemination, before any clinics were offering the procedure.

Now Laura and Pat, these two militant dykes, were determined to adopt an abused kid away from a heterosexual mother to whom they were not related, and to take the fight to the courts if necessary. Ann Bernard was right there to help them, as was Becky, who went to Detroit and brought the baby back to California. Surrounded by positive attention, the little red-headed girl, at first pale and hollow-eyed, quickly caught up developmentally. Laura and Pat brought their confidence and their enthusiastic extended families to the custody hearing. The hearing didn't last long, as the judge looked at the crowd of relatives filling the court—black, white, Irish, Mexican, young, old—all testifying to their eagerness to become aunts, uncles, grandparents, and cousins to this little girl, and to support the two courageous and caring women who proposed to raise her. The team brought Cassidy home in triumph. Laura and Pat's friends helped in many ways. Wendy and I kept Cassidy at our house every Friday night so the still-in-love couple could step out on the town.

POSITIVE AND NEGATIVE FORCES

Positive new currents, such as health services and support groups—especially AA—designed specifically for women and the gay and lesbian community, were giving promise to a quality of life for individuals in those communities that was unknown in the past. But the movement at large was fragmenting, and twisting around to bite itself, partly from pressures within and partly from the country turning sharply right. The contortions were as often birth pangs as they were death throes. A woman, Elaine Brown, was leading the Black Panther Party and had helped elect Oakland's first black mayor, Lionel Wilson. But at the same time, rumors increasingly held that the Panthers in Oakland were acting more and more like a drug gang than like political revolutionaries. I wasn't sure what to believe.

At the end of 1978, violence erupted on an enormous scale. In Guyana, over nine hundred people, almost seventy percent of them black, killed themselves in what appeared to be a mass suicide at Jonestown—the alleged social utopia created by Jim Jones, the paranoid, white, authoritarian leader of the cult-like People's Temple, which was headquartered in San Francisco. I was in the Oakland airport when a few of the survivors came home, and will never forget how disassociated they looked.

In the years following the Jonestown massacre, Pat Parker wrote what is in my opinion her best work, a thirteen-page poem called "Jonestown," which drew from her deep feelings about suicide. As a child she had heard her parents declaring the impossibility that her mother's brother Dave had killed himself while in the hands of the local police. Parker translated the intensely held truth of his murder into the emphatic chorale for her poem: "Black folks do *not* / Black folks do *not* / Black folks do *not* commit suicide."

The shock of the Jonestown tragedy had barely subsided in the headlines when, ten days later, the first openly gay person elected to office in California, San Francisco City Council member Harvey Milk, was assassinated, along with the city's liberal mayor, George Moscone, by another council member, Dan White. The jury delivered an extremely light sentence to White, and the gay community exploded in days of rioting, giving a big push to the consolidation of the gay rights movement.

Amidst the turmoil yet already out of it, I sat on the ground in my garden, where the flowers opened for every visitor and the life-bringing rain landed indiscriminately on everyone. My emotions, revved up by a certainty that the FBI was following me everywhere, started to calm down. My body began to recover from overwork, industrialism, and separatism and I was again, as I had been as a child, in love with the world, determined to write for everyone, to accept love from everyone. I also continue to understand that separatism is a brilliant tactic, and it worked for us very well, as I believe nothing else could have. Separatism focused our warrior energy, and enabled our strategies. Out of the strength, the loving and tumultuous cauldrons of our households, came public institutions that supported women's voices. The generation following us would have unimaginable freedoms, as the separatist groove, having been laid down, would continue to impact people throughout the eighties. Marriage changed, as did warfare; men challenged the fatalistic expectation that they would die on the battlefield just as women came out against mandatory sex and slavery in marriage. The draft was dropped and to great extent so was the word "obey" from the bride's marital vows.

We had also set out to discover who we were as dykes and to make it possible to lead meaningful, loving lives. As a result, we had succeeded in helping to mobilize a mass movement that proceeded to spread around the globe. And so the decade of Gay Women's Liberation and radical lesbians/ feminists charting maps and kicking open doors drew to a close. What we had put in place would now transform and flower, or die.

Gays and lesbians had instigated a strong movement that would challenge all four walls holding homosexual oppression in place: the attitude of psychology that pathologized us; the laws and courts that criminalized us and stole our children; the liberation movements that both rejected and used us; and, perhaps most basic to it all, those powerful religious leaders who condemned, ostracized, endangered, and scapegoated us.

But there were still problems to puzzle out. Remedies to create. What remained for me was the certainty that so long as patriarchal religions held sway and made the definitions, neither women nor gay people would ever have permanent access to states of liberation. Unless we could challenge the major origin stories told in mass culture, we could always be pushed back into repression. Science was no help in changing the stories. It was hopeful that the American Psychiatric Association in 1973, due to gay movement pressure, had dropped the classification of homosexuality as a mental illness. But if not a crime or an illness, what was it? A choice, a "lifestyle"? Some entirely different ideas needed to arise, ideas and models that could incorporate antiracism, class issues, and ecology as well. New philosophical positions were needed. As Alice had often said, quoting Ursula Le Guin, "When action proves unprofitable, gather information." Ecofeminism was surfacing, pushed along by Susan

Griffin's fresh take in *Woman and Nature*, and Charlene Spretnak's *The Politics of Women's Spirituality*. New spiritually and politically integrated voices, like those of Cherríe Moraga, Gloria Anzaldúa, and many more women of color, prepared to take center stage. New questions would be raised.

Changing Winds

The dragons of conflict had raged, and had inflicted wounds of distrust. As tightly bound in loyalty and courage as we had been, we were now split apart and some would scatter. Still mad at Alice for taking a position against FEN, I would not talk to her for two or three years. Outraged at the vehement movement split over FEN and the Diana Press vandalism, Susan Griffin, carrying great moral authority, stood in front of a large gathering of Bay Area women and chided the crowd: "We must stop trashing each other. This must stop now." I sat silently weeping in the back.

Yet I was also relieved. Perhaps the tension would let up and I could have control of my life. Perhaps I could go out into a bigger world, as this one was feeling painfully small. Perhaps I could find some help for my emotional fragility, which had not lessened.

By 1980 Wendy and I were 35 and 40 years old, respectively, and both at loose ends with the press gone and no new enterprise to engage us. It was a time to travel and make new friends. We had grown close to her family at last. Social support for parents and friends of lesbians and gays (PFLAG) enabled them to better understand their children. We went to the East Coast often, especially when Joe Cadden became ill and eventually passed away. We traveled around New York state, visited Adrienne Rich in the hospital recovering from one of her frequent operations for severe arthritis, and on another occasion we had lunch at the quixotic "carriage house" she and her longtime love Michelle Cliff shared in Montague, NY.

Another time we were at Wendy's mother's apartment in Manhattan. Two charming, compelling women, Blanche Wiesen Cook and Clare Coss were standing in the living room, talking to Vivian about Blanche's three-book project on Eleanor Roosevelt. I was fortunate to have more contact with them later in California, and we became lifelong friends.

On several occasions Wendy and I visited a movement organizer named Ann Shellabarger, who lived across the Bay in Tiburon, and had contributed money to a few of our projects, including the High Risk album. I had the wild idea that we should expand the press collective by buying a freighter, staffed only with women, that would travel the world from port to port, exchanging our books for goods that women had produced. Wendy, Shellabarger, and I went so far as to go down to the docks of Oakland and clamber up and down the iron ladders on an old freighter that was for sale. Though nothing further came of this notion, we stayed friends with her, and later worked with her and Paula Wallace on an early women's film festival they put together. There were so few woman-centered films at that time that one we selected was about mother lions! (Needless to say, the film didn't get such a great reception from the audience.) Shellabarger also owned a twenty-foot sailboat, and, to Wendy's special delight, we went out on the Bay to crew for her. I too loved that day, learning to know the wind in a new way, as the ocean's breath and as a possible friend that would help you in your travels, provided you paid attention to its purposefulness and whimsy.

The Shellabarger family had left their daughter some rather strange property. It was wonderful acreage, but in the process of building what was to be a grand mansion, the father had run out of money after completing only a modest coach house for guests and servants. Ann had stayed on living in the coach house; she also had a generous orchard, with dozens of European plum trees. One summer afternoon, Wendy and I were avidly picking the fruits, using a ladder that leaned on a high tree limb. As the late afternoon sun sent an amber gleam through the leaves, I was standing about twenty feet up reaching ambitiously for one last fat purple orb. Unfortunately the bucket, loaded with heavy fruits, hung suspended from that same skinny arm in a miscalculation of the mechanics of weight distribution, mass, height, and the stability of ladders.

As the slender ladder began its slow, inevitable tip, Wendy saw me trying to fly, and moved. She was quite a distance away, yet she managed to break my fall by going into a dramatic baseball slide just in time for me to land full length on her body, in her strong arms instead of on earth and stones. She was bruised but I was saved broken bones. This is one example of how we were together; though the dynamic sometimes shifted, in my memory it was mostly I who climbed and fell, she who tried to be there to catch.

Increasingly, various small but debilitating illnesses robbed me of everyday life, and I would be in bed, throwing up or coughing or recovering from sunburn—every week something. I also was hiding just how withdrawn and paranoid I had become. Wendy would sit with me, trying to get me to talk about what was going on inside. But I was mute, could not bear to tell her that many days I went out to shop or visit someone, but drove around lost, pulling over to the side of the road crying. I really *was* lost; my road had been washed out by stormy, willful winds coming from new directions. I couldn't tell anyone that my mind was shutting down, my attention wandering away during conversations. I nodded in the right places, faking alertness. Though frightened about what was happening to me, I kept it secret. And then I left.

Breaking an intensely close relationship, a fourteen-year relationship, is a terrible act that devastates both parties, but especially the one who is left, who has no agency. Wendy did not deserve to have me leave with no explanation. And I didn't know how to talk from inside myself. To say, "I am so crazy I'm scaring myself. I have to get out of this movement. I have to find some help. And I have to do the rest of my work."

I really needed to leave, to find a good therapist or two, and explore my connections to spirituality. And I was so dependent on having a lover that I jumped into another relationship before telling Wendy I was leaving. If only I'd had the skill to break up gracefully as so many other lesbians did, maintaining lifelong friendships. But I did not have that skill, and left a rift between us that lasted for years.

Breaking up an iconic couple was also difficult for our community to accept. Pat was extremely upset, accused Wendy of driving me away. Others expressed their anger with me, as though I had no right to begin a new life. "I hate you," one movement friend wrote. "I feel like you've abandoned us." People approached me on the street, "What have you done to Wendy?" I finally burst out to one of them, "Women have won the right to divorce, and that includes me!"

But eventually the bitterness faded, the love flooded back into us. From the moment Wendy had sent her mysterious telegram, we were on course to have a love that thrived within a greater, communal love, a bond that enabled us to ride the wild storms of passion to achievements no one we knew had ever imagined. And a love that truly would never end.

CROSSROADS

Pat and I had also each reached a crossroads in our lives. Following the adoption of Cassidy, she became the medical director of the Oakland Feminist Health Center. This was a white-collar job at last, and it would allow her to own a house and have a family. She eventually moved to a suburb about twenty-five miles from Oakland with her last and most devoted lover, Marty Campbell. They adopted a daughter, Anastasia Parker-Campbell. Due to these choices, Pat's time was accounted for, and her writing did not develop much further because she didn't have the thousands of hours necessary to write prose.

In 1978 Olivia Records launched "The Varied Voices of Black Women," a tour of the Northeast that included Parker, Linda Tillery, Vicki Randle (who would later spend fourteen years as a drummer and vocalist with The Tonight Show band), pianist-composer Mary Watkins, and vocalist-composer-performance artist Gwen Avery. The inclusion of Parker, a political poet, on the tour encouraged more lesbians of color to take a public stand about their sexual orientation. This tour brought many more invitations to the participants as it gave them higher national profiles early in their careers.

Olivia Records wanted to sweep me into their lineup of performers, but I resisted. I did not want to become an entertainer, or in any way be dependent on pleasing an audience. I wanted to write serious nonfiction books that would add to the dialogues about women, gay and lesbian people, social justice, and culture. It sounds a little silly to me now (couldn't I have done both?), yet I can see this was a fork in the road and I took the one that led straight to the writing of prose books and complicated, book-length poems. Not that I gave up readings, I would do hundreds of them, but they remained secondary, and increasingly less overtly political. My occupation as a writing teacher and performing artist was not so exacting of my time. And every penny I got went directly into buying the vast, concentrated hours I needed for research and writing.

Four generous women set me on the lifesaving path of teaching. Diane di Prima gave me my first teaching experience in 1975 when I filled in for her at a YWCA writing workshop. Rachel Guido deVries, founder of the Women's Writers Center in Cazenovia, New York, and Beverly Tannenbaum and Katharyn Machan of the Feminist Women's Writing Workshops in Ithaca asked me to teach at their programs; a few years later I began to be invited annually.

At last I had the beginnings of an occupation, and a way to tour on the East Coast. Colleges and universities began to invite me to speak for money, especially following a gig gotten for me by—who else?—Diane di Prima, who said she would not go to a conference at a college in Wyoming unless Audre and I were also invited. Then within a short period of time I was given two sums of money, one from *American Poetry Review* for "A Woman Is Talking to Death," the other a grant from the National Endowment for the Arts. Suddenly it became possible to write longer works. The notes I had been gathering for years began to jump into focus. Charlene Spretnak, editor of *The Politics of Women's Spirituality*, asked for an article on menstruation and culture. I was also collecting every scrap of information I could find about terms such as dyke, faggot, butch, femme, drag as chapters of my cultural story of gay people, *Another Mother Tongue,* rose into view like undersea creatures from the national subconscious.

Women Surfacing from Underground—Almost

I was convinced that the political needed to be spiritual, in the sense of being deeply connected to the preciousness of each life, because when it wasn't, when it lost sight of love, common humanity, and the need for humility in the face of our capacity to do harm, political activism made terrible mistakes. One sunny afternoon in Oakland I sat across a table from someone who was on the verge of doing just that.

Wendy and I had not seen three of the Weather Underground women for more than a year (though prior to that we had visited Judith Bissell in prison several times after attending her hearing when she was arrested in Houston in 1977). It was spring of 1980, and Wendy and I were eating lunch with one of the Weather Underground women, Kathy Boudin, who was in disguise, still underground. We were trying to persuade her to surface, as President Carter was offering amnesty for underground radicals. We were feeling optimistic about her chances because Kathy had just told us that she was pregnant. We talked about babies, birthing, midwives, and diets. Was she taking good care of herself? Oh, yes, changing eating habits and getting more sleep. But her nails were bitten close; I had noticed this each time we met, and always thought she chewed on herself mercilessly.

We were in a Mandarin Chinese restaurant on College Avenue in Oakland eating spicy Szechuan food. The more we talked the more the gleaming white tablecloth seemed to stretch across a widening gap between us; there was tension as we leaned forward. Would she surface? She didn't answer, looked down at her hands, then back at us with her intense eyes. I remembered that she had wanted to become a doctor before she became a Weatherman. "There is one more action I need to do," she said finally. "Something that has been planned for a long time."

Our hearts fell. She wasn't going to turn away from the violent, male-dominated tactics of the underground men, tactics we did not support. She seemed trapped. What action could she be planning? Of course she didn't say, but by the following year I would know just how fierce the trap was for her.

Most of the other underground people had surfaced, including a couple of our friends. We went to visit them at their apartment one evening. In low voices they told us that an FBI van was parked down the block, recording every word we said. Here was my chance. I existed in a constant state of anxiety, a certainty that I would never live to write all my ideas down. So after they gave this warning, I began to speak compulsively, telling all the details of my idea for a grand women's and gay people's cultural history book. (I would later actually write three books based on some of what I said that night.) I went on and on for well over an hour, until all eyes were glazed with overload. Even if I did not live to write it all down, at least it was recorded and existed, somewhere, in some archive.

Swirling

In the aftermath of the demise of the press, our group swirled off in various directions. Coletta eventually dismantled what was left of the shards of the press and became involved in women's spirituality, going into business for herself as a consultant, moving to New Mexico. Becky became lovers for a time with Ann Bernard; after they broke up Ann fled the organic food co-op scene in Berkeley to the countryside, where she lived "off the grid" without running water or electricity for sixteen years, emerging to become a spiritual advisor to women in northern California, having changed her name to "Montanna Jones." Becky somehow slipped economically and became homeless for two years. Too ashamed to come to any of us for help she slid into a daze, until she was hospitalized for pneumonia, and a nurse fell in love with her, and pulled her back into civilization. Laura and Parker continued running the Oakland Feminist Women's Health Center for a decade. During the 1979 Iranian revolution, Laura Brown went to Iran to support the revolution and talk to Kurdish women about all-women's households. She was captured by the conservative government, accused of spying, and held in a notorious prison for six months. Typical of the warrior stances taken by our generation, she described her altercations with the male guards as "fighting." Not "they beat me." When she returned she decided to have a baby, and thus raised two daughters, Cassidy and Lela.

Wendy continued with her art and graphic design, running her own business. One day she went on a blind date, who turned out to be Barbara, the doctor who had treated Von in her last few weeks of life and a former Army colonel. They have now been together twenty-three years and have sailed their 42-foot boat in many of the world's waters. Willyce Kim got a job at UC Berkeley, eventually becoming a head librarian. Martha Shelley left the movement, found a suitable worker's advocacy occupation and a long time love; she recently published a highly readable novel centering on the historical figure of Jezebel. Sandi Ajida tried unsuccessfully to kick her heroin habit; she was walking down the street in New York City in 1981 when someone mugged her, hitting her so hard she had a concussion, and a few days later, she died. Evan Rubin, whose compelling stories I had included in *True to Life Adventure Stories* and who was a lesbian activist in Los Angeles, vanished in the early 1980s, with friends saying she had most probably committed suicide. Linda Tillery went on to have a very successful multinational musical career. Pat Norman ran for office in San Francisco in the 1980s, and was the first open lesbian appointed to the San Francisco Department of Public Health, working with LGBT people. She later fell in love with a woman with whom she would raise six children. Anne Leonard raised three daughters, aided by lesbian friends, and was able to send one of her girls to college. Jane Lawhon got a law degree and a career representing unions, especially the California Nurses Association. Karen Garrison became co-director and senior policy analyst of the Oceans Program at the Natural Resources Defense Council. She spearheaded the 1999 Marine Life Protection Act, which led, among other things, to California setting aside four areas of protected coastline, or "oceanic parks," to maintain and restore intact ecosystems.

Red Arobateau, who taught us karate in the early days of Gay Women's Liberation, opened a storefront church and preached the Christian gospel. She wrote and published dozens of novels, most notably *Lucy & Mickey*, and continued painting; eventually Red transitioned, saying that as a transman he had finally found a community that felt like home. Barbara Hoke became partners with a woman realtor (who had once been an FBI agent) and sold houses to working-class lesbians, acquiring a tiny one for herself in a modest part of town. Sandy Boucher took part in anti-nuke protests of the early 1980s, traveled to Sri Lanka and became a Buddhist in preparation for writing her books. Max Dashu traveled widely giving lectures and selling her artwork, and became a women's spirituality teacher.

Alice, Carol, and Natalie continued running A Woman's Place, refusing to update any procedures, holding even the most mundane information in their heads, and maddening the younger women who came to help them, while steadfastly holding their brilliant educational vision in place. In 1983 a younger group with Marxist ideology, but little experience, took them to court and took the bookstore away from them. At the time, Carol told me, "We left them with two years of inventory, so the bookstore will stay open for two years. Since they have no idea what women want to read, they won't order correctly, and will have to close." She was, as she almost always was, perfectly correct. Undaunted, the triumvirate took their situation to the community, who raised enough cash for them to rent another space on Telegraph Avenue. They called their charming, den-like space "Mama Bears" and put in a coffee bar with tables and a tiny performance space. Just in time for all of us drama queens to have a great grassroots sounding board for our newest work, and for thousands of women to engage with women-centered knowledge and community.

We had started as a movement within the larger civil rights and antiwar movements. As Sandy Boucher has pointed out to me, by the end of the seventies, this larger movement didn't exist anymore; instead, there were many small groups working in different ways. "And the media," she said, "began saying the movement was dead." Her own experience seemed to affirm that.

> I was looking around, where were the people who used to go with me to this and that? Now they were preparing for their careers; there was professionalism. Like, in the battered women's centers, they began hiring people with psychotherapist degrees; you couldn't just show up to help anymore, take a position and take leadership.

The women's movement of course went on, though morphing into different forms. Women continued to advocate for and contribute to each other's well-being. Poets and other performers continued to do benefits, raising money for a multitude of causes. Women continued to share with each other. One day someone knocked on my door on Ninth Avenue. I opened to find Laura Tow, the founder of Breakaway, which trained women for jobs, and who had organized a few readings for me in Berkeley. Now she handed me a check.

"I just got an inheritance," she said, "and can't think of anyone I would rather share it with than you." Astonished and grateful, I accepted the offering. After she left I read the number: a thousand dollars, which in that economy would give me months of time to work on my projects.

In my writing I was exploring ways to get everyone I knew into the great stories that society tells about itself. In *The Cell*, which we had staged at Antioch College, everyone in the gymnasium was accounted for, except for me—I had not written myself into the play. I had been correcting for that ever since—as all of us cultural workers were doing, writing ourselves and those like us who had been excluded or overlooked into the social stories, into the histories and the theories about humanity.

I was going to do everything in my power to get women acknowledged as culture-makers. I knew how much devastation lay beneath that simple phrase, "left out of the story." At the same time another idea was tugging at my sleeve, one that would soon demand my full attention, again from an internal certainty: that gay and lesbian people had been erased from history, yet have valid, and in some cultures, valued places in cultural stories, beyond simply being tolerated.

As did other movement poets like Audre, Adrienne, and Susan, I would write my ideas out extensively in prose. We greatly extended our philosophical voices, would invent new forms and push beyond the limitations of theory without losing the necessity for change, for new maps of new territory. The 1980s were a flowering of the potential developed in the 1970s, even as that decade also contained a pullback from freedom to practices of control. Along with the national sharp turn to the right, there was an intentional, pervasive move to increase the wealth and power of the upper classes.

One exciting weekend in Boston, several of us lesbian poets celebrated Ely Bulkin and Joan Larkin's anthology *Lesbian Poetry* with a packed reading from the high pulpit of a venerable eighteenth-century church. That same weekend I was offered a contract by Beacon Press, for whom I would write two prose books attempting to restore gay people and women to the status of culture-makers: *Another Mother Tongue: Gay Words, Gay Worlds* and *Blood, Bread, and Roses: How Menstruation Created the World*. That weekend I was also invited to a meeting at the new Kitchen Table Women of Color Press, which Barbara Smith was putting in place, along with Audre Lorde, Cherríe Moraga, Hattie Gossett and many other women of color. Throughout the eighties and into the nineties, Kitchen Table would change the dialogues around feminism, lesbianism, and racism.

Malvina Hoffman's heads were nodding inside my subconscious, pleased with my progress; however, by now I knew that the idea of "all" humanity co-existing happily in one room was a beautiful illusion. I had come to understand that any interaction requires a comprehension that there are power dynamics working between nearly any two people. There are differences, both obvious and hidden, which, to borrow from what Parker said in her poem, "For the white person who wants to know how to be my friend," *you must forget and you must never forget.*

I had gotten to know and learn from some of the most interesting people I could imagine, and many more were about to arrive. In the 1980s I would remain avidly pro-woman yet again know wonderful men—Robert Gluck, Steve Abbott, Tede Mathews, Jack Foley, Bill Vartnaw. People were writing to me about my poetry from colleges, and also from deep inside the sinister walls of women's prisons. I was in dialogue with feminists, gay men, artists, intellectuals, and hard hats from Germany, Australia, Canada, Italy, India, Japan, New Zealand, Argentina, England, and beyond. My heroine Ursula Le Guin would take me to dinner; many gay men struggling with AIDS would write letters about how much it meant that I included them in my research.

At the women's conference in Houston we had heard a new song, "The Old Woman Song," with the line, "I want to live to be an old woman," written by Michal Brody and performed by a Chicago women's band. The crowd cheered with wild enthusiasm, perhaps for the same reason I did. The lyrics broke the grip of the warrior fatalism that had held me for a decade. Like Parker, I never believed we would live to be thirty, or forty. Now we could try for quality of life. This also meant that I could follow my poet's heart into the mythology of Helen, the archetype of love in the West, and write book-length poems about her.

In 1981 I would see the dreadful news that Kathy Boudin had left her baby with a babysitter in order to drive the getaway vehicle for members of the Black Liberation Army who had killed three people during the robbery of a Brink's truck in New York state. She would serve twenty-three years, and later told her son that she and his father had made a terrible mistake and felt great remorse about the lives that had been lost. Marilyn Buck was also part of this misguided action, was arrested later, and spent her life in prison.

Sometime later, I would touch a name on the Black Wall of Vietnam casualties. And read in the Vietnam War Memorial book of names that my friend from Howard University, Larry Jones, had died in combat in 1968.

WINDS OF THE FUTURE

Despite all the walls our militant part of the movement had broken through, and all that had been brought to consciousness by 1980, my most pressing and interesting questions had not yet been answered. What does it *mean* to be gay or lesbian? Do we have a significance to our societies now? *What would it mean if the world loved women?* Would it be a more peaceful world? A world more protective of the needs of nature? Wouldn't women think more of ourselves if we knew what contributions women have made to culture? Why don't we know about these matters? Why are we left out of the origin stories of science and religion? And how could I, a sporadically educated, working-class dyke person with a medium sized (though continually erupting) reputation as a poet, possibly hope to make a viable contribution to any of these significant lines of questioning? Was I really going to become a philosopher poet, and develop a philosophy? My sense of internal certainty said "Yes."

I wonder sometimes what our country would be like if feminism, ecology, equality, the ending of imperial wars, and other values of our revolutionary generation had prevailed. Climate change, as the People's Park rebellion presaged, is coming rapidly to produce economic disaster and unrest throughout the world. What if economic justice, creating a new kind of economy by funding women's small businesses, placing real power in the hands of working-class women and their families, developing and publishing our best ideas, mythologies, and images in well-distributed mass forms, making childcare a priority, spreading organic gardening instead of fast foods, making rape and forced pregnancy crimes against both humanity and nature, asking that "love" be continually redefined to maintain its troth with truth and social care… What if those values had swept over the country at the opening of the 1980s?

What I would eventually learn is that the wave we had set in motion will never stop, that the tenets we had held of a simple revolution are both subtle and crucial. Because the writing, thinking, arts, and processes we created interacted with the major cultural institutions and power structures of our time, we were able to make changes. Gender issues are part of prime time news. The sufferings of soldiers are no longer taken for granted, though still not adequately addressed (nor is the habit of war and the devastation it brings to civilian populations); the denial of rights to women is addressed in world organizations; the necessity to end racism is understood by many millions more people as crucial to achieve peace. Gay organizations stand for the rights of sexual orientation and gender definitions all over the world, and the rights of transgender people are beginning to be recognized. As I write, polls say that the majority of U.S. people favor marriage equality for LGBT people. The worst superstitions of patriarchal religion are being challenged for the harm they bestow on women and children. Younger generations of men are seeking to be better parents and partners. The Sacred Feminine is being articulated as nature herself—a multi-gendered matrix of life—and the biblical and scientific injunctions to grab and devour her are now challenged and are up for renegotiation.

At the same time, global capitalism has never been more threatening to human life on earth. Every generation must reinvent the movements and methods that ensure its survival, building on what went before, and creating what needs to manifest. Determining the difference between going for ideas and going for what feels wrong, every generation creates its own simple revolutions, creates its own structures and theories.

For much of my lesbian generation, the structure was a house, and the purpose was to nurture bonds of love. A house is like a theory, functioning as a structure to help keep us safe as we sally out into the wind-torn world. A house, like a theory, can sustain and also constrict possibility. In the story I have told I see a trail of living spaces that grew more substantial the more a feminist and lesbian movement developed. A house, in my life and in the lesbian movement, came to mean a place where love between women can be cherished, and can make a mark on the world. The trail in my life began in the little unsuccessful room-of-my-own on Jewel's porch, to Von and I having no space at all to be in love with each other, to my "house arrest" in the service, and the roommate dutifully spying on me. The trail widened with Von's metaphorically profound house of rebellion, with walls but no furniture, then on to the love-saturated mattresses on floors that kept Wendy and I tangled in each othe's arms, and whose spareness enabled all the adventurous freedom anyone cou crucial lesson of the collective lesbian households was that a "house to address a number of unmet needs for love and caring that we individual, in their origin. Extending outward from the base o: women began to occupy public space in the women-owned book and presses, at the music festivals, and much more.

Likewise, various social theories—Marxism, socialism, black nationalism, and eventually feminism—served as structures that spurred us to foment rebellion on a number of fronts, yet the limitations of each one required us to step outside its framework in order to lift our noses to the air, to find for ourselves which way the wind blows, and be original in creating methods responsive to our own lived needs. We have to be both "home and wanderer," as Adrienne wrote. We need the structure but only if we also have our senses tuned to the wind, that wise talkative migrant.

The wind in the Bay Area is a daily experience, and because it's mostly the onshore breathing of the ocean, it has a complexity to it. In the evenings, and sometimes in the mornings as well, the ocean breath is a cloud of fog, a fractal being that pours through the low places in the coastal mountains, softly flooding across certain urban or forest areas with its enveloping, diffuse, cool grey light. Nearly every afternoon, the wind whips up, stirring the trees to a talkative wildness, whisking up the busy streets of the Mission and across the Bay through all the local cities, waking everyone up. Hats blow off, people wrap their arms around their waists and make remarks about needing to remember to always carry a jacket. Nothing stays the same for very long; renewal is the song of the air.

The moving air stirs up questions: What else can we think, how deeply can we feel, what more can we know, what different ways can we act—these thoughts are in the restless breath of the wind. The air also moves when people talk together. Perhaps this breath is what drives the notion of a simple revolution more than anything: the wind that shows up every day, relentless and faithfully working away, cleaning up and rearranging, yet always asking the questions: What needs doing, who best can do this, how do I take care of myself in the midst of changes, what is my stake in this, how much pressure needs to be exerted, who has been left out, how do we stay centered, especially centered in love, while redefining what feels like "everything"?

> Everyone wants Love to be his own,
> to be her own.
> But what is it that Love wants,
> what does Love want to know?
> Everyone wants Love to follow them
> down their road.
> Where is it that Love wants to go?*

*from *The Queen of Swords*, 1987

ACKNOWLEDGEMENTS

I HEARTILY THANK everyone who assisted with this project, including those who gave time and attention for interviews: Sandy Boucher, Laura K. Brown, Wendy Cadden, Blanche Wiesen Cook, Tee Corinne, Clare Coss, Max Dashu, Alix Dobkin, Nancy Feinstein, Cynth Fitzpatrick, Karen Garrison, Naomi Groeschel, Barbara Hoke, Patricia Jackson, Montanna Jones, Jane Lawhon, Anne Leonard, Barbara Price, Coletta Reid, Martha Shelley, Linda Tillery, and Mary Watkins.

I thank those who contributed photos, letters, or other information: Francine Kady Butler, Cathy Cade, Karlene Faith, Lenn Keller, Willyce Kim, Lee Kissman, Joan Larkin, Ruth Mountaingrove, Pat Norman, Beth (Oglesby) Rimanoczy, Carol Seajay, John Oliver Simon, Lisbet Tellefsen, Karla Tonella, Laura Tow, Chana Wilson, and many others. Thanks to Katrina Rahn and her excellent library staff at Sofia University.

I am grateful for assistance that made this project possible: Generous grants from the Thanks Be to Grandmother Winifred Foundation and Horizons Foundation. I thank my two excellent research assistants, Gregory Gajus, who persistently connected me to my past, and Akhila Elizabeth Kohlsar, who found my early article in a 1966 issue of *Sexology Magazine* at the UC Santa Cruz library, among many other services. I thank Paul Roy of Sofia University for his encouragement, for allowing me to take a partial leave, and for making research assistance available. For assisting with two interviews, thanks to Jean Weisinger.

For reading early versions of the manuscript and giving invaluable comments thanks to: Kris Brandenburger, Dianne Jenett, Anya de Marie, and Anne Carol Mitchell.

For encouragement I thank: Blackberri, Jeanne Cordova, Iris (Brenda) Crider, Lillian Faderman, Jack and Adele Foley, D'vorah Grenn, Jack and Peggy Grove, Mel Kettner, Lynda Koolish, Ed May, Betty De Shong Meador, Janet Rubenstein, Richard Taggett, and many others. Special thanks to Joan Pinkvoss for rich discussions about the "simple revolution" and what that might mean.

Avotcja Jiltonilro deserves much gratitude for her yearly "Tribute to Pat Parker" community performances at La Peña in Berkeley. Credit also should go to Haley Ravenswing and Lisbet Tellefsen for organizing "Sister Comrade, celebrating the lives of Audre Lorde and Pat Parker." Thanks to Dianne Jenett and D'vorah Grenn for organizing "A Tribute to Judy Grahn," and to Aunt Lute Books and panel members who contributed to "A Simple Revolution" events.

Some of this autobiographical material was published earlier: "Ground Zero" in *The Whole World Is Watching*, Harold Adler, ed.; "Widows" in *A Woman Like That*, Joan Larkin, ed.; "Riding the Dragon's Breath" in *Contemporary Authors Autobiography Series*, Vol. 29, Gale Research Group. Excerpts from the manuscript appeared as blog postings on Aunt Lute's online site, "A Simple Revolution."

Finally, much gratitude to Aunt Lute's astutely conscientious editors Joan Pinkvoss, Lisa Hogeland, Gina Gemello, Shay Brawn, Kara Owens, and to assistant editors, Erin Petersen and Ellen French.

Rights to reprint Pat Parker's work are held by Anastasia Dunham-Parker-Brady.

ABOUT THE AUTHOR

JUDY GRAHN

is an internationally known poet, writer, and social theorist. Her poetry collections include *Edward the Dyke and Other Poems* (1971), *She Who* (1977), *The Work of a Common Woman* (1978), *The Queen of Swords* (1987), and *love belongs to those who do the feeling* (2008), among others. In addition to poetry, Grahn has written extensively on what it means to be a lesbian and a lesbian writer. In *Another Mother Tongue: Gay Words, Gay Worlds* (1984) she explores queer meanings, while *The Highest Apple: Sappho and the Lesbian Poetic Tradition* (1985) focuses on the ways poetry has served as a vehicle for establishing a lesbian literary tradition. Her novel, *Mundane's World* (1988), constructs an imagined world centered around women's spiritual and social practices. In 2009, *The Judy Grahn Reader*, representing all phases of Grahn's writing career, was published by Aunt Lute Books.

Her work has won several awards, including an American Book Review Award, American Book Award, Stonewall (American Library) Award, Lifetime Achievement Award (in Lesbian Letters), and a Founding Foremothers of Women's Spirituality Award. In 1997 the Publishing Triangle, an association of lesbians and gay men in publishing, established an award in her name: The Judy Grahn Award, recognizing the best non-fiction book of the year that resonates themes and issues affecting lesbian lives.

Judy Grahn currently serves as Executive Core Faculty and Co-director for the Women's Spirituality Master's Program at Sofia University in Palo Alto, California. She also teaches Creative Inquiry and Creative Writing in the Writing, Consciousness, and Creative Inquiry Program at the California Institute of Integral Studies in San Francisco, where she earned her Ph.D. in Integral Studies with an emphasis in Women's Spirituality.

Aunt Lute Books is a multicultural women's press that has been committed to publishing high quality, culturally diverse literature since 1982. In 1990, the Aunt Lute Foundation was formed as a non-profit corporation to publish and distribute books that reflect the complex truths of women's lives and to present voices that are underrepresented in mainstream publishing. We seek work that explores the specificities of the very different histories from which we come, and the possibilities for personal and social change.

Please contact us if you would like a free catalog of our books or if you wish to be on our mailing list for news of future titles. You may buy books from our website, by phoning in a credit card order, or by mailing a check with the catalog order form.

Aunt Lute Books
P.O. Box 410687
San Francisco, CA 94141
415.826.1300

www.auntlute.com
books@auntlute.com

This book would not have been possible without the kind contributions of the Aunt Lute Founding Friends:

Anonymous Donor   Diana Harris
Anonymous Donor   Phoebe Robins Hunter
Rusty Barcelo   Diane Mosbacher, M.D., Ph.D.
Marian Bremer   Sara Paretsky
Marta Drury   William Preston, Jr.
Diane Goldstein   Elise Rymer Turner